C4.5:
PROGRAMS
FOR
MACHINE
LEARNING

THE MORGAN KAUFMANN SERIES IN MACHINE LEARNING

Edited by Pat Langley

Machine learning studies the mechanisms through which intelligent systems improve their performance over time. Research on this topic explores learning in many different domains, employs a variety of methods, and aims for quite different goals, but the field is held together by its concerns with computational mechanisms for learning. The Morgan Kaufmann series in machine learning includes monographs and edited volumes that report progress in this area from a wide variety of perspectives. The series is produced in cooperation with the Institute for the Study of Learning and Expertise, a nonprofit corporation devoted to research on machine learning.

READINGS IN MACHINE LEARNING
Jude W. Shavlik (University of Wisconsin) and
Thomas G. Dietterich (Oregon State University)

COMPUTATIONAL MODELS OF SCIENTIFIC DISCOVERY AND
THEORY FORMATION
Edited by Jeff Shrager (Xerox Palo Alto Research Center) and
Pat Langley (NASA Ames Research Center)

CONCEPT FORMATION: KNOWLEDGE AND EXPERIENCE IN
UNSUPERVISED LEARNING
Edited by Douglas H. Fisher, Jr. (Vanderbilt University),
Michael J. Pazzani (University of California, Irvine), and
Pat Langley (NASA Ames Research Center)

MACHINE LEARNING METHODS FOR PLANNING
Edited by Steven Minton (NASA Ames Research Center)

C4.5: PROGRAMS FOR MACHINE LEARNING
J. Ross Quinlan (University of Sydney)

C4.5: PROGRAMS FOR MACHINE LEARNING

J. ROSS QUINLAN

MORGAN KAUFMANN PUBLISHERS

Amsterdam   Boston   Heidelberg   London   New York   Oxford
Paris   San Diego   San Francisco   Singapore   Sydney   Tokyo

Sponsoring Editor: *Michael B. Morgan*
Production Manager: *Yonie Overton*
Production Editor: *Carol Leyba*
Editorial Coordinator: *Douglas Sery*
Copy Editor: *John Hammett*
Proofreader: *Gary Morris*
Cover Design: *Jo Jackson and Pat O'Connell*
Composition: *SuperScript Typography*

Cover art is from *The Celtic Art Source Book* by Courtney Davis,
© 1988, and is reproduced with permission from Cassell Publishers,
London, England.

Morgan Kaufmann Publishers, Inc.
Editorial Office:
2929 Campus Drive, Suite 260
San Mateo, CA 94403

Library of Congress Cataloging-in-Publication Data
Quinlan, J. R. (John Ross), 1943–
    C4.5 : programs for machine learning / J. Ross Quinlan.
      p. cm.—(Morgan Kaufmann series in machine learning)
    Includes bibliographical references and index.
    ISBN 1-55860-238-0
    1. Machine learning. 2. Algorithms. 3. Electronic digital
computers—Programming. I. Title. II. Series.
    Q325.5.Q56 1993
    006.3'1—dc20   92-32653
                                                        CIP

Table of Contents

Preface

C4.5 has its origins in Hunt's *Concept Learning Systems* by way of ID3. While visiting Stanford University in 1978, I was fortunate to sit in on an engrossing graduate course taught by Donald Michie that included a challenging assignment—to learn a complete and correct rule for deciding whether one side in a simple chess endgame was lost two-ply. Most of the class used Ryszard Michalski's INDUCE system, a then-recent method of learning classifiers from data, but I decided to write a CLS-like program for comparison. That program evolved into ID3 which led in turn to C4.5, the subject of this book.

In the last fourteen years many modifications have been incorporated, some of which have been abandoned subsequently, so that my published papers do not give an accurate (or even consistent) account of C4.5 *circa* 1992. This book is meant to rectify that situation by providing a definitive description of the system right down to the level of code, together with notes on how to use it effectively.

I would like to take this opportunity to thank many people. Earl Hunt supervised my doctoral research (on quite another topic) and, in the process, helped me to appreciate heuristic algorithms. As mentioned above, Donald Michie started me down the ID3 track; his comments and suggestions over many years have done much to shape the current system. Ivan Bratko, Peter Gacs, Pat Langley, and Ron Rivest also contributed important insights. Bill Simpson read an earlier version of the code and added some very helpful documentation. William Cohen, Andrea Danyluk, Tom Dietterich, Phil Hammond, and an anonymous reviewer drew attention to errors and omissions in the first draft of this book and helped to make it more comprehensible (I hope).

Many of the ideas embodied in the system were crystallized during sabbaticals at the Heuristic Programming Project, Stanford University, and at the Artificial Intelligence Laboratory, MIT; special thanks to Edward Feigenbaum and Patrick Winston, respectively, for making these visits possible.

The University of California, Irvine, maintains a repository of machine learning databases, some of which are used as examples in this book. The librarians to date, David Aha and Patrick Murphy, deserve the gratitude of the whole field.

My research has been funded by grants from the Australian Research Council, without whose enduring support C4.5 would not have been built.

Ross Quinlan
Sydney, June 1992

CHAPTER 1

Introduction

Most applications of artificial intelligence to tasks of practical importance are based on constructing a model of the knowledge used by a human expert. This approach, which has had a major impact only since the early 1980s, is illustrated by numerous case studies reported in *The Rise of the Expert Company* [Feigenbaum, McCorduck, and Nii, 1988]. In some cases, the task that an expert performs can be thought of as *classification*—assigning things to categories or classes determined by their properties. For instance, Feigenbaum *et al.* cite a system developed by American Express to assist credit authorizers. The primary properties for this application are details of a proposed transaction and the particular customer's credit history, and the classes correspond to a recommendation to approve or to decline the transaction. Less obviously, an in-house expert system at Texas Instruments (TI) that helps in the preparation of capital expenditure proposals can also be viewed as classification-based; each item on the proposal must be judged to be consistent or inconsistent with TI's policies. Of course, many medical diagnosis tasks involve classification. At the Garvan Institute of Medical Research, the more than six thousand thyroid assay reports produced each year are drafted by an expert system. A particular assay might contain several diagnostic comments, but the process can be thought of as a sequence of small decisions as to whether each of the seventy-odd possible diagnostic comments is relevant to the assay in question. Each such decision is conceptually a yes/no classification based on properties that include the assay measurements and background information such as the source of the assay.

In a classification model, the connection between classes and properties can be defined by something as simple as a flowchart or as complex and unstructured as a procedures manual. If we restrict discussion to executable models—those that can be represented as computer programs— there are two very different ways in which they can be constructed. On one hand, the model might be obtained by interviewing the relevant expert or experts; most knowledge-based systems have been built this way, despite the well-known difficulties attendant on this approach [Michie,

1987, 1989]. Alternatively, numerous recorded classifications might be examined and a model constructed inductively, by generalizing from specific examples.

This book describes a set of computer programs that construct classification models of the second kind, i.e., by discovering and analyzing patterns found in such records. Their collective name is C4.5, which is also the name of the principal program, a descendant of an earlier program of mine called ID3. Not all classification tasks lend themselves to this inductive approach, let alone to the particular induction methods embodied in these programs, so it seems helpful to review the key requirements:

- *Attribute-value description:* The data to be analyzed must be what is sometimes called a flat file—all information about one object or *case* must be expressible in terms of a fixed collection of properties or *attributes*. Each attribute may have either discrete or numeric values, but the attributes used to describe a case must not vary from one case to another. This restriction rules out domains in which objects have inherently variable structure; for instance, it is hard to imagine an attribute-value description of a complete medical history, because such histories vary in the type and quantity of information contained in them.[1]

- *Predefined classes:* The categories to which cases are to be assigned must have been established beforehand. In the terminology of machine learning, this is *supervised* learning, as contrasted with unsupervised learning in which appropriate groupings of cases are found by analysis. Fisher, Pazzani, and Langley [1991] provide a thorough treatment of this latter task.

- *Discrete classes:* This requirement has to do with the categories to which cases are assigned. The classes must be sharply delineated—a case either does or does not belong to a particular class—and there must be far more cases than classes. Some learning tasks are not of this kind. One group of tasks that does not have discrete classes is concerned with prediction of continuous values such as the price of gold or the temperature at which an alloy will melt. Similar tasks in which a continuous-valued class is broken into vague categories such as hard, quite hard, flexible, quite soft, soft should be

---

1. For an illustration of analogous methods for dealing with structured data, see Quinlan [1990c].

approached with caution. Friedman [1988] and Breiman, Friedman, Olshen, and Stone [1984] describe analogous methods for handling continuous classes.

- *Sufficient data:* Inductive generalization proceeds by identifying patterns in data, as noted above. The approach founders if valid, robust patterns cannot be distinguished from chance coincidences. As this differentiation usually depends on statistical tests of one kind or another, there must be sufficient cases to allow these tests to be effective. The amount of data required is affected by factors such as the numbers of properties and classes and the complexity of the classification model; as these increase, more data will be needed to construct a reliable model. A simple model can sometimes be identified in a handful of cases, but a detailed classification model usually requires hundreds or even thousands of training cases.

- *"Logical" classification models:* The programs construct only classifiers that can be expressed as decision trees or sets of production rules. These forms, illustrated in the next section, essentially restrict the description of a class to a logical expression whose primitives are statements about the values of particular attributes. One common form of classification model which does not satisfy this requirement is the *linear discriminant* [Nilsson, 1965] in which weighted contributions of attributes are combined arithmetically and compared to a threshold; the corresponding descriptions of classes are thus arithmetic rather than logical. We will return to the issue of matching classification tasks to model-building methodologies in Chapter 10.

We will now consider a small example, intended to illustrate both the kind of classification task to which C4.5 can be applied and the "look and feel" of its two principal component programs.

1.1 Example: Labor negotiation settlements

The University of California at Irvine maintains a publicly accessible library of datasets that have been used in machine learning experiments.[2] One of these, provided by Stan Matwin of the University of Ottawa, concerns the outcome of Canadian contract negotiations in 1987–1988. To quote from the information provided with the data:

---

2. More information on how to access these databases can be obtained by contacting ml-repository@ics.uci.edu.

Creators: *Collective Bargaining Review*, monthly publication, Labour Canada, Industrial Relations Information Service, Ottawa, Ontario, K1A 0J2, Canada, (819) 997-3117. The data includes all collective agreements reached in the business and personal services sector for locals with at least 500 members (teachers, nurses, university staff, police, etc.) in Canada in 87 and first quarter of 88.... The data was used to learn the description of an acceptable and unacceptable contract. The unacceptable contracts were either obtained by interviewing experts, or by inventing near misses.

Each case, then, concerns one contract. Sixteen properties have been used to describe each case although, as is common, some properties are not applicable to some cases. The outcome of each case is given as **good** or **bad** depending on whether the agreement was judged to be acceptable or otherwise. From these cases, a learning system must construct a classification model that relates the acceptability of a contract to the values of the recorded properties. This model should be general, so that it could be used to predict the acceptability of contracts other than those used in its construction.

Let us follow this task through the stages of preparing input for C4.5 and interpreting its output. All tasks to be processed by the system need a brief name; this one has been called **labor-neg**. The first step is to define the classes and attributes by preparing a file **labor-neg.names**, shown in Figure 1–1. The file specifies the classes (in this example, **good** and **bad**), then the name and description of each attribute. Some attributes, such as **duration** and **wage increase first year**, have numeric values and are described just as **continuous**; others, such as **cost of living adjustment** and **vacation**, have a small set of possible values that are listed explicitly in any order.

The next step is to provide information on the individual cases. This involves spelling out the attribute values for each case, separated by commas, and followed by the case's class. Three of the cases are

```
1, 2.0, ?, ?, none, 38, none, ?, ?, yes, 11, average, no, none, no, none, bad.
2, 4.0, 5.0, ?, tcf, 35, ?, 13, 5, ?, 15, generous, ?, ?, ?, ?, good.
2, 4.3, 4.4, ?, ?, 38, ?, ?, 4, ?, 12, generous, ?, full, ?, full, good.
```

with unknown or inapplicable attribute values indicated by question marks. The first case has duration 1 year, a 2% wage increase in the first year, inapplicable increases in the second and third years, no cost of living adjustment, and so on.

```
good, bad.

duration:                          continuous.
wage increase first year:          continuous.
wage increase second year:         continuous.
wage increase third year:          continuous.
cost of living adjustment:         none, tcf, tc.
working hours:                     continuous.
pension:                           none, ret_allw, empl_contr.
standby pay:                       continuous.
shift differential:                continuous.
education allowance:               yes, no.
statutory holidays:                continuous.
vacation:                          below average, average, generous.
longterm disability assistance:    yes, no.
contribution to dental plan:       none, half, full.
bereavement assistance:            yes, no.
contribution to health plan:       none, half, full.
```

Figure 1–1. File defining labor-neg classes and attributes

There are 57 cases like this in the dataset. A decision must now be made: Are all the cases to be provided to the system, or should some be reserved to test the accuracy of the resulting classifier? In this illustration, 40 of the cases have been selected randomly to form a *training set* from which the classifier will be constructed, reserving 17 cases as a *test set*. The training cases are placed in the file labor-neg.data, the test set in labor-neg.test.

1.1.1 Decision trees

We commence with the program C4.5 from which the whole system derives its name. This program generates a classifier in the form of a *decision tree*, a structure that is either

- a *leaf*, indicating a class, or

- a *decision node* that specifies some test to be carried out on a single attribute value, with one branch and subtree for each possible outcome of the test.

A decision tree can be used to classify a case by starting at the root of the tree and moving through it until a leaf is encountered. At each nonleaf decision node, the case's outcome for the test at the node is determined and attention shifts to the root of the subtree corresponding to this outcome. When this process finally (and inevitably) leads to a leaf, the class of the case is predicted to be that recorded at the leaf.

The UNIX command

c4.5 -f labor-neg -u

invokes C4.5, with the -f option giving the task name and the -u option indicating that the classifier is to be tested on unseen cases. The output of the decision-tree generator in this instance appears in Figure 1–2. After a preamble recording the options used and the number of training cases read, the output gives the decision tree generated from the cases. This tree can be paraphrased as

> *if wage increase first year* $\leq$ 2.5 *then*
>> *if working hours* $\leq$ 36 *then class good*
>> *else if working hours* > 36 *then*
>>> *if contribution to health plan is none then class bad*
>>> *else if contribution to health plan is half then class good*
>>> *else if contribution to health plan is full then class bad*
>> *else if wage increase first year* > 2.5 *then*
>>> *if statutory holidays* > 10 *then class good*
>>> *else if statutory holidays* $\leq$ 10 *then*
>>>> *if wage increase first year* $\leq$ 4 *then class bad*
>>>> *else if wage increase first year* > 4 *then class good*

(Since this structure may not look much like a tree, it is also shown in the more usual graph form in Figure 1–3.) The numbers in parentheses following each leaf will be discussed in detail in Chapter 4 but, as a rough guide, they indicate the number of training cases associated with each leaf and the number of them misclassified by the leaf.

The program also contains heuristic methods for simplifying decision trees, with the aim of producing more comprehensible structures without compromising accuracy on unseen cases. The next section of the output gives the simplified tree; in this example, the entire left-most branch has been replaced by a leaf.

After presenting the simplified tree, the output shows how both the original and simplified trees perform on the training set from which they were constructed. The original tree of 12 nodes (7 leaves and 5 decision nodes) misclassifies one of the 40 training cases. The simplified tree also misclassifies just 1 training case, but the program predicts that

C4.5 [release 5] decision tree generator   Fri Dec 6 13:33:54 1991

Options:
        File stem <labor-neg>
        Trees evaluated on unseen cases

Read 40 cases (16 attributes) from labor-neg.data

Decision Tree:

wage increase first year ≤ 2.5 :
    working hours ≤ 36 : good (2.0/1.0)
    working hours > 36 :
        contribution to health plan = none: bad (5.1)
        contribution to health plan = half: good (0.4/0.0)
        contribution to health plan = full: bad (3.8)
wage increase first year > 2.5 :
    statutory holidays > 10 : good (21.2)
    statutory holidays ≤ 10 :
        wage increase first year ≤ 4 : bad (4.5/0.5)
        wage increase first year > 4 : good (3.0)

Simplified Decision Tree:

wage increase first year ≤ 2.5 : bad (11.3/2.8)
wage increase first year > 2.5 :
    statutory holidays > 10 : good (21.2/1.3)
    statutory holidays ≤ 10 :
        wage increase first year ≤ 4 : bad (4.5/1.7)
        wage increase first year > 4 : good (3.0/1.1)

Tree saved

Evaluation on training data (40 items):

Before Pruning		After Pruning		
Size	Errors	Size	Errors	Estimate
12	1 (2.5%)	7	1 (2.5%)	(17.4%) <<

Evaluation on test data (17 items):

Before Pruning		After Pruning		
Size	Errors	Size	Errors	Estimate
12	3 (17.6%)	7	3 (17.6%)	(17.4%) <<

(a)	(b)	<–classified as
10	1	(a): class good
2	4	(b): class bad

Figure 1–2. Output of C4.5 on labor-neg data

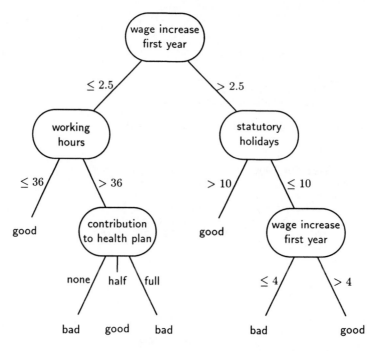

Figure 1–3. labor-neg decision tree in graph form

it will have a much higher error rate of 17.4% on unseen cases. (The cryptic "<<" mark focuses attention on the key results; it is also used when extracting these results from output files during cross-validation experiments, described in Chapter 9.)

All the above has been carried out without examining the test cases in file labor-neg.test. The file of 17 cases is read at this point and each case classified by the original and simplified trees. The original tree misclassifies 3 of the 17 unseen cases, as does the simplified tree. (The actual error rate on this test set is very close indeed to the predicted value of 17.4%, but the predictions are not usually as accurate as this!) The final part of the output is a *confusion matrix* for the simplified tree on the test cases, showing how the misclassifications were distributed. There are 11 test cases of class **good**, 10 of which are correctly classified as **good** while 1 is misclassified as **bad**. Similarly, 4 of the 6 test cases of class **bad** are correctly classified by the simplified tree and 2 are misclassified as **good**.

1.1.2 Production rules

The purpose of constructing classification models is not limited to the development of accurate predictors, although this is certainly a keyconcern.

Another principal aim is that the model should be intelligible to human beings.

In our small example, the simplified decision tree is so compact that it can be readily understood. When classification tasks become more intricate, however, even simplified trees can grow to unwieldy proportions. As an illustration, the simplified decision tree for a particular four-piece chess endgame has 158 nodes and would require more than three pages to reproduce here. This tree, although extremely accurate, is too complex to be understood by anyone! Donald Michie writes of a similar chess classification model:

> Recent results have shown that programs constructed by systems such as Quinlan's ID3 can be, in one sense, "super-programs" and at the same time quite incomprehensible to people.... The ID3-synthesised program clearly qualifies as a super-program. Further and perhaps alarmingly, however hard they try, chess experts cannot understand it. Even though it constitutes a complete and correct description, it does not qualify as a *concept expression*. [Michie 1986, p. 233]

Several ways of surmounting this comprehension barrier have been explored. Shapiro [1987], for instance, breaks down a single large tree into a hierarchy of small trees; his *structured induction* approach can lead to trees that, individually and collectively, are easier to understand. C4.5 uses a different means of achieving the same goal by reexpressing a classification model as *production rules*, a format that appears to be more intelligible than trees.

The programs use a simplified form of production rule $L \rightarrow R$ in which the left-hand side L is a conjunction of attribute-based tests and the right-hand side R is a class. One of the classes is also designated as a default. To classify a case using a production rule model, the ordered list of rules is examined to find the first whose left-hand side is satisfied by the case. The predicted class is then the one nominated by the right-hand side of this rule. If no rule's left-hand side is satisfied, the case is predicted to belong to the default class.

C4.5RULES examines the (original) decision tree produced by the C4.5 program and derives from it a set of production rules of the form above. In our example, the command

c4.5rules -f labor-neg -u

(where the options have the same meanings as previously), produces the output shown in Figure 1–4. After a similar preamble, the program

C4.5 [release 5] rule generator   Fri Dec 6 13:34:20 1991

  Options:
    File stem <labor-neg>
    Rulesets evaluated on unseen cases

Read 40 cases (16 attributes) from labor-neg

Processing tree 0

Final rules from tree 0:

Rule 5:
    wage increase first year > 2.5
    statutory holidays > 10
    -> class good [93.0%]

Rule 4:
    wage increase first year > 4
    -> class good [90.6%]

Rule 3:
    wage increase first year $\leq$ 4
    statutory holidays $\leq$ 10
    -> class bad [87.1%]

Rule 2:
    wage increase first year $\leq$ 2.5
    working hours > 36
    -> class bad [85.7%]

Default class: good

Evaluation on training data (40 items):

Rule	Size	Error	Used	Wrong		Advantage		
5	2	7.0%	19	0	(0.0%)	0 (0|0)		good
4	1	9.4%	3	0	(0.0%)	0 (0|0)		good
3	2	12.9%	10	0	(0.0%)	5 (5|0)		bad
2	2	14.3%	4	0	(0.0%)	4 (4|0)		bad

Tested 40, errors 0 (0.0%)   <<

    (a) (b) <-classified as

     26   (a): class good
        14 (b): class bad

Evaluation on test data (17 items):

Rule	Size	Error	Used	Wrong		Advantage		
5	2	7.0%	9	1	(11.1%)	0 (0|0)		good
4	1	9.4%	3	1	(33.3%)	0 (0|0)		good
3	2	12.9%	1	0	(0.0%)	1 (1|0)		bad
2	2	14.3%	3	0	(0.0%)	3 (3|0)		bad

Tested 17, errors 2 (11.8%)   <<

    (a) (b) <-classified as

     11   (a): class good
     2   4 (b): class bad

Figure 1–4. Result of postprocessing to rules

generates four rules from the 12-node decision tree of Figure 1–2. The
first of them,

    Rule 5:

        wage increase first year > 2.5
        statutory holidays > 10
        -> class good [93.0%]

can be broken down as follows. The rule number (here 5) is arbitrary,
being derived from the order of leaves in the original tree, and just serves
to identify the rule. The left-hand side contains two tests and a case
that satisfies both of them is classified as **good**, the class identified by
the right-hand side of the rule. The program also predicts that this
classification will be correct for 93% of unseen cases that satisfy this
rule's left-hand side. After listing three similar rules, the program selects
good as the default class for this domain.

The set of rules is now evaluated on the training cases from which
the tree was constructed, with the performance of each rule displayed
separately. The statistics for the first rule (Rule 5) are

Rule	Size	Error	Used	Wrong		Advantage		
5	2	7.0%	19	0	(0.0%)	0 (0|0)		good

This rule, with two tests in its left-hand side and a predicted error rate
of 7%, was used 19 times in classifying the training cases. All of the
cases that satisfied the rule's left-hand side did in fact belong to class
good, so there were no errors on this set. The section headed **Advantage**
shows what would happen if this rule were omitted from the list. Each
entry of the form a $(b|c)$ indicates that, if the rule were omitted, b cases
now classified correctly by this rule would be classified incorrectly, and
c cases now misclassified by this rule would be correctly classified by the
subsequent rules and the default; the net benefit of retaining the rule is
thus $a = b - c$. There are no training cases that satisfy the left-hand
side of both Rule 5 and another rule, so all cases that it covers would be
correctly classified by the default rule anyway. Nevertheless, the rule is
retained as it constitutes part of the description of class **good**.

Following the report on each rule there is a summary and a confusion
matrix showing where the misclassifications of the training cases occur.

The rules are derived from examination only of the decision tree and
the training cases from which it was developed. The production rule
classification model is now evaluated on the unseen test cases in file
labor-neg.test. The performance of each rule is summarized as above.
On the whole, the production rule classification model has two errors
on the test cases versus three for the decision tree classifier, and so it

performs slightly better on these cases. (The numbers are too small, however, to differentiate reliably between the models' performance.)

This small domain has illustrated two principal programs of the system, those that generate decision trees and production rules. The remaining programs allow interactive classification of cases using decision-tree or production rule classifiers developed by the programs and provide some help for conducting experiments.

1.2 Other kinds of classification models

We have now seen examples of decision trees and sets of production rules, the forms in which C4.5 expresses classification models. Before we head off into several chapters worth of detail on these formalisms and associated algorithms, it seems sensible to give at least a thumbnail sketch of some other approaches to learning classifiers from the same kind of data.

1.2.1 Instance-based classifiers

One way to classify a case is to recall a similar case whose class is known and to predict that the new case will have the same class. This philosophy underlies instance-based systems, which classify unseen cases by referring to similar remembered cases. An instance-based classifier thus circumvents the need for symbolic theories.

The central issues in instance-based systems are:

- What training cases should be remembered? If all cases are saved, the classifier can become unwieldy and slow. The ideal would be to retain prototypical cases that, together, summarize all the important information, an approach that can be observed in medical and legal textbooks. Aha, Kibler, and Albert [1991] describe strategies for deciding when a new case ought to be retained.

- How can the similarity of cases be measured? If all the attributes are continuous, we can compute the distance between two cases as the square root of the sum of squares of attribute differences, perhaps first scaling attributes so that their contributions are comparable. When some attributes are nonordinal, however, the interpretation of this distance becomes more problematic. Moreover, if there are many irrelevant attributes, two similar cases may appear to be quite dissimilar because they have different values of unimportant attributes.

Stanfill and Waltz [1986] have developed a context-sensitive method for scaling attributes so that distance measures of this kind are more robust.

- How should the new case be related to remembered cases? Two alternatives are to use the single most similar remembered case, or to use several similar cases with predictions weighted by their differing degrees of similarity.

1.2.2 Neural networks

Nilsson [1965] encapsulates early artificial intelligence work in pattern recognition in which Rosenblatt, Widrow, and others attempted to construct classifiers based on neuron-like threshold units. This approach petered out rather quickly because the assemblies of these units that could be effectively "trained" were suitable only for a limited range of learning tasks. Since the mid-1980s, there has been an explosive reawakening of interest in classifiers of this kind, triggered primarily by the development of new training methods [Hinton, 1986; McClelland and Rumelhart, 1988].

In its modern form, a neural network consists of units connected by links, as illustrated in Figure 1–5. Three kinds of units are distinguished: input units, such as A and B, that introduce information from the environment to the network; output units, such as E, that give the result; and all other units, such as C and D, that are "hidden" from the environment. Each link has an associated weight and some units have a bias that appears below the unit. To process a case, the input units are first assigned numbers between 0 and 1 representing the attribute values. Each unit's input I is determined as the sum of the weighted output of the units connected into it, plus the unit's bias, and the unit's output determined as

$$\frac{1}{e^{-I} + 1}$$

which ranges from 0 to 1 as I ranges from $-\infty$ to ∞. For example, if unit A had the value 0 while unit B had the value 1, the input to unit C would be $0 \times 5.7 + 1 \times 5.7 + (-2.2) = 3.5$ and its output would be 0.97. This output in turn becomes an input to unit E, with weight 6.5.

The values of the network weights and biases are learned through repeated examination of the training cases. The deviation of each output unit's output from its correct value for the case is *back-propagated* through the network; all relevant connection weights and unit biases are

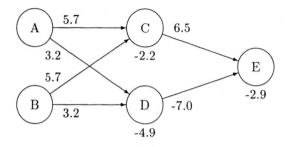

Figure 1–5. A neural network for XOR

adjusted, using gradient descent, to make the actual output closer to the target. Training continues until the weights and biases stabilize.

Networks can be used to predict real values, not just classes. In a classification context, however, the predicted class is encoded in some way. For instance, if the number of classes lies between 2^{b-1} and 2^b so that b bits are required to identify a class, each of b output units can be made to represent one bit of the class code. Alternatively, one output unit can be associated with every class. See Dieterich, Hild, and Bakiri [1989] for a discussion of the impact of such coding schemes.

1.2.3 Genetic algorithms

Yet another classification formalism is derived from an evolutionary model of learning [Holland, 1986]. A genetic classifier consists of a population of classification elements that compete to make the prediction. Elements that perform poorly are discarded while more successful elements proliferate, producing variants of themselves. On the Darwinian analogy of "survival of the fittest," the population should improve over time.

A simple form of genetic classifier for discrete attributes is described by Wilson [1987]. Each element consists of

- a *taxon* specifying, for each attribute, either a particular value that must be matched by a case, or a "don't care";

- a predicted class; and

- a strength.

Whenever a case is to be classified, each element is inspected to determine whether the case matches the element by having the required values for all attributes. One of the matched elements is then selected randomly, but with probability proportional to the element strengths, and the selected element determines the predicted class. During training, element strengths are adjusted to reward correct predictions and/or to penalize errors. The whole population periodically undergoes an upheaval in which weak elements die and new elements are created. This latter process occurs as a result of mutation, in which random changes are made to an element's taxon, and breeding, in which two elements combine to give a new element whose taxon is provided partly by each parent.

[Aside: The three formalisms above are all *distributed*—their classification performance does not depend critically on any small part of the model. Some remembered cases can be forgotten, some weights or links corrupted, or some elements discarded, without destroying the performance of the model. In contrast, symbolic models such as decision trees are much more susceptible to small alterations.]

1.2.4 Machine learning and statistics

For a statistician, the above description of instance-based classifiers would immediately call to mind the familiar *k-nearest-neighbor* method for classifying unseen cases. In fact, statistics has given rise to a multitude of classification methods, many of which are presented concisely in Hunt [1975]. How do these methods differ from those explored in machine learning?

In some cases there is no difference: CART [Breiman *et al.*, 1984], a very well-respected system for building decision trees, was developed by statisticians. As a general rule, however, statistical techniques tend to focus on tasks in which all the attributes have continuous or ordinal values. Many of them are also *parametric*, assuming some form for the model and then finding appropriate values for the model's parameters from the data. For instance, a linear classifier assumes that class can be expressed as a linear combination of the attribute values, then finds the particular linear combination that gives the best fit over the training cases. Maximum likelihood classifiers often assume that attribute values are normally distributed, then use the training data to determine the distribution means, variances, and covariances [Shepherd, Piper, and Rutovitz, 1988]. (Some authors have even grouped neural networks with parametric statistical procedures since training a network usually means finding appropriate values for predetermined weights and biases.)

This book hardly mentions classical statistical classification techniques. Anyone with an important classification problem would be well-advised to try common statistical methods in addition to those described here. Many authors have compared statistical and learning algorithms over collections of "typical" datasets; see, for example, Weiss and Kulikowski [1991].

1.3 What lies ahead

The next few chapters outline the algorithms that underpin C4.5, including some features that were not relevant to the simple example in Section 1.1. The algorithm descriptions are intended to give a broad-brush view of how the programs work, leaving detailed discussion to the code itself. This group of chapters ends with Chapter 9, which covers the various options that can be used to modify the behavior of the programs and provides a complete user manual for the system.

The last couple of chapters return to more general issues in the construction of classification models. Chapter 10 isolates some features of classification tasks themselves that might suggest whether logic-based models are likely to be appropriate. Finally, Chapter 11 discusses facilities that C4.5 *doesn't* have, but from which it might benefit.

More than half of the book is taken up by the source listing of the programs that make up the system. It may seem odd to print this sort of material but, following the lead of books like *Explorations in Parallel Distributed Processing* [McClelland and Rumelhart, 1988] and *Numerical Recipes in C* [Press, Flannery, Teukolsky, and Vetterling, 1988], I feel that the C-language code is the final specification of the system. There are many small heuristics and programming wrinkles that, individually, are too small to rate a mention in the overview chapters, yet, collectively, they contribute a great deal to the performance of the system. In other words, if you need to understand the system in depth, this must involve you in reading the code.

Unfortunately, the code itself has evolved like Topsy over a period of seven years or so. A complete rewrite would certainly shorten and clarify it, but at the cost of delaying publication by several months. As an intermediate step, the programs have been formatted to make them more readable and further assistance is provided in the form of brief notes on the data structures, descriptions of files, and an alphabetic index of routines.

## CHAPTER 2

Constructing Decision Trees

If any algorithm can be said to have fundamental importance in this software, it is the process of generating an initial decision tree from a set of training cases. The original idea goes back to the work of Hoveland and Hunt in the late 1950s, culminating in the pioneering book *Experiments in Induction* [Hunt, Marin, and Stone, 1966] that describes extensive experiments with several implementations of *concept learning systems* (CLS). Other research workers have arrived independently at the same, or similar, methods; in particular, Friedman [1977] lays the foundations for the famous CART system [Breiman *et al.*, 1984]. This same algorithm also underpins ID3 [Quinlan, 1979, 1983a, 1986b], PLS1 [Rendell, 1983], ASSISTANT 86 [Cestnik, Kononenko, and Bratko, 1987], and their commercial counterparts such as ExTran.

2.1 Divide and conquer

The skeleton of Hunt's method for constructing a decision tree from a set T of training cases is elegantly simple. Let the classes be denoted $\{C_1, C_2, \ldots, C_k\}$. There are three possibilities:

- T contains one or more cases, all belonging to a single class C_j:
  The decision tree for T is a leaf identifying class C_j.

- T contains no cases:
  The decision tree is again a leaf, but the class to be associated with the leaf must be determined from information other than T. For example, the leaf might be chosen in accordance with some background knowledge of the domain, such as the overall majority class. C4.5 uses the most frequent class at the parent of this node.

- T contains cases that belong to a mixture of classes:
  In this situation, the idea is to refine T into subsets of cases that are, or seem to be heading towards, single-class collections of cases. A *test T10* is chosen, based on a single attribute, that has one or more mutually exclusive outcomes $\{O_1, O_2, \ldots, O_n\}$. T is partitioned into subsets $T_1, T_2, \ldots, T_n$, where T_i contains all the cases in T that have

outcome O_i of the chosen test. The decision tree for T consists of a decision node identifying the test, and one branch for each possible outcome. The same tree-building machinery is applied recursively to each subset of training cases, so that the ith branch leads to the decision tree constructed from the subset T_i of training cases.

2.1.1 An illustration

The successive division of the set of training cases proceeds until all the subsets consist of cases belonging to a single class. My favorite illustration of the process involves the small training set of Figure 2–1 in which there are four attributes and two classes. The cases have been grouped on the first attribute outlook to simplify the following discussion.

Outlook	Temp ($^\circ F$)	Humidity (%)	Windy?	Class
sunny	75	70	true	Play
sunny	80	90	true	Don't Play
sunny	85	85	false	Don't Play
sunny	72	95	false	Don't Play
sunny	69	70	false	Play
overcast	72	90	true	Play
overcast	83	78	false	Play
overcast	64	65	true	Play
overcast	81	75	false	Play
rain	71	80	true	Don't Play
rain	65	70	true	Don't Play
rain	75	80	false	Play
rain	68	80	false	Play
rain	70	96	false	Play

Figure 2–1. A small training set

Since these cases do not all belong to the same class, the divide-and-conquer algorithm attempts to split them into subsets. We have not yet discussed the way a test is chosen but, for this example, suppose that the test is outlook with three outcomes, outlook = sunny, outlook = overcast and outlook = rain. The middle group contains only cases of class Play but the first and third subsets still have mixed classes. If the first subset were further divided by a test on humidity, with outcomes humidity $\leq$ 75 and humidity $>$ 75, and the third subset by a test on windy, with outcomes windy = true and windy = false, each of the subsets would now

Partition of cases:

outlook = sunny:
humidity ≤ 75:

Outlook	Temp (°F)	Humidity (%)	Windy?	Decision
sunny	75	70	true	Play
sunny	69	70	false	Play

humidity > 75:

Outlook	Temp (°F)	Humidity (%)	Windy?	Decision
sunny	80	90	true	Don't Play
sunny	85	85	false	Don't Play
sunny	72	95	false	Don't Play

outlook = overcast:

Outlook	Temp (°F)	Humidity (%)	Windy?	Decision
overcast	72	90	true	Play
overcast	83	78	false	Play
overcast	64	65	true	Play
overcast	81	75	false	Play

outlook = rain:
windy = true:

Outlook	Temp (°F)	Humidity (%)	Windy?	Decision
rain	71	80	true	Don't Play
rain	65	70	true	Don't Play

windy = false:

Outlook	Temp (°F)	Humidity (%)	Windy?	Decision
rain	75	80	false	Play
rain	68	80	false	Play
rain	70	96	false	Play

Corresponding decision tree:

outlook = sunny:
humidity ≤ 75: Play
humidity > 75: Don't Play
outlook = overcast: Play
outlook = rain:
windy = true: Don't Play
windy = false: Play

Figure 2–2. Final partition of cases and corresponding decision tree

contain cases from a single class. The final divisions of the subsets and the corresponding decision tree are shown in Figure 2–2.

2.2 Evaluating tests

This toy example depends a great deal on the choice of appropriate tests, which we have apparently extracted from thin air. *Any* test that divides T in a nontrivial way, so that at least two of the subsets $\{T_i\}$ are not empty, will eventually result in a partition into single-class subsets, even if all or most of them contain a single training case. However, the tree-building process is not intended merely to find any such partition, but to build a tree that reveals the structure of the domain and so has predictive power. For that, we need a significant number of cases at each leaf or, to put it another way, the partition must have as few blocks as possible. Ideally, we would like to choose a test at each stage so that the final tree is small.

Since we are looking for a compact decision tree that is consistent with the training set, why not explore all possible trees and select the simplest? Unfortunately, the problem of finding the smallest decision tree consistent with a training set is NP-complete [Hyafil and Rivest, 1976]. A staggering number of trees would have to be examined—for example, there are more than 4×10^6 decision trees that are consistent with the tiny training set of Figure 2–1!

Most decision tree construction methods, including the one described in the previous section, are nonbacktracking, *greedy* algorithms. Once a test has been selected to partition the current set of training cases, usually on the basis of maximizing some local measure of progress, the choice is cast in concrete and the consequences of alternative choices are not explored. This is surely another inducement to try to make the choice well.

2.2.1 Gain criterion

Suppose again we have a possible test with n outcomes that partitions the set T of training cases into subsets $T_1, T_2, \ldots, T_n$. If this test is to be evaluated without exploring subsequent divisions of the T_i's, the only information available for guidance is the distribution of classes in T and its subsets. Since we will frequently need to refer to class distributions in this section, some notation will help. If S is any set of cases, let *freq*(C_i, S) stand for the number of cases in S that belong to class C_i. We will also use the standard notation in which $\mid S \mid$ denotes the number of cases in set S.

Hunt's original CLS experiments considered several rubrics under which a test might be assessed. Most of these were based on class frequency criteria. For example, CLS1 was restricted to problems with two classes, positive and negative, and preferred tests with an outcome whose associated case subset contained

- only positive cases; or, failing that,

- only negative cases; or, failing these,

- the largest number of positive cases.

Even though his programs used simple criteria of this kind, Hunt suggested that an approach based on information theory might have advantages [Hunt *et al.*, 1966, p. 95]. When I was building the forerunner of ID3, I had forgotten this suggestion until the possibility of using information-based methods was raised independently by Peter Gacs.

The original ID3 used a criterion called *gain*, defined below. The information theory that underpins this criterion can be given in one statement: The information conveyed by a message depends on its probability and can be measured in bits as minus the logarithm to base 2 of that probability. So, for example, if there are eight equally probable messages, the information conveyed by any one of them is $-\log_2(1/8)$ or 3 bits.

Imagine selecting one case at random from a set S of cases and announcing that it belongs to some class C_j. This message has probability

$$\frac{\mathit{freq}(C_j, S)}{|S|}$$

and so the information it conveys is

$$-\log_2\left(\frac{\mathit{freq}(C_j, S)}{|S|}\right)\ \text{bits}.$$

To find the expected information from such a message pertaining to class membership, we sum over the classes in proportion to their frequencies in S, giving

$$\mathit{info}(S) = -\sum_{j=1}^{k} \frac{\mathit{freq}(C_j, S)}{|S|} \times \log_2\left(\frac{\mathit{freq}(C_j, S)}{|S|}\right)\ \text{bits}.$$

When applied to the set of training cases, $\mathit{info}(T)$ measures the average amount of information needed to identify the class of a case in T. (This quantity is also known as the *entropy* of the set S.)

Now consider a similar measurement after T has been partitioned in accordance with the n outcomes of a test X. The expected information requirement can be found as the weighted sum over the subsets, as

$$info_X(T) = \sum_{i=1}^{n} \frac{|T_i|}{|T|} \times info(T_i).$$

The quantity

$$gain(X) = info(T) - info_X(T)$$

measures the information that is gained by partitioning T in accordance with the test X. The *gain criterion*, then, selects a test to maximize this information gain (which is also known as the *mutual information* between the test X and the class).

As a concrete illustration, consider again the training set of Figure 2–1. There are two classes, nine cases belonging to Play and five to Don't Play, so

$$info(T) = -9/14 \times \log_2(9/14) - 5/14 \times \log_2(5/14) = 0.940 \text{ bits.}$$

(Remember, this represents the average information needed to identify the class of a case in T.) After using outlook to divide T into three subsets, the result is given by

$$
\begin{aligned}
info_X(T) &= 5/14 \times (-2/5 \times \log_2(2/5) - 3/5 \times \log_2(3/5)) \\
&\quad + 4/14 \times (-4/4 \times \log_2(4/4) - 0/4 \times \log_2(0/4)) \\
&\quad + 5/14 \times (-3/5 \times \log_2(3/5) - 2/5 \times \log_2(2/5)) \\
&= 0.694 \text{ bits.}
\end{aligned}
$$

The information gained by this test is therefore $0.940 - 0.694 = 0.246$ bits. Now suppose that, instead of dividing T on the attribute outlook, we had partitioned it on the attribute windy. This would have given two subsets, one with three Play and three Don't Play cases, the other with six Play and two Don't Play cases. The similar computation is

$$
\begin{aligned}
info_X(T) &= 6/14 \times (-3/6 \times \log_2(3/6) - 3/6 \times \log_2(3/6)) \\
&\quad + 8/14 \times (-6/8 \times \log_2(6/8) - 2/8 \times \log_2(2/8)) \\
&= 0.892 \text{ bits}
\end{aligned}
$$

for a gain of 0.048 bits, which is less than the gain resulting from the previous test. The gain criterion would then prefer the test on outlook over the latter test on windy.

2.2.2 Gain ratio criterion

For some years the selection of a test in ID3 was made on the basis of the gain criterion. Although it gave quite good results, this criterion has a serious deficiency—it has a strong bias in favor of tests with many outcomes. We can see this by considering a hypothetical medical diagnosis task in which one of the attributes contains a patient identification. Since every such identification is intended to be unique, partitioning any set of training cases on the values of this attribute will lead to a large number of subsets, each containing just one case. Since all of these one-case subsets necessarily contain cases of a single class, $info_X(T) = 0$, so information gain from using this attribute to partition the set of training cases is maximal. From the point of view of prediction, however, such a division is quite useless.

The bias inherent in the gain criterion can be rectified by a kind of normalization in which the apparent gain attributable to tests with many outcomes is adjusted. Consider the information content of a message pertaining to a case that indicates not the class to which the case belongs, but the outcome of the test. By analogy with the definition of $info(S)$, we have

$$split\ info(X) = -\sum_{i=1}^{n} \frac{|T_i|}{|T|} \times \log_2 \left(\frac{|T_i|}{|T|} \right)$$

This represents the potential information generated by dividing T into n subsets, whereas the information gain measures the information relevant to classification that arises from the same division. Then,

$$gain\ ratio(X) = gain(X)/split\ info(X)$$

expresses the proportion of information generated by the split that is useful, i.e., that appears helpful for classification. If the split is near-trivial, split information will be small and this ratio will be unstable. To avoid this, the *gain ratio* criterion selects a test to maximize the ratio above, subject to the constraint that the information gain must be large—at least as great as the average gain over all tests examined.

It is apparent that the patient identification attribute will not be ranked highly by this criterion. If there are k classes, as before, the numerator (information gain) is at most $\log_2(k)$. The denominator, on the other hand, is $\log_2(n)$ where n is the number of training cases, since every case has a unique outcome. It seems reasonable to presume that the number of training cases is much larger than the number of classes, so the ratio would have a small value.

To continue the previous illustration, the test on outlook produces three subsets containing five, four, and five cases respectively. The split information is calculated as

$$-5/14 \times \log_2(5/14) - 4/14 \times \log_2(4/14) - 5/14 \times \log_2(5/14)$$

or 1.577 bits. For this test, whose gain is 0.246 (as before), the gain ratio is 0.246 / 1.577 = 0.156.

In my experience, the gain ratio criterion is robust and typically gives a consistently better choice of test than the gain criterion [Quinlan, 1988b]. It even appears advantageous when all tests are binary but differ in the proportions of cases associated with the two outcomes. However, Mingers [1989] compares several test selection criteria and, while he finds that gain ratio leads to smaller trees, expresses reservations about its tendency to favor unbalanced splits in which one subset T_i is much smaller than the others.

2.3 Possible tests considered

A criterion for evaluating tests provides a mechanism for ranking a set of proposed tests so that the most favorable-seeming test can be chosen. This presumes, of course, that there is some way of generating possible tests.

Most classifier-building systems define a form for possible tests and then examine all tests of this form. Conventionally, a test involves just one attribute, because this makes the tree easier to understand and sidesteps the combinatorial explosion that results if multiple attributes can appear in a single test.[3]

C4.5 contains mechanisms for proposing three types of tests:

- The "standard" test on a discrete attribute, with one outcome and branch for each possible value of that attribute.

- A more complex test, based on a discrete attribute, in which the possible values are allocated to a variable number of groups with one outcome for each group rather than each value. Tests of this form, discussed in Chapter 7, must be invoked by an option.

- If attribute A has continuous numeric values, a binary test with outcomes $A \le Z$ and $A > Z$, based on comparing the value of A against a threshold value Z.

---

3. The use of more complex tests is discussed in Chapter 10; see Breiman *et al.* [1984] and Utgoff and Brodley [1991] for illustrations.

All these tests are evaluated in the same way, looking at the gain ratio (or, optionally, the gain) arising from the division of the training cases that they produce. It has also proved useful to introduce a further constraint: For any division, at least two of the subsets T_i must contain a reasonable number of cases. This restriction, which avoids near-trivial splits of the training cases, comes into play only when the set T is small. (The default minimum number of cases is 2, but this can be changed via an option as described later.)

2.4 Tests on continuous attributes

It might seem that tests on continuous attributes would be difficult to formulate, since they contain arbitrary thresholds. This is not so: The method for finding such tests can be described very concisely. This algorithm for finding appropriate thresholds against which to compare the values of continuous attributes was drawn to my attention by Paterson and Niblett [1982], although the same strategy appears also in Breiman *et al.* [1984].

The training cases T are first sorted on the values of the attribute A being considered. There are only a finite number of these values, so let us denote them in order as $\{v_1, v_2, \ldots, v_m\}$. Any threshold value lying between v_i and v_{i+1} will have the same effect of dividing the cases into those whose value of the attribute A lies in $\{v_1, v_2, \ldots, v_i\}$ and those whose value is in $\{v_{i+1}, v_{i+2}, \ldots, v_m\}$. There are thus only $m - 1$ possible splits on A, all of which are examined. (It might seem expensive to examine all $m - 1$ such thresholds, but, when the cases have been sorted as above, this can be carried out in one pass, updating the class distributions to the left and right of the threshold on the fly.)

It is usual to choose the midpoint of each interval as the representative threshold, the ith such being

$$\frac{v_i + v_{i+1}}{2}.$$

C4.5 differs in choosing the largest value of A in the entire training set that does not exceed the midpoint above, rather than the midpoint itself, as the threshold; this ensures that all threshold values appearing in trees and/or rules actually occur in the data.

To illustrate this threshold-finding process, we return briefly to the labor negotiation data discussed in Chapter 1 and the attribute **wage increase first year**. There are 15 distinct values of this attribute in the

40 training cases, with 14 associated thresholds, but the largest value is excluded because it splits off only 1 training case. Figure 2–3 shows the values of gain ratio and gain resulting from divisions based on the 13 possible thresholds. Both gain and gain ratio happen to peak at the same threshold in this instance, but the peak for gain ratio is more clearly defined. As the figure shows, the best threshold for the wage increase first year gives a division into values up to 2.5 on the one hand, and higher values on the other; this division gives a greater gain ratio value than any other test and so becomes the root of the decision tree.

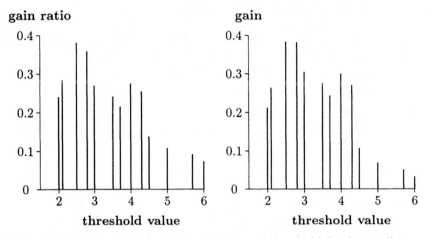

Figure 2–3. Gain ratio and gain as a function of threshold for the attribute wage increase first year, labor negotiation data.

One point should be made here: Whereas most of the operations required to construct a given decision tree grow linearly with the number of training cases, sorting d continuous values grows as $d \times \log(d)$. The time required to construct a decision tree from a large training set can be dominated by the sorting of continuous attributes as a prelude to examining possible thresholds on them. Several authors, notably Catlett [1991b], have discussed mechanisms for ameliorating this computational impost.

## CHAPTER 3

Unknown Attribute Values

The basic algorithm for constructing decision trees, described in the previous chapter, contains a hidden assumption: that the outcome of a test for any case can be determined. This assumption comes into play when partitioning a set T of training cases into subsets $\{T_i\}$ associated with the outcomes of the selected test, and in a similar implicit partitioning during the evaluation of possible tests. Further, classifying a case using a decision tree, as outlined in Section 1.1, requires taking the branch appropriate to the case at each decision node. Since every test is based on a single attribute, the outcome of a test cannot be determined unless the value of that attribute is known.

It is an unfortunate fact of life that data often has missing attribute values. This might occur because the value is not relevant to a particular case, was not recorded when the data was collected, or could not be deciphered by the person responsible for putting the data into machine-readable form. For example, I have carried out numerous experiments with thyroid assay data from the Garvan Institute of Medical Research. Each case concerns one patient referral and includes information provided by the referring physician as well as the results of requested laboratory measurements. In one batch of three thousand cases, many cases failed to specify the age and/or sex of the patient, even though this information is usually relevant to interpretation; this is presumably an example of incomplete data collection. More than 30% of the cases were missing some information, usually assays that were not requested and so were probably irrelevant to interpretation. Such incompleteness is typical of real-world data.

We are then left with a choice: Either a significant proportion of available data must be discarded and some test cases pronounced unclassifiable, or the algorithms must be amended to cope with missing attribute values. In most situations the former course is unacceptable as it weakens the ability to find patterns. To address the second alternative, three questions must be answered:

- Selection of a test on which to partition the training set is made on the basis of heuristic criteria such as *gain* or *gain ratio*. If two tests use attributes with different numbers of unknown values, how should this be taken into account when weighing their relative desirability?

- Once a test has been selected, training cases with unknown values of the relevant attribute cannot be associated with a particular outcome of the test, and so cannot be assigned to a particular subset T_i. How should these cases be treated in the partitioning?

- When the decision tree is used to classify an unseen case, how should the system proceed if the case has an unknown value for the attribute tested in the current decision node?

Several authors have developed different answers to these questions, usually based either on filling in missing attribute values (with the most probable value or a value determined by exploiting interrelationships among the values of different attributes), or on looking at the probability distribution of values of attributes. More common approaches are compared empirically in Quinlan [1989], leading to the general conclusion that some approaches are clearly inferior, but no one approach is uniformly superior. The treatment of missing attribute values in C4.5 that is described below has proved satisfactory for the sort of data that I use, but several alternative schemes employed by other systems are probably just as good.

3.1 Adapting the previous algorithms

3.1.1 Evaluating tests

Modification of the criteria for choosing tests is relatively straightforward because they are derived from the notion of information. Recall that the *gain* of a test measures the information about class membership that can be expected from partitioning the training cases, calculated by subtracting the expected information required to ascertain the class of a case after the partition from the same quantity before partition. It is evident that a test can provide no information about the class membership of cases whose value of the test attribute is unknown.

As in Section 2.2, let T be a training set and X a test based on some attribute A, and suppose that the value of A is known in fraction F of the cases in T. Let $info(T)$ and $info_X(T)$ be calculated as before, except that only cases with known values of A are taken into account. The definition of *gain* can reasonably be amended to

$$
\begin{aligned}
gain(X) \;\; &= \;\; \text{probability } A \text{ is known} \times (info(T) - info_X(T)) \\
&\quad + \text{probability } A \text{ is not known} \times 0 \\
&= \;\; F \times (info(T) - info_X(T))
\end{aligned}
$$

or, in other words, the apparent gain from looking at cases with known values of the relevant attribute, multiplied by the fraction of such cases in the training set.

Similarly, the definition of *split info*(X) can be altered by regarding the cases with unknown values as an additional group. If a test has n outcomes, its split information is computed as if the test divided the cases into $n + 1$ subsets.

3.1.2 Partitioning the training set

A test can be selected from the possible tests as before, using the modified definitions of *gain* and *split info*. If the test X with outcomes $O_1, O_2, \ldots, O_n$ that is finally chosen has unknown outcomes on some of the training cases, the concept of partitioning must be generalized.

In this situation, C4.5 follows ASSISTANT [Cestnik *et al.*, 1987] in adopting a probabilistic approach. When a case from T with known outcome O_i is assigned to subset T_i, this indicates that the probability of that case belonging in subset T_i is 1 and in all other subsets is 0. When the outcome is not known, however, only a weaker probabilistic statement can be made. We therefore associate with each case in each subset T_i a *weight* representing the probability that the case belongs to each subset. If the case has a known outcome, this weight is 1; if the case has an unknown outcome, the weight is just the probability of outcome O_i at this point. Each subset T_i is now a collection of possibly fractional cases so that $|T_i|$ should be reinterpreted as the sum of the fractional weights of the cases in the set.

Of course, the training cases in T might have had nonunit weights to start with, since T might be one subset of an earlier partition. So, in general, a case from T with weight w whose outcome is not known is assigned to each subset T_i with weight

$$
w \times \text{probability of outcome } O_i.
$$

The latter probability is estimated as the sum of the weights of cases in T known to have outcome O_i, divided by the sum of the weights of the cases in T with known outcomes on this test.

3.1.3 Classifying an unseen case

A similar approach is taken when the decision tree is used to classify a case. If a decision node is encountered at which the relevant attribute value is unknown, so that the outcome of the test cannot be determined, the system explores all possible outcomes and combines the resulting classifications arithmetically. Since there can now be multiple paths from the root of a tree or subtree to the leaves, a "classification" is a class distribution rather than a single class. When the total class distribution for the unseen case has been established in this way, the class with the highest probability is assigned as "the" predicted class.

3.2 Play/Don't Play example again

To clarify the effect of these modifications, we return to the training set of Figure 2–1 and suppose that the value of the attribute outlook for the case

outlook = overcast, temperature = 72°, humidity = 90%, windy = true

were unknown (denoted by "?") rather than overcast. When we restrict our attention to the 13 remaining cases whose value for outlook is known, we get the following frequencies:

	Play	Don't Play	Total
outlook = sunny	2	3	5
overcast	3	0	3
rain	3	2	5
Total	8	5	13

Using the corresponding relative frequencies to compute the quantities relevant to the assessment of a test on outlook, we have

$$
\begin{aligned}
info(T) &= -8/13 \times \log_2(8/13) - 5/13 \times \log_2(5/13) \\
&= 0.961 \text{ bits} \\
info_X(T) &= 5/13 \times (-2/5 \times \log_2(2/5) - 3/5 \times \log_2(3/5)) \\
&\quad + 3/13 \times (-3/3 \times \log_2(3/3) - 0/3 \times \log_2(0/3)) \\
&\quad + 5/13 \times (-3/5 \times \log_2(3/5) - 2/5 \times \log_2(2/5)) \\
&= 0.747 \text{ bits} \\
gain(X) &= 13/14 \times (0.961 - 0.747) \\
&= 0.199 \text{ bits}.
\end{aligned}
$$

The gain for this test is slightly lower than the previous value of 0.246 bits. The split information, however, is still determined from the entire training set and is larger, since there is an extra category for unknown outcome that has to be taken into account:

$$-5/14 \times \log_2(5/14) \quad \text{(for sunny)}$$
$$-3/14 \times \log_2(3/14) \quad \text{(for overcast)}$$
$$-5/14 \times \log_2(5/14) \quad \text{(for rain)}$$
$$-1/14 \times \log_2(1/14) \quad \text{(for ``?'')}$$

which comes to 1.809 bits instead of the previous 1.577 bits. The gain ratio value thus drops from 0.156 to 0.110.

When the 14 training cases are partitioned by this test, the 13 cases for which the value of outlook are known present no problem. The remaining case is assigned to *all* blocks of the partition, corresponding to outlooks sunny, overcast and rain, with weights 5/13, 3/13, and 5/13 respectively.

We now focus on the first such subset of cases corresponding to outlook = sunny, namely

Outlook	Temp ($°F$)	Humidity (%)	Windy?	Decision	Weight
sunny	75	70	true	Play	1
sunny	80	90	true	Don't Play	1
sunny	85	85	false	Don't Play	1
sunny	72	95	false	Don't Play	1
sunny	69	70	false	Play	1
?	72	90	true	Play	5/13

If this subset is partitioned further by the same test on humidity as in Figure 2–2, the class distributions in the subsets are

$$\text{humidity} \leq 75 \quad \text{2 class Play,} \quad \text{0 class Don't Play}$$
$$\text{humidity} > 75 \quad \text{5/13 class Play,} \quad \text{3 class Don't Play}$$

The first consists of cases of the single class Play. The second still contains cases from both classes but the program can find no test that sensibly improves on the situation. Similarly, the subset corresponding to outlook = rain cannot be partitioned into single-class subsets. The decision tree has much the same structure as before,

```
outlook = sunny:
|     humidity ≤ 75: Play (2.0)
|     humidity > 75: Don't Play (3.4/0.4)
outlook = overcast: Play (3.2)
outlook = rain:
|     windy = true: Don't Play (2.4/0.4)
|     windy = false: Play (3.0)
```

but the numbers at the leaves, of the form (N) or (N/E), now become important. N is the sum of the fractional cases that reach the leaf; in the second form, E is the number of cases that belong to classes other than the nominated class.[4] So

$$\text{Don't Play (3.4/0.4)}$$

means that 3.4 (fractional) training cases reached this leaf, of which 0.4 did not belong to class Don't Play.

We now investigate what happens when this tree is used to classify another case with sunny outlook, temperature 70°, unknown humidity, and windy false. The outlook value ensures this case moves to the first subtree, but it is not possible now to determine whether humidity ≤ 75. However, we can see that

- if the humidity were less than or equal to 75%, the case would be classified as Play, and

- if the humidity were greater than 75%, the case would be classified as Don't Play with probability 3/3.4 (88%) and Play with probability 0.4/3.4 (12%).

At the time the tree was constructed, the partitions for these outcomes contained 2.0 and 3.4 cases respectively. The conditional conclusions are combined with the same relative weights, 2.0/5.4 and 3.4/5.4, so that the final class distribution for this case is

Play: $2.0/5.4 \times 100\% + 3.4/5.4 \times 12\% = 44\%$
Don't Play: $3.4/5.4 \times 88\% = 56\%$

3.3 Recapitulation

It is possible to get enmeshed in details of calculations like these, thereby losing sight of the fundamental simplicity of the approach. C4.5 assumes

---

4. E has a slightly different meaning for a pruned tree, as explained in the next chapter.

that unknown test outcomes are distributed probabilistically according to the relative frequency of known outcomes. A (possibly fractional) case with an unknown test outcome is divided into fragments whose weights are proportional to these relative frequencies, with the result that a single case can follow multiple paths in the tree. This applies equally when the training cases are divided during the construction of a tree and when the tree is used to classify cases.

It is interesting to compare this approach with that taken in CART. Whenever a test is chosen, CART finds another test called a *surrogate split* whose partition of the training cases is most similar to that of the original test. If a case's outcome of the original test is not known, the outcome of the surrogate is used instead; if this is unknown too, the next best surrogate is invoked, and so on. This method does not call for individual cases to be fragmented and so is more efficient. It depends, however, on being able to find suitably accurate surrogate splits, which seems unlikely in domains where tests have different numbers of outcomes and where there is little correlation between attributes.

CHAPTER 4

Pruning Decision Trees

The recursive partitioning method of constructing decision trees described in Chapter 2 will continue to subdivide the set of training cases until each subset in the partition contains cases of a single class, or until no test offers any improvement. The result is often a very complex tree that "overfits the data" by inferring more structure than is justified by the training cases.

This effect is readily seen in the extreme example of random data in which the class of each case is quite unrelated to its attribute values. I constructed an artificial dataset of this kind with ten attributes, each of which took the value 0 or 1 with equal probability. The class was also binary, yes with probability 0.25 and no with probability 0.75. One thousand randomly generated cases were split into a training set of 500 and a test set of 500. From this data, C4.5's initial tree-building routine produces a nonsensical tree of 119 nodes that has an error rate of more than 35% on the test cases.

This small example illustrates the twin perils that can come from too gullible acceptance of the initial tree: It is often extremely complex, and can actually have a higher error rate than a simpler tree. For the random data above, a tree consisting of just the leaf no would have an expected error rate of 25% on unseen cases, yet the elaborate tree is noticeably less accurate. While the complexity comes as no surprise, the increased error attributable to overfitting is not intuitively obvious. To explain this, suppose we have a two-class task in which a case's class is inherently indeterminate, with proportion $p \geq 0.5$ of the cases belonging to the majority class (here no). If a classifier assigns all such cases to this majority class, its expected error rate is clearly $1 - p$. If, on the other hand, the classifier assigns a case to the majority class with probability p and to the other class with probability $1 - p$, its expected error rate is the sum of

- the probability that a case belonging to the majority class is assigned to the other class, $p \times (1 - p)$, and

- the probability that a case belonging to the other class is assigned to the majority class, $(1 - p) \times p$

35

which comes to $2 \times p \times (1 - p)$. Since p is at least 0.5, this is generally greater than $1 - p$, so the second classifier will have a higher error rate. Now, the complex decision tree bears a close resemblance to this second type of classifier. The tests are unrelated to class so, like a symbolic pachinko machine, the tree sends each case randomly to one of the leaves. We would expect the leaves themselves to be distributed in proportion to the class frequencies in the training set. Consequently, the tree's expected error rate for the random data above is $2 \times 0.25 \times 0.75$ or 37.5%, quite close to the observed value.

It may seem that this discussion of random classifiers and indeterminate classes is a far cry from real-world induction tasks. This is not so: Tasks are often at least partly indeterminate because the attributes do not capture all information relevant to classification. Again, when the training set has been split many times so that tests are selected from examination of a small subset of cases, several tests may appear equally promising and choosing a particular one of them has elements of randomness. In my experience, almost all decision trees can benefit from simplification.

A decision tree is not usually simplified by deleting the whole tree in favor of a leaf, as was done in the random data example. Instead, the idea is to remove parts of the tree that do not contribute to classification accuracy on unseen cases, producing something less complex and thus more comprehensible.

4.1 When to simplify?

There are basically two ways in which the recursive partitioning method can be modified to produce simpler trees: deciding not to divide a set of training cases any further, or removing retrospectively some of the structure built up by recursive partitioning.

The former approach, sometimes called *stopping* or *prepruning*, has the attraction that time is not wasted assembling structure that is not used in the final simplified tree. The typical approach is to look at the best way of splitting a subset and to assess the split from the point of view of statistical significance, information gain, error reduction, or whatever. If this assessment falls below some threshold, the division is rejected and the tree for the subset is just the most appropriate leaf. However, as Breiman *et al.* point out, such stopping rules are not easy to get right—too high a threshold can terminate division before the benefits of subsequent splits become evident, while too low a value results in little simplification.

At one stage, I used a stopping criterion based on the χ^2 test of statistical significance [Quinlan, 1986a]. The results were quite satisfactory in some domains but were uneven, so I abandoned this approach; C4.5, like CART, now follows the second path. The divide-and-conquer process is given free rein and the overfitted tree that it produces is then pruned. The additional computation invested in building parts of the tree that are subsequently discarded can be substantial, but this cost is offset against benefits due to a more thorough exploration of possible partitions. Growing and pruning trees is slower but more reliable.

Pruning a decision tree will almost invariably cause it to misclassify more of the training cases. Consequently, the leaves of the pruned tree will not necessarily contain training cases from a single class, a phenomenon we have encountered in the previous chapter. Instead of a class associated with a leaf, there will again be a *class distribution* specifying, for each class, the probability that a training case at the leaf belongs to that class. This modification can slightly alter the determination of the most probable class for an unseen case. The fact that there is a distribution rather than a single class becomes important when we discuss the certainty of prediction (Chapter 8).

4.2 Error-based pruning

Decision trees are usually simplified by discarding one or more subtrees and replacing them with leaves; as when building trees, the class associated with a leaf is found by examining the training cases covered by the leaf and choosing the most frequent class. In addition, C4.5 allows replacement of a subtree by one of its branches. Both operations are illustrated in Figure 4–1 that shows a decision tree derived from congressional voting data[5] before and after pruning. (For the unpruned tree, recall that the (N) or (N/E) appearing after a leaf indicates that the leaf covers N training cases, E erroneously; similar numbers for the pruned tree are explained below.) The subtree

---

5. This dataset, collected by Jeff Schlimmer, records the votes of all United States congressmen on 16 key issues selected by the *Congressional Quarterly Almanac* for the second session of 1984. It is available in the University of California, Irvine data library.

Original decision tree:

```
physician fee freeze = n:
|   adoption of the budget resolution = y: democrat (151)
|   adoption of the budget resolution = u: democrat (1)
|   adoption of the budget resolution = n:
|   |   education spending = n: democrat (6)
|   |   education spending = y: democrat (9)
|   |   education spending = u: republican (1)
physician fee freeze = y:
|   synfuels corporation cutback = n: republican (97/3)
|   synfuels corporation cutback = u: republican (4)
|   synfuels corporation cutback = y:
|   |   duty free exports = y: democrat (2)
|   |   duty free exports = u: republican (1)
|   |   duty free exports = n:
|   |   |   education spending = n: democrat (5/2)
|   |   |   education spending = y: republican (13/2)
|   |   |   education spending = u: democrat (1)
physician fee freeze = u:
|   water project cost sharing = n: democrat (0)
|   water project cost sharing = y: democrat (4)
|   water project cost sharing = u:
|   |   mx missile = n: republican (0)
|   |   mx missile = y: democrat (3/1)
|   |   mx missile = u: republican (2)
```

After pruning:

```
physician fee freeze = n: democrat (168/2.6)
physician fee freeze = y: republican (123/13.9)
physician fee freeze = u:
|   mx missile = n: democrat (3/1.1)
|   mx missile = y: democrat (4/2.2)
|   mx missile = u: republican (2/1)
```

Figure 4–1. Decision tree before and after pruning

```
adoption of the budget resolution = y: democrat
adoption of the budget resolution = u: democrat
adoption of the budget resolution = n:
    education spending = n: democrat
    education spending = y: democrat
    education spending = u: republican
```

has been replaced by the leaf **democrat**, the subtree

```
synfuels corporation cutback = n: republican
synfuels corporation cutback = u: republican
synfuels corporation cutback = y:
    duty free exports = y: democrat
    duty free exports = u: republican
    duty free exports = n:
        education spending = n: democrat
        education spending = y: republican
        education spending = u: democrat
```

has become the leaf **republican**, and the subtree

```
water project cost sharing = n: democrat
water project cost sharing = y: democrat
water project cost sharing = u:
    mx missile = n: republican
    mx missile = y: democrat
    mx missile = u: republican
```

has been replaced by the subtree at its third branch.

Suppose that it was possible to predict the error rate of a tree and of its subtrees (including leaves). This would immediately suggest the following simple pruning rationale: Start from the bottom of the tree and examine each nonleaf subtree. If replacement of this subtree with a leaf, or with its most frequently used branch, would lead to a lower predicted error rate, then prune the tree accordingly, remembering that the predicted error rate for all trees that include this one will be affected. Since the error rate for the whole tree decreases as the error rate of any of its subtrees is reduced, this process will lead to a tree whose predicted error rate is minimal with respect to the allowable forms of pruning.

How can we predict these error rates? It is clear that error rate on the training set from which the tree was built (*resubstitution error*, in the terminology of Breiman *et al.*) does not provide a suitable estimate; as far as the training set is concerned, pruning always increases error. In the tree of Figure 4–1, the first replaced subtree separates 1 Republican from 167 Democrats (with no errors on the training set), so pruning this subtree to the leaf democrat causes one of the training cases to be misclassified. The second subtree misclassifies 7 training cases when sorting out 11 Democrats and 112 Republicans, but this increases to 11 errors when the tree is replaced by the leaf republican.

This search for a way of predicting error rates leads once again to two families of techniques. The first family predicts the error rate of the tree and its subtrees using a new set of cases that is distinct from the training set. Since these cases were not examined at the time the tree was constructed, the estimates obtained from them are clearly unbiased and, if there are enough of them, reliable. Examples of such techniques are:

- *Cost-complexity* pruning [Breiman *et al.*, 1984], in which the predicted error rate of a tree is modeled as the weighted sum of its complexity and its error on the training cases, with the separate cases used primarily to determine an appropriate weighting.

- *Reduced-error* pruning [Quinlan, 1987e], which assesses the error rates of the tree and its components directly on the set of separate cases.

The drawback associated with this family of techniques is simply that some of the available data must be reserved for the separate set, so the original tree must be constructed from a smaller training set. This may not be much of a disadvantage when data is abundant, but can lead to inferior trees when data is scarce. One way around this problem is to use a *cross-validation* approach. In essence, the available cases are divided into C equal-sized blocks and, for each block, a tree is constructed from cases in all the other blocks and tested on cases in the "holdout" block. For moderate values of C, the assumption is made that the tree constructed from all but one block will not differ much from the tree constructed from all data. Of course, C trees must be grown instead of just one. See Breiman *et al.* [1984] and Chapter 9 for more on cross-validation.

The approach taken in C4.5 belongs to the second family of techniques that use only the training set from which the tree was built. The raw resubstitution estimate of error rate is adjusted to reflect this estimate's bias. In earlier work, I developed a method called *pessimistic* pruning, inspired by a statistical correction, that effectively increased the number of errors observed at each leaf by 0.5 [Quinlan, 1987e]. C4.5 now employs a far more pessimistic estimate as follows.

When N training cases are covered by a leaf, E of them incorrectly, the resubstitution error rate for this leaf is E/N. However, we can regard this somewhat naively as observing E "events" in N trials. If this set of N training cases could be regarded as a sample (which, of course, it is not), we could ask what this result tells us about the probability of an event (error) over the entire population of cases covered by this leaf. The probability of error cannot be determined exactly, but has itself a (posterior) probability distribution that is usually summarized by a pair of confidence limits. For a given confidence level CF, the upper limit on this probability can be found from the confidence limits for the binomial distribution; this upper limit is here written $U_{CF}(E, N)$[6]. Then, C4.5 simply equates the predicted error rate at a leaf with this upper limit, on the argument that the tree has been constructed to minimize the observed error rate. Now, this description does violence to statistical notions of sampling and confidence limits, so the reasoning should be taken with a large grain of salt. Like many heuristics with questionable underpinnings, however, the estimates that it produces seem frequently to yield acceptable results.

To simplify the accounting, error estimates for leaves and subtrees are computed assuming that they were used to classify a set of unseen cases of the same size as the training set. So, a leaf covering N training cases with a predicted error rate of $U_{CF}(E, N)$ would give rise to a predicted $N \times U_{CF}(E, N)$ errors. Similarly, the number of predicted errors associated with a (sub)tree is just the sum of the predicted errors of its branches.

4.3 Example: Democrats and Republicans

To illustrate what is happening, we will return to the example in Figure 4–1. The subtree

education spending = n: democrat (6)
education spending = y: democrat (9)
education spending = u: republican (1)

has no associated errors on the training set. For the first leaf, $N = 6$, $E = 0$, and (using C4.5's default confidence level of 25%), $U_{25\%}(0, 6) = 0.206$, so the predicted number of errors if this leaf were used to classify 6 unseen cases is 6×0.206. For the remaining leaves, $U_{25\%}(0, 9) = 0.143$ and $U_{25\%}(0, 1) = 0.750$, so the number of predicted errors for this subtree is given by

$$6 \times 0.206 + 9 \times 0.143 + 1 \times 0.750 = 3.273.$$

---

6. The upper and lower limits are symmetrical, so that the probability that the real error rate exceeds $U_{CF}(E, N)$ is $CF/2$.

If the subtree were replaced by the leaf democrat, it would cover the same 16 cases with one error, so the corresponding predicted errors come to

$$16 \times U_{25\%}(1, 16) = 16 \times 0.157 = 2.512.$$

Since the existing subtree has a higher number of predicted errors, it is pruned to a leaf.

The subtree immediately above this now looks like

adoption of the budget resolution = y: democrat (151)
adoption of the budget resolution = u: democrat (1)
adoption of the budget resolution = n: democrat (16/1)

The number of predicted errors for this subtree is

$$151 \times U_{25\%}(0, 151) + 1 \times U_{25\%}(0, 1) + 2.512 \text{ (from above)}$$

which comes to 4.642. If this subtree were replaced by the leaf democrat, the predicted errors would be $168 \times U_{25\%}(1, 168) = 2.610$. The predicted error rate for the leaf again is lower than that for the subtree, so this subtree is also pruned to a leaf.

4.4 Estimating error rates for trees

The numbers (N/E) at the leaves of the pruned tree in Figure 4–1 can now be explained. As before, N is the number of training cases covered by the leaf. E is just the number of predicted errors if a set of N unseen cases were classified by the tree.

The sum of the predicted errors at the leaves, divided by the number of cases in the training set, provides an immediate estimate of the error rate of the pruned tree on unseen cases. For this tree, the sum of the predicted errors at the leaves is 20.8 for a training set of size 300. By this estimate, then, the pruned tree will misclassify 6.9% of unseen cases.

The summary of results on the training cases and a set of test cases appears in Figure 4–2. For this particular dataset, the error rate of the pruned tree is higher than that of the unpruned tree for the training data, but, as hoped, the pruned tree has a lower error rate than the original tree on the unseen cases. The estimate here of 6.9% turns out to be somewhat high as the observed error rate on unseen cases is 3%. On a ten-way cross-validation, however, the average actual and predicted error rates on unseen cases, 5.3% and 5.6% respectively, are much closer.

Evaluation on training data (300 items):

Before Pruning		After Pruning		
Size	Errors	Size	Errors	Estimate
25	8(2.7%)	7	13(4.3%)	(6.9%)

Evaluation on test data (135 items):

Before Pruning		After Pruning		
Size	Errors	Size	Errors	Estimate
25	7(5.2%)	7	4(3.0%)	(6.9%)

Figure 4–2. Results with congressional voting data

## CHAPTER 5

From Trees to Rules

As we saw in the previous section, it is often possible to prune a decision tree so that it is both simpler and more accurate. Even though the pruned trees are more compact than the originals, they can still be cumbersome, complex, and inscrutable. If we want our classifiers to provide insight as well as accurate predictions on unseen cases, there is still some way to go!

Large decision trees are difficult to understand because each node has a specific context established by the outcomes of tests at antecedent nodes. The decision tree of Figure 5–1 concerning the detection of hypothyroid conditions was generated from data supplied by the Garvan Institute of Medical Research in Sydney. The last node that tests TT4 measured, giving class compensated hypothyroid if the answer is t, does not suggest that the presence of TT4 among the requested assays is sufficient to diagnose compensated hypothyroidism! This test makes sense only when read in conjunction with the outcomes of earlier tests. Every test in the tree has a unique context that is crucial to its understanding and it can be very difficult indeed to keep track of the continually changing context while scanning a large tree.

Another complication arises because the structure of the tree may cause individual subconcepts to be fragmented. Consider the simple artificial task in which there are four binary attributes, F, G, J, and K, and two classes, yes and no. Every class yes case has either F and G both with value 1, or J and K with value 1, as expressed by the decision tree in Figure 5–2. The tree contains two identical subtrees that test for J and K both being 1. This single subconcept has been split so that it appears twice in the tree, which makes the tree more difficult to understand. The replication is not just an aberration of this particular tree—any tree for this concept must necessarily split either the F=G=1 subconcept or the J=K=1 subconcept. There are only two ways to get around this problem: defining new, more task-specific attributes such as F=G=1, as FRINGE [Pagallo and Haussler, 1990] does, or moving away from the decision tree representation of classifiers. This section focuses on the latter approach.

```
TSH ≤ 6 : negative
TSH > 6 :
    FTI ≤ 64 :
        TSH measured = f: negative
        TSH measured = t:
            T4U measured = f:
                TSH ≤ 17 : compensated hypothyroid
                TSH > 17 : primary hypothyroid
            T4U measured = t:
                thyroid surgery = f: primary hypothyroid
                thyroid surgery = t: negative *
    FTI > 64 :
        on thyroxine = t: negative
        on thyroxine = f:
            TSH measured = f: negative
            TSH measured = t:
                thyroid surgery = t: negative
                thyroid surgery = f:
                    TT4 > 150 : negative
                    TT4 ≤ 150 :
                        TT4 measured = f: primary hypothyroid
                        TT4 measured = t: compensated hypothyroid
```

Figure 5–1. Decision tree for hypothyroid conditions

```
F = 0:
    J = 0: no
    J = 1:
        K = 0: no
        K = 1: yes
F = 1:
    G = 1: yes
    G = 0:
        J = 0: no
        J = 1:
            K = 0: no
            K = 1: yes
```

Figure 5–2. Simple decision tree for F=G=1 or J=K=1

In any decision tree, the conditions that must be satisfied when a case is classified by a leaf can be found by tracing all the test outcomes along the path from the root to that leaf. In the tree of Figure 5–2, the deepest yes leaf is associated with the outcomes F=1, G=0, J=1, and K=1; any case that satisfies these conditions will be mapped to that yes leaf. We could thus write, "If F=1 and G=0 and J=1 and K=1 then the class is yes," which suddenly has the form of the ubiquitous production rule [Winston, 1992]. In fact, if the path to each leaf were to be transformed into a production rule of this form, the resulting collection of rules would classify cases exactly as the tree does. As a consequence of their tree origin, the "if" parts of the rules would be mutually exclusive and exhaustive, so the order of the rules would not matter.

We are going to focus on production rules for some pages, so we should establish a more precise basis for talking about them. A rule such as the above will be written

> **if** F=1
>   G=0
>   J=1
>   K=1
> **then** class yes

with the understanding that the conditions making up the rule antecedent are to be interpreted as a conjunction. We will say that a rule *covers* a case if the case satisfies the rule's antecedent conditions.

5.1 Generalizing single rules

Rewriting the tree to a collection of rules, one for each leaf in the tree, would not result in anything much simpler than the tree, since there would be one rule for every leaf. However, we can see that the antecedents of individual rules may contain irrelevant conditions. In the rule above, the conclusion is unaffected by the values of F and G. The rule can be generalized by deleting these superfluous conditions without affecting its accuracy, leaving the more appealing rule

> **if** J=1
>   K=1
> **then** class yes.

How can we decide when a condition should be deleted? Let rule R be of the form if A then class C

and a more general rule R^-

if A^- then class C,

where A^- is obtained by deleting one condition X from the conditions A. The evidence for the importance of condition X must be found in the training cases used to construct the decision tree. Each case that satisfies the shorter antecedent A^- either does or does not belong to the designated class C, and does or does not satisfy condition X. The numbers of cases in each of these four groups can be organized into a 2×2 *contingency table*:

	Class C	Other Classes
Satisfies condition X	Y_1	E_1
Does not satisfy condition X	Y_2	E_2

Since we are looking only at cases that satisfy A^-, those that satisfy condition X as well are covered by the original rule R. There are $Y_1 + E_1$ such cases, E_1 of them being misclassified by R since they belong to some class other than C. Similarly, those cases that satisfy A^- but not X would be covered by the generalized rule R^- but not by the original rule. There are $Y_2 + E_2$ of them with E_2 errors. Since R^- also covers all cases that satisfy R, the total number of cases covered by R^- is $Y_1 + Y_2 + E_1 + E_2$.

My first experiments with simplifying rules, reported in Quinlan [1987c], used a test of significance on this contingency table to decide whether condition X should be deleted. The idea is that condition X is retained only when the division of these cases exposed by the contingency table is extremely unlikely to have happened by chance. This significance test is retained as an option in the system, but I have obtained improved results using a pessimistic estimate of the accuracy of rules R and R^- on unseen cases.

As noted when we discussed pruning, a leaf covering N training cases with E errors is very unlikely to have an error rate as low as E/N when it classifies unseen cases. Instead of the resubstitution estimate E/N, we estimated the leaf's true error rate as the upper limit $U_{CF}(E, N)$ of the confidence interval for this rate for some specified confidence level CF. The same approach can be used here: The estimate of the error rate of rule R can be set to $U_{CF}(E_1, Y_1 + E_1)$ and that of rule R^- to the corresponding $U_{CF}(E_1 + E_2, Y_1 + Y_2 + E_1 + E_2)$. If the pessimistic error rate of rule R^- is no greater than that of the original rule R, then it makes sense to delete condition X.

Of course, more than one condition may have to be deleted when a rule is generalized. Rather than looking at all possible subsets of conditions that could be deleted, the system carries out a straightforward greedy elimination: While one or more conditions can be deleted as above, that condition is removed that produces the lowest pessimistic error rate of the generalized rule. As with all greedy searches, there is no guarantee that minimizing pessimistic error rate at each step will lead to a global minimum. The system could probably be improved by carrying out an exhaustive search when the number of conditions is small, and using some approach such as simulated annealing (discussed later in this chapter) when it is not. However, the greedy search seems to work reasonably well in practice, and is relatively fast—an important consideration, because this generalization is carried out many times.

To illustrate what is going on, we return to the hypothyroid decision tree in Figure 5–1. In particular, the asterisked leaf near the middle of the tree corresponds to the initial rule

> **if** TSH > 6
> FTI ≤ 64
> TSH measured = t
> T4U measured = t
> thyroid surgery = t
> **then** class negative

that covers three of the training cases, two of which actually belong to class negative, i.e., $Y_1 = 2$ and $E_1 = 1$. Using the default certainty factor, the upper limit of the error rate on this rule $U_{25\%}(1,3)$ is 69%. Now we observe what happens if we were to drop each of the conditions in this rule, as shown in Table 5–1. Deleting any of the first four conditions gives a rule whose pessimistic error rate is no higher than the original rule.

Table 5–1. Possible conditions to delete (stage 1)

Condition Deleted	$Y_1 + Y_2$	$E_1 + E_2$	Pessimistic Error Rate
TSH > 6	3	1	55%
FTI ≤ 64	6	1	34%
TSH measured = t	2	1	69%
T4U measured = t	2	1	69%
thyroid surgery = t	3	59	97%

The lowest pessimistic error rate is obtained by deleting the condition FTI $\leq$ 64; when this is done, the system computes revised values if the remaining conditions were to be deleted, giving the situation shown in Table 5–2. Again it is possible to delete conditions without increasing the pessimistic error rate of the rule. The best condition to delete is the first, giving a more general rule with a pessimistic error rate of 8%, and the process continues. The final rule contains just one condition:

if thyroid surgery = t
then class negative

This much-simplified rule covers 35 of the training cases with only one error and has a pessimistic error rate of 7%.

Table 5–2. Possible conditions to delete (stage 2)

Condition Deleted	$Y_1 + Y_2$	$E_1 + E_2$	Pessimistic Error Rate
TSH > 6	31	1	8%
TSH measured = t	6	1	34%
T4U measured = t	7	1	30%
thyroid surgery = t	44	179	82%

5.2 Class rulesets

The rule generalization process is repeated for each path in the unsimplified decision tree. The rules derived from some paths may have an unacceptably high error rate or may duplicate rules derived from other paths, so the process usually yields fewer rules than the number of leaves in the tree.

One complication caused by generalization is that the rules cease to be mutually exclusive and exhaustive; there will be cases that satisfy the conditions of more than one rule or, if inaccurate rules are discarded, of no rules. A full production rule interpreter must specify how these cases are to be classified. In the latter situation, it is conventional to define a fallback or *default* rule that comes into play when no other rule covers a case. Deciding what to do in the former situation is usually called *conflict resolution* and the scheme adopted in C4.5 is perhaps the simplest possible: The rules are ordered and the first rule that covers a case is taken as the operative one. We thus need some method for establishing the priority of rules and for deciding on a default classification.

In earlier work [Quinlan, 1987e], I developed a scheme for ranking all rules and for selecting a subset of them, all as a composite operation. Although this worked reasonably well, the resulting sets of rules were still difficult to understand—the order of rules was important, but seemed arbitrary. Following a suggestion from Donald Michie, I altered the algorithm so that all rules for a single class appear together and these class subsets, rather than the rules themselves, are ordered. This grouping makes the rule sets more intelligible and has the advantage that the order of rules for a particular class is unimportant.

Suppose that, from the set of all rules developed earlier, we were to select a subset S of rules to cover a particular class C. The performance of this subset can be summarized by the number of training cases covered by S that do not belong to class C (the *false positives*), and the number of class C training cases that are not covered by any rule in S (the *false negatives*). The worth of the subset S of rules is assessed using the Minimum Description Length (MDL) Principle [Rissanen, 1983] in a manner similar to that described in Quinlan and Rivest [1989]. This provides a basis for offsetting the accuracy of a theory (here, a subset of rules) against its complexity.

This use of the MDL Principle is disarmingly simple: A Sender and a Receiver both have identical copies of a set of training cases, but the Sender's copy also specifies the class of each case while the Receiver's copy lacks all class information. The Sender must communicate this missing information to the Receiver by transmitting a classification theory together with exceptions to this theory. The Sender may choose the complexity of the theory he sends—a relatively simple theory with a substantial number of exceptions, or a more complete theory with fewer exceptions. The MDL Principle states that the best theory derivable from the training data will minimize the number of bits required to encode the total message consisting of the theory together with its associated exceptions.

The information being transmitted here is the identity of the training cases belonging to class C, using some encoding scheme for the theory (subset S of rules) and exceptions. The scheme used by the system is approximate, since it attempts to find a lower limit on the number of bits in any encoding rather than choosing a particular encoding. The general idea can be summarized as follows:

- To encode a rule, we must specify each condition in its left-hand side. The right-hand side need not be encoded, since all rules in the subset concern the same class C. There is one small complication: The conditions must be sent in some order, but the order does not matter since the conditions are *and*ed together. If there are x conditions in the left-hand side, there are $x!$ possible orderings that could be sent, all of them equivalent from the point of view of specifying the rule. Therefore, the bits required to send any particular ordering must be reduced by a "credit" of $\log_2(x!)$.

- Encoding a set of rules requires the sum of the bits to encode each rule, less a similar credit for rule ordering (since all orderings of rules for a single class are equivalent).

- Exceptions are encoded by indicating which of the cases covered by the rules S are false positives and which of those not covered are false negatives. If the rules cover r of the n training cases, with fp false positives and fn false negatives, the number of bits required to encode the exceptions is

$$\log_2\left(\binom{r}{fp}\right) + \log_2\left(\binom{n-r}{fn}\right).$$

The first term is the bits needed to indicate the false positives among the cases covered by the rules and the second term gives a similar expression for identifying the false negatives among the uncovered cases.

The worth of a particular subset S is measured by the sum of the encoding lengths for rules and exceptions—the smaller the sum, the better the theory represented by S.

In practice, encoding schemes often tend to overestimate the number of bits required to encode a theory relative to sets of exceptions. This can be explained in part by the fact that sets of attributes are often redundant, so that different theories can be functionally identical. Since the role of a theory for a class is to identify a subset of the training cases, different sets of rules that denote the same subset of cases are interchangeable, even though they may have quite different encodings. Following Quinlan and Rivest [1989], the system compensates for this effect by using a weighted sum

exception bits + W × theory bits,

where W is a factor less than one. Now, an appropriate value of W will depend on the probability of two theories describing the same collection of cases, which in turn will depend on the degree of redundancy in the attributes. C4.5 uses a default value of 0.5, which can be further reduced by the -r option (Chapter 9) when it seems likely that the attributes have an unusual degree of overlap. (Fortunately, the algorithm does not seem to be particularly sensitive to the value of W.)

The task, then, is to find a subset S of the rules for class C that minimizes this total encoding. This is similar to the rule-generalization task discussed above—finding a subset of the conditions that minimizes the rule's pessimistic error rate—but, whereas the greedy elimination approach used there is reasonably satisfactory, hill-climbing does not seem to work well here. Instead, the system considers all possible subsets of the rules for a class, if there are not too many of them, and uses simulated annealing to find a good subset otherwise. For the latter, the system repeatedly picks one of the rules randomly and considers including it in the subset S (if it is not already there), or deleting it (if it is). This action will produce a change ΔB in the total bits to encode the subset plus exceptions and, if this change is beneficial, it is automatically accepted. If the action increases total coding length so that ΔB is positive, the change to S is accepted with probability $e^{-\Delta B/K}$ where K is a kind of synthetic temperature. By gradually reducing K as changes are explored, the system tends to converge on a set of rules with near-minimum encoding. (Simulated annealing is discussed in detail in Press *et al.* [1988].)

The selection of rule subsets is again illustrated by the hypothyroid domain with rules for class **primary hypothyroid**. For this class, the decision tree obtained from 2,514 training cases gives three rules whose (unmeaningful) identity numbers happen to be 4, 5, and 7. Table 5–3 summarizes the analysis of the eight possible subsets of these rules. The last row of the table can be explained as follows:

- The coding cost for the set of three rules is the sum of the coding costs for the individual rules, less the ordering credit. The individual rules have coding costs of 17.1, 19.8, and 15.7 bits respectively and, since there are 3! ways of ordering them, the theory cost is $17.1 + 19.8 + 15.7 - \log_2(6)$.

- There are four false positive cases among the 66 cases covered by these rules, and two false negative cases among the remaining 2,448 cases, so the exception coding requires $\log_2(\binom{66}{4}) + \log_2(\binom{2448}{2})$ bits. Using the default value $W = 0.5$, the total coding cost is then $41.0 + 0.5 \times 49.9$.

Table 5–3. Coding costs for rule subsets

Theory		Exceptions			Total
Rules included	Coding cost	False positive	False negative	Coding cost	coding cost
-	0.0	0	64	425.8	425.8
{4}	17.1	2	12	116.8	125.3
{5}	19.8	1	6	63.9	73.8
{7}	15.7	1	61	411.8	419.6
{4, 5}	35.8	3	5	64.6	82.5
{4, 7}	31.7	3	9	97.8	113.6
{5, 7}	34.4	2	3	42.1	59.3
{4, 5, 7}	49.9	4	2	41.0	65.9

In this example, the subset consisting of rules 5 and 7 gives the smallest total encoding cost—although the addition of rule 4 decreases the cost to encode exceptions, the reduction is outweighed by the additional cost of encoding the theory.

5.3 Ranking classes and choosing a default

After a subset of the rules to represent each class has been decided, the only steps remaining are to settle on an ordering for the classes and to select a default class. Both operations are relatively simple.

Recall that the subset of rules selected for each class will usually cause false positive errors, since they will cover some cases that do not belong to that particular class. When deciding on an order for classes, it seems sensible to defer those classes whose rulesets commit many false positive errors; earlier subsets might then have (correctly) covered some of these cases before they are so misclassified. The class subsets are examined and the class whose rule subset has fewest false positive errors becomes the first class. The false positives on the remaining training cases are recomputed, the next class selected, and so on.

One reasonable choice for the default class would be that which appears most frequently in the training set. However, the default class will be used only when a case is not covered by any selected rules, so these rules should play some part in determining it. The system simply chooses as the default that class which contains the most training cases not covered by any rule, resolving ties in favor of the class with the higher absolute frequency.

After the class order and default class have been established, the composite ruleset is subject to one final polishing process. If there are one or more rules whose omission would actually reduce the number of classification errors on the training cases, the first such rule is discarded and the set checked again. This step is designed to allow a final global scrutiny of the ruleset as a whole, in the context of the way it will be used.

In our hypothyroid example, the situation after rulesets have been established for each class is summarized in Table 5–4. The rules for compensated hypothyroid, with no false positives, are placed first, followed by the rule subset for primary hypothyroid, and finally the rules for class negative. There are 8 compensated hypothyroid training cases that are not covered by any rule, more than the number for any other class, so this becomes the default class. In the final ruleset (shown in Figure 5–3), the predicted accuracy of each rule appears in square brackets. These rules represent a more human-friendly theory than the original decision tree of Figure 5–1, and yet the rules are just as accurate as the tree: Both give just eight errors (0.6%) when classifying 1,258 unseen cases.

Table 5–4. Performance of class rulesets, hypothyroid

Class	Generalized Rules	Rules Selected	Cases Covered	False positives	False negatives
negative	6	5	2319	2	3
primary	3	2	66	2	3
compensated	2	1	120	0	9

5.4 Summary

This chapter has been rather solid going, containing many algorithms and heuristics. The key ideas are:

- Every path from the root of an unpruned tree to a leaf gives one initial rule. The left-hand side of the rule contains all the conditions established by the path, and the right-hand side specifies the class at the leaf.

- Each such rule is simplified by removing conditions that do not seem helpful for discriminating the nominated class from other classes, using a pessimistic estimate of the accuracy of the rule.

> **if** on thyroxine = f
> thyroid surgery = f
> TSH > 6
> TT4 ≤ 150
> FTI > 64
> **then** class compensated hypothyroid [98.9%]
>
> **if** thyroid surgery = f
> TSH > 6
> FTI ≤ 64
> **then** class primary hypothyroid [95.6%]
>
> **if** on thyroxine = f
> TT4 measured = f
> TSH > 6
> **then** class primary hypothyroid [45.3%]
>
> **if** TSH ≤ 6
> **then** class negative [99.9%]
>
> **if** on thyroxine = t
> FTI > 64
> **then** class negative [99.5%]
>
> **if** TSH measured = f
> **then** class negative [99.5%]
>
> **if** TT4 > 150
> **then** class negative [99.4%]
>
> **if** thyroid surgery = t
> **then** class negative [92.7%]
>
> **if** none of the above
> **then** class compensated hypothyroid

Figure 5–3. Final rules for hypothyroid example

- For each class in turn, all the simplified rules for that class are sifted to remove rules that do not contribute to the accuracy of the set of rules as a whole.

- The sets of rules for the classes are then ordered to minimize false positive errors and a default class is chosen.

This process leads to a production rule classifier that is usually about as accurate as a pruned tree, but more easily understood by people.

CHAPTER 6

Windowing

When I started work on ID3 in the late 1970s, computers with virtual memory were uncommon and programs were usually subject to size restrictions. The training sets of those early experiments were quite large—one had 30,000 cases described by 24 attributes—and exceeded my memory allowance on the machine I was using. Consequently, there was a need to explore indirect methods of growing trees from large datasets.

The method adopted was quite straightforward. A subset of the training cases called a *window* was selected randomly and a decision tree developed from it. This tree was then used to classify the training cases that had not been included in the window, usually with the result that some of them were misclassified. A selection of these *exceptions* was then added to the initial window, and a second tree, constructed from the enlarged training set, was tested on the remaining cases. This cycle was repeated until a tree built from the current window correctly classified all the training cases outside the window. Quite commonly, the window ended up containing only a small fraction of the training cases. The final window can be thought of as a screened set of training cases that contains all the "interesting" ones, together with sufficient "ordinary" cases to guide the tree-building.

Since those early experiments, the windowing strategy has evolved in several minor ways. Rather than picking training cases randomly to form the initial window, C4.5 biases the choice so that the distribution of classes in the initial window is as uniform as possible. This sampling strategy seems to lead to better initial trees when the distribution of classes in the training set is very unbalanced. Secondly, where ID3 used a fixed ceiling on the number of exceptions that could be added at each cycle, C4.5 includes at least half of them in the next window, thereby attempting to speed convergence on a final tree. Thirdly, the program can now stop before the tree correctly classifies all cases outside the window if it appears that the sequence of trees is not becoming more accurate. For domains in which classification is affected by noise or indeterminacy, early termination is meant to prevent the inexorable growth of the window until it includes almost all the training cases.

6.1 Example: Hypothyroid conditions revisited

The windowing process is illustrated on the hypothyroid data discussed in the previous chapter. When C4.5 is invoked with the windowing option, the growth of the window is summarized by the output segment in Figure 6–1. For the first cycle, the initial window contains 502 of the 2,514 training cases. The tree developed from this window contains 15 nodes and misclassifies 5 of the training cases in the window and 15 other training cases. When these latter 15 cases are added to the window, the tree found at the second cycle contains 19 nodes and misclassifies 29 of the other training cases, apparently a step in the wrong direction. When these 29 cases are added to the window, however, the decision tree of 21 nodes misclassifies only 8 cases in the window and none outside it, so the process terminates. The final window contains only 546 cases, or 22% of the training set, yet the final decision tree is almost identical to the tree of Figure 5–1 in the previous chapter that was developed from all the training cases. The 546 screened cases apparently contain as much information as the complete training set of 2,514!

Cycle	Tree size	—Objects— window	other	window	rate	other	rate	total	rate
1	15	502	2012	5	1.0%	15	0.7%	20	0.8%
2	19	517	1997	8	1.5%	29	1.5%	37	1.5%
3	21	546	1968	8	1.5%	0	0.0%	8	0.3%

Figure 6–1. Effect of windowing using hypothyroid data

6.2 Why retain windowing?

These days, even an inexpensive workstation will happily run processes that are much larger than its (large) physical memory. Since windowing was introduced to overcome memory limits that no longer pose any problems, its retention in the system needs some justification.

6.2.1 Faster construction of trees (sometimes)

The datasets used in my early experiments were largely free of noise and indeterminism: A tree could usually be found that correctly classified all training cases. In this kind of classification domain, windowing can quickly converge on a final tree and so lead to computational speedup.

The University of California, Irvine, data library includes a collection of 8,124 mushroom descriptions, each classified as poisonous or edible. There is a middle-sized decision tree of 31 nodes that correctly classifies all of the training cases. When this data is used with the default windowing parameters, the initial window gives a tree that correctly classifies all the other cases, so the final tree is arrived at on the first cycle. The speedup in this example is not great—a 15% improvement—but in other domains with larger training sets, windowing has reduced the time required to construct a decision tree by a factor of three [Catlett, 1991b].

For most real-world classification domains, however, the use of windowing slows down the process of building a tree. When the final tree has a significant error rate on the whole training set, windowing generally requires many cycles to converge.

6.2.2 More accurate trees

While windowing can be justified on efficiency grounds for some unusual domains, its principal benefit is that it can lead to more accurate trees. Jason Catlett's experiments cited above show that the use of a uniform-class sample for the initial window can result in better choice of thresholds for continuous attributes. This same biased sample can also help in the selection of tests of discrete attributes at higher levels in the tree. It seems worthwhile to try windowing with any domain in which the classes are quite unbalanced, and in which it should be possible to develop a very accurate decision tree.

Another contribution to accuracy, though, comes from a rather unexpected quarter. The initial window is still selected randomly, subject to making the class distributions as uniform as possible. Different initial windows generally lead to different initial trees, with different exceptions, and so on. So, even though the training set is unchanged, the use of windowing can often allow different final trees to be constructed. This potential for multiple trees provides the basis for two features not found in ID3, namely:

- Growing several alternative trees and selecting as "the" tree the one with the lowest predicted error rate; and

- Growing several trees, generating production rules from all of them, then constructing a single production rule classifier from all the available rules.

It often turns out that the final classifier obtained in this way is more accurate than one obtained via a single tree. The downside is that growing n trees requires n times as long as developing one of them, and selecting a collection of production rules from many possible rules also requires more computation.

6.3 Example: The multiplexor

A good illustration of these potential advantages of windowing is provided by the pathological *multiplexor* task [Wilson, 1987]. A case is described by a series of bits, the first a of which constitute an address (from 0 to $2^a - 1$), followed by one data bit for each address. There are two classes, yes and no, and a case is of class yes if the data bit corresponding to the address is 1. Consider, for instance, the situation when $a = 3$. There are three address bits $a_0 a_1 a_2$ followed by eight data bits $d_0 d_1 d_2 \ldots d_7$, so case 01001101001 belongs to class yes since 010 = 2 and d_2 is 1. This classification domain is unusually awkward since all attribute selection criteria seem to lead to a nonsensical initial division that tests a data bit rather than an address bit [Quinlan, 1988a].

For this 11-bit multiplexor, five training set sizes 100, 200, ..., 500 were chosen and five training sets of each size generated randomly (with replacement). A large set of 1,000 test cases was also generated randomly. Each training set was processed by C4.5 in three modes:

- standard mode, in which a single tree was generated from all training cases;

- windowing mode, producing a single tree; and

- windowing mode, growing ten trees and (automatically) selecting one of them.

The program C4.5RULES was also used to generate a ruleset in each case. Table 6–1 shows, for each training set size, the average error rate of the trees on the 1,000 unseen cases and Table 6–2 gives the same information for the rulesets. As expected, the error rate of a single tree grown without windowing declines as the number of training cases increases. When a single tree is grown with windowing, the error rates on the unseen test cases decline more rapidly; the improvement is even more rapid when ten trees are grown using windowing and the final tree selected on the basis of its predicted error rate. The same pattern appears in the results for rulesets—the use of windowing gives more accurate classifiers and rulesets extracted from ten trees are better than rulesets extracted from a single tree. This is one domain in which production rule classifiers are generally more accurate than decision trees for training sets containing more than 100 cases.

Table 6–1. Error rates on multiplexor task (trees)

Training Cases	Without Windowing	Windowing, Single Tree	Windowing, Ten Trees
100	35.4%	36.0%	34.4%
200	24.4%	24.6%	16.9%
300	18.5%	13.9%	11.6%
400	17.9%	9.4%	5.7%
500	13.2%	8.0%	6.3%

Table 6–2. Error rates on multiplexor task (rules)

Training Cases	Without Windowing	Windowing, Single Tree	Windowing, Ten Trees
100	36.4%	36.0%	26.0%
200	18.3%	18.7%	9.2%
300	7.4%	4.3%	1.7%
400	3.5%	0.0%	0.6%
500	0.5%	0.0%	0.0%

Not all domains exhibit this same improvement with windowing [Wirth and Catlett, 1988]. Even here, the higher accuracy on unseen cases was achieved at a cost: Developing a single tree by windowing takes almost twice as long as generating a tree from all the training cases in one pass, and producing ten trees takes ten times as long again. My own experience with windowing shows that it rarely leads to a less accurate final tree, it sometimes gives a better final tree, but it usually takes longer. Constructing multiple trees *always* takes longer, but occasionally it can be worth the effort, particularly if the trees are to be reprocessed to give a production rule classifier.

## CHAPTER 7

Grouping Attribute Values

When the divide-and-conquer algorithm discussed in Chapter 2 chooses to split the training set on a discrete-valued attribute, it generates a separate branch and subtree for each possible value of that attribute. This is usually appropriate—the differences in class distribution that led to this attribute being selected suggest that training cases associated with each value of the attribute ought to be treated separately. If there are many such values, however, this approach raises two concerns:

- One consequence of partitioning the training set into numerous subsets is that each subset is small.

- If discrete attributes vary markedly in their numbers of values, can we be sure that selection criteria such as gain ratio are assessing them equitably?

The first concern is that the useful patterns in the subsets may become undetectable through an insufficiency of data. The second is more subtle: The gain ratio criterion measures the ratio of information relevant to classification that is provided by the division (the information gain) to the information produced by the division itself (the split information). The denominator of this ratio grows rapidly as the number of subsets increases. The gain ratio criterion is heuristic in nature and, while experimental evidence suggests that it usually leads to good choices of splitting attribute, the form of the criterion biases it against attributes with many values.

If we wish to reduce the number of outcomes from testing a multivalued attribute, one or more outcomes must be associated with a collection of attribute values rather than a single value. Collections of attribute values associated with a single branch will be referred to as *value groups*, not to be confused with subsets of training cases. In previous work on finding attribute value groups, the partition has often been forced all the way to a binary split. The original CLS [Hunt *et al.*, 1966] selects one distinguished value of the splitting attribute for one branch and lumps all other values together for the other branch. CART also uses binary splits, but selects a group of values for both branches. Rather than forcing binary splits, C4.5 associates a value group with each of a variable number of branches.

In some domains, appropriate groups of attribute values can be determined from domain knowledge. Consider the case of an attribute denoting a chemical element.

- The periodic table groups elements into families such as the halogens and the noble metals.

- At room temperature, each element is either a solid, a liquid, or a gas.

- Some elements conduct electricity, some do not.

Any or all of these groupings of the elements may be relevant to the classification task at hand. Where such well-established groupings are known beforehand, it makes sense to provide this information to the system by way of additional attributes, one for each potentially relevant grouping. So, in this case, we might add a true-false attribute to indicate whether the original attribute was a conductor, another multivalued attribute to give its periodic table family, another three-valued attribute to indicate its state, and so on.

The rest of this chapter is about finding reasonable groupings of attribute values from the data itself. If the attribute has n values then there are $2^{n-1} - 1$ nontrivial binary partitions of these values, so even these two-way splits cannot be explored exhaustively for values of n larger than 15 or so. It turns out here that binary splits have a great advantage in some circumstances. Breiman *et al.* [1984] prove that, if there are just two classes, it is possible to order the values so that the best partition is one of the "cuts" of this sequence—instead of $2^{n-1} - 1$ possibilities, only $n-1$ need to be examined. (This result is so appealing that, even when there are more than two classes, Breiman *et al.* group them into two superclasses for the purpose of finding attribute value groups.) Against the requirement for binary splits is the argument that they can force artificial divisions—some partitions are inherently multivalued, as illustrated by medical *triage*.

7.1 Finding value groups by merging

C4.5 uses another greedy algorithm to find groups of attribute values; as usual, this means that the groups that are found may not be optimal in any sense. Since additional attributes defining all sensible groups of attribute values may have been included, or one-branch-per-value trees might be required for other reasons, this process is carried out only when the -s option is specified.

The method used is based on iterative merging of value groups. The initial value groups are just the individual values of the attribute under consideration and, at each cycle, C4.5 evaluates the consequences of merging every pair of groups. (Any division of the attribute values into attribute groups is reflected in the split of the training cases by that attribute, and so in the corresponding split information and gain.) The process continues until just two value groups remain, or until no such merger would produce a better partition of the training cases.

The partition arising from any particular collection of value groups is evaluated as before by whatever selection criterion is in force. Under the default gain ratio criterion, merging two groups of attribute values results in fewer subsets of training cases and a corresponding reduction of the split information. If the reduction in information gain is not substantial, the final gain ratio figure may be increased. However, if the optional gain criterion is used, the repeated merging always produces a split with at most the same gain, so merging is forced to continue until only two value groups remain.

There is a certain amount of fine print in the implementation of this simple hill-climbing algorithm. The code must ensure that the split induced by the value groups satisfies the requirement for at least two subsets to contain the minimum number of cases. Additionally, the final split should have at least half the gain of the original multivalued split, by analogy with the similar condition on the gain ratio criterion. This renders the code more complex than might be expected.

7.2 Example: Soybean diseases

The algorithm for finding attribute value groups is illustrated in Table 7–1, using Michalski's well-known soybean data in which there are 35 attributes, 19 classes, and 683 training cases [Michalski and Chilausky, 1980]. For this illustration we focus on the attribute stem canker with four values: none, below soil, above soil, and above 2nd node. The first section of Table 7–1 shows the key parameters of the partition into four groups based on these individual values. The second section exhibits the outcomes of all possible pairwise combinations of these one-value groups. The last combination has the highest gain ratio value and, since this is an improvement on the initial value, above soil and above 2nd node are

Table 7–1. Exploration of stem canker value groups

Attribute Value Groups	Split Inf. (bits)	Split Gain (bits)	Gain Ratio
{none},{below soil},{above soil},{above 2nd node}	1.677	0.853	0.509
{none, below soil},{above soil},{above 2nd node}	1.403	0.609	0.434
{none, above soil},{below soil},{above 2nd node}	1.419	0.638	0.450
{none, above 2nd node},{below soil},{above soil}	0.909	0.358	0.394
{none},{below soil, above soil},{above 2nd node}	1.567	0.813	0.519
{none},{below soil, above 2nd node},{above soil}	1.456	0.704	0.484
{none},{below soil},{above soil, above 2nd node}	1.467	0.780	0.531
{none, below soil},{above soil, above 2nd node}	1.194	0.535	0.448
{none, above soil, above 2nd node},{below soil}	0.621	0.214	0.345
{none},{below soil, above soil, above 2nd node}	1.233	0.639	0.518

merged. When a similar pairwise merger of the remaining three value groups is examined, with the results shown in the third section of Table 7–1, it is apparent that all the splits have a lower gain ratio value than the current one. The merging of attribute values then stops, leaving three groups of values for this attribute. If stem canker were selected as the splitting attribute at this point, there would be three branches and three subtrees: one for none, one for below soil, and the third for the pair of values above soil and above 2nd node.

7.3 When to form groups?

The remaining question is when to invoke the process of finding attribute value groups. One approach would be to carry out the analysis before the tree-building process commences, either adding new attributes with the reduced numbers of values or using them in place of the original attributes from which they were formed. However, it seems likely that the most appropriate division of an attribute's values into value groups will not remain constant but will reflect the contexts established in different parts of the tree. Although the "do-it-once" approach is economical from a computational point of view, it is probably too crude.

Alternatively, the value groups for a multivalued discrete attribute could be determined after it had been chosen as the splitting attribute. The trouble with this approach, brought out by Table 7–1, is that the gain ratio value of an attribute changes as the value groups are merged.

Because the split information in the denominator is large, an attribute with numerous values may have such a low gain ratio value that it is quite unlikely to be chosen as the best splitting attribute, even though its gain ratio after forming value groups might be much higher. In brief, this would address the first concern of over-division but would not help with the equity problem raised by the second.

Since both these approaches have apparent defects, C4.5 chooses the remaining option of last resort and finds value groups of multivalued attributes each time that possible splits of the training cases are being evaluated. At this time, the best groupings are determined for each multivalued discrete attribute and its gain ratio or gain calculated using the partition induced by the value groups. This continual redetermination of value groups can require a substantial increase in computation, especially for domains in which many discrete attributes have many possible values—another reason for leaving value group formation as an option rather than the default.

For the soybean data mentioned above, the -s option increases cpu time by nearly 70%. A ten-way cross-validation shows that identifying value groups does not have much benefit for this domain—the pruned trees are actually less accurate, while the corresponding production rulesets improve only marginally.

7.4 Example: The Monk's problems

The Monk's problems are three artificial tasks designed to test learning algorithms [Thrun *et al.*, 1991]. Constructed tasks like these are often unlike real learning problems in having simple, exact solutions, but findings from such tasks, if interpreted with caution, can illustrate the suitability of learning methods for finding different types of theories.

The following is taken from the description provided with the data:

The MONK's problems are a collection of three binary classification problems over a six-attribute discrete domain.... The attributes may take the following values:

$$
\begin{array}{ll}
\text{attribute\#1:} & \{1,\,2,\,3\} \\
\text{attribute\#2:} & \{1,\,2,\,3\} \\
\text{attribute\#3:} & \{1,\,2\} \\
\text{attribute\#4:} & \{1,\,2,\,3\} \\
\text{attribute\#5:} & \{1,\,2,\,3,\,4\} \\
\text{attribute\#6:} & \{1,\,2\}
\end{array}
$$

Thus, the six attributes span a space of $432 = 3 \times 3 \times 2 \times 3 \times 4 \times 2$ examples. The "true" concepts underlying each MONK's problem are given by:

M1: (attribute#1 = attribute#2) or (attribute#5 = 1)

M2: (attribute#n = 1) for *exactly two* choices of n in $\{1,2,\ldots,6\}$

M3: (attribute#5 = 3 and attribute#4 = 1) or (attribute#5 $\neq$ 4 and attribute#2 $\neq$ 3).
    M3 has 5% additional noise (misclassifications) in the training set.

Each problem has a specified set of training cases and the entire 432 possible cases are used to test classifiers generated by the learning algorithms.

Decision trees generated by C4.5 do not include tests of the form "attribute#1 = attribute#2," "exactly two attributes have their first value," or even "attribute#5 $\neq$ 4." When these are spelled out in terms of standard tests on discrete attributes, the target concepts above become far less concise: A standard decision tree for the second concept, for instance, has 296 leaves. As a result, C4.5 in standard mode is not well suited to these problems. (We return to the issue of C4.5's suitability for tasks in Chapter 10.) However, the tasks bring out the usefulness of being able to test groups of values and to convert decision trees to production rules. Table 7–2 shows error rates (on the complete test set) for standard decision trees, rules obtained from these trees, trees generated using the -s option to find groupings of attribute values, and rules extracted from these latter trees. The target concept for the first problem cannot be expressed succinctly by a standard decision tree, but the production rule formalism is more attuned to this task. Thus, while the decision trees themselves are very inaccurate, the production rules generated from them capture the concept exactly. When the -s option is used to invoke tests on groups of attribute values, both the decision trees

Table 7–2. Error rates on the Monk's problems

	Monk's Problem		
	M1	M2	M3
Standard decision trees	24.3%	35.0%	2.8%
Production rules	0.0%	34.7%	3.7%
Trees generated with -s	0.0%	29.6%	0.0%
Production rules	0.0%	32.9%	0.0%

and production rules are error-free. The second problem, for which the target concept requires exactly two attributes to have the value 1, is just plain difficult to express either as trees or as rules. Value grouping helps slightly, but all classifiers generated by the programs are very poor. A standard decision tree for the third target concept is nearly exact. When value grouping is invoked, a test "attribute#5 $\neq$ 4" can be captured by "attribute#5 in {1,2,3}"; C4.5 is then able to identify the exact target concept, even though the training cases contain a few misclassifications.

7.5 Uneasy reflections

All methods of grouping the values of discrete attributes seem to be based on the notion of optimizing the splitting criterion. For example, the approach described above tries to find the attribute value groups that yield a partition of the training cases with maximum gain ratio value. Two groups will tend to be merged if the training cases associated with each group have similar class distributions. For this scheme, the best situation arises when there are two groups whose associated training cases have identical distributions; merging these groups causes a reduction in split information, since there are fewer subsets, and does not affect gain, so gain ratio is increased.

However, this is a flimsy foundation on which to base formation of value groups, since it assumes implicitly that sets of training cases with similar class distributions will give rise to similar decision trees. Merging two value groups makes sense only if the decision tree is simplified as a consequence; i.e., the decision tree for the training cases associated with the merged groups is simpler than the sum of the separate trees for the cases associated with each group in turn. When stated baldly like this, the assumption seems implausible unless, as in the Monk's problems, the benefit of such grouping is both substantial and immediately apparent. I have the lingering suspicion that a method for deciding on value groupings after constructing a standard tree would give better results.

CHAPTER 8

Interacting with Classification Models

The chapters thus far have discussed principally the methods used to construct classification models and to evaluate their accuracy (by comparing predicted class to known class on unseen test cases). This sort of activity, dealing as it does with statistical numbers of cases, is quite different from the use of a model as a decision-making aid. In the latter context, all attention is focused on a single case whose real class is not known. Since the goal here is to provide as much help as possible to the person using the model, it seems fruitful to allow more flexibility in describing the case and to provide more information about the prediction.

This chapter outlines programs that interact with classification models of either the decision tree or rule-based variety. While they have the same purpose, the different model types are handled by separate programs. The programs extend the simple methods for using decision trees and production rulesets described so far, with two goals:

- To permit the use of imprecise information about attribute values; and

- To characterize the degree of certainty associated with the predicted most likely class and its alternatives.

Beware: There is no well-founded or even commonly accepted approach to either issue. The discussion here should be regarded as illustrative and speculative, rather than definitive.

8.1 Decision tree models

We start with the program consult that interprets decision trees. As our example, we return to the decision tree for hypothyroid conditions (Figure 5–1). Where this tree is pruned as described in Chapter 4, the result is the very similar tree of Figure 8–1.

```
TSH ≤ 6 : negative
TSH > 6 :
    FTI ≤ 64 :
        TSH measured = f: negative
        TSH measured = t:
            T4U measured = f: compensated hypothyroid
            T4U measured = t:
                thyroid surgery = f: primary hypothyroid
                thyroid surgery = t: negative
    FTI > 64 :
        on thyroxine = t: negative
        on thyroxine = f:
            TSH measured = f: negative
            TSH measured = t:
                thyroid surgery = t: negative
                thyroid surgery = f:
                    TT4 > 150 : negative
                    TT4 ≤ 150 :
                        TT4 measured = f: primary hypothyroid
                        TT4 measured = t: compensated hypothyroid
```

Figure 8–1. Pruned decision tree for hypothyroid conditions

8.1.1 Class distributions

Part of the transcript that results when this tree is used to classify a sample case is:

```
TSH: 8.8
FTI: 75
on thyroxine: f
TSH measured: t
thyroid surgery: f
TT4: 148
TT4 measured: t

Decision:
    compensated hypothyroid CF = 0.99 [ 0.97 - 1.00 ]
    primary hypothyroid CF = 0.01 [ 0.00 - 0.03 ]
```

Since the consult program is interactive, information entered by the user appears in italics to differentiate it from prompts and output generated by the program. In this example, the program gives the prompt TSH:, the user keys in the value *8.8*, the program prompts for FTI value, and so on. After asking for the values of six attributes, the program gives the predicted classification under the heading Decision. The first thing to notice is that two possible classifications are suggested for this case, each characterized by an estimate of its certainty factor (CF) and bounds for same in the style of INFERNO [Quinlan, 1983b]. The program gives compensated hypothyroid as the most likely class with probability somewhere between 0.97 and 1, the best guess being 0.99. Another class, primary hypothyroid, comes a rather distant second with probability 0.01.

According to the decision tree of Figure 8–1, this case should have been classified as compensated hypothyroid, so where do the certainty factors and the second class come from? To answer this question, it is necessary to know that 127.4 of the 2,514 training cases found their way to this leaf.[7] Roughly 99% of them belong to class compensated hypothyroid, 1% to class primary hypothyroid, and insignificant fractions to the other classes. The first class is in the overwhelming majority and so is properly associated with this leaf, but there is a small but noteworthy presence of primary hypothyroid, which the interpreter points out.

In Chapter 4, we calculated a predicted number of errors at a leaf using U_{CF} rather than the number of erroneous training examples. The same strategy can be adopted here, in which case the error rate at the leaf grows from 1% to 3%. The program takes this as the lower bound on the proportion of cases of class compensated hypothyroid at this leaf, giving a predicted confidence interval for this class of [0.97–1.00]. In general, the lower bound of the confidence interval for each class is determined by U_{CF}, while the upper bound is computed as $1 - S$, where S is the sum of the lower bounds for all other classes. (Note that the meaning of the bounds is deliberately vague; they do not represent 1 standard error limits or probability limits to any confidence level.)

Essentially, the interpreter program is exploiting information on class distributions at the leaves. Breiman *et al.* [1984] carry this one stage further by growing special *class probability trees* so as to increase the informativeness of these distributions. Since they have observed no significant advantage in doing so, however, I prefer to use the information that comes as a by-product of the standard tree-growing routines.

---

7. The nonintegral number is caused by fractional apportionment of cases with unknown outcomes of tests, as described in Chapter 3.

8.1.2 Imprecise values

The information about attribute values in the above transcript fragment was precise: TSH exactly 8.8, on thyroxine definitely false, and so on. Such precise information is sometimes unavailable and we must do as best we can with the imperfect information to hand. The program allows for two common kinds of imprecision in supplying attribute values:

- Discrete attributes can be described by a probability distribution over their possible values. Instead of a single value, a response may be a series of values, each followed by a colon and a probability. If some values do not appear in this list, any unassigned probability is shared among them.

- Continuous attributes can be specified by a range rather than a single value. The response consists of two numbers, denoting the lower and upper limits of the range, separated by a hyphen.

Continuing the example above, let us suppose that the value of **on thyroxine** was not known with certainty, but it was thought to be false with 90% probability (and thus true with 10% probability). This can be expressed by the input f:0.90. With this change, the transcript becomes:

TSH: *8.8*
FTI: *75*
on thyroxine: *f:0.90*
TSH measured: *t*
thyroid surgery: *f*
TT4: *148*
TT4 measured: *t*

Decision:
    compensated hypothyroid CF = 0.89 [0.88 - 0.90]
    negative CF = 0.10 [0.10 - 0.12]
    primary hypothyroid CF = 0.01 [0.00 - 0.03]

Although **compensated hypothyroid** is still the most probable class, it is much less certain—class **negative** is now a real possibility.

Indefinite attribute values like this are handled in a manner similar to unknown values (Chapter 3). The outcome of the test on thyroxine is not known with certainty, so all outcomes are investigated. However, the results are then combined in proportion to each outcome's given probability, rather than the relative frequency of the outcome in the training set at this point. For this example, the approximate class probability distributions and combining weights are:

	compensated hypothyroid	primary hypothyroid	negative
on thyroxine = f (0.90)	0.99	0.01	-
t (0.10)	-	-	1.00

giving the estimated certainty factors that appear in the transcript.

Continuous attributes specified by a range rather than a single value can be used to provide a similar probability distribution over outcomes, under the assumption that the value is uniformly distributed in the specified range. If a continuous attribute A is used in a test, with outcomes $A \leq Z$ and $A > Z$, the probability of the first outcome is the proportion of the range that is less than or equal to threshold Z. If Z has a value of 12, for example, and the specified range is 10–15, the probability associated with the "$\leq$" outcome is 2/5.

Of course, the value of an attribute may still be given as unknown or irrelevant, denoted by "?." The probabilities of the outcomes are then assessed by the relative frequencies in the relevant training set, as described in Chapter 3.

8.1.3 Soft thresholds

The decision tree of Figure 8–1 contains three tests on continuous attributes, in each of which a value is compared against a threshold. Such a test acts as a switch that refers a case being classified to one or other of the subtrees, which may not resemble each other at all. Sending a case down one path or the other is reasonable when an attribute value lies clearly to one side of the threshold; if the value lies close to the threshold, however, so that small changes can move the value across the threshold, insignificant differences might produce radically different classifications. In some areas this might be entirely appropriate—thresholds on critical mass or saturation of a queue exhibit this sort of behavior—but in many domains it introduces unwarranted discontinuity. In the decision tree above, changing FTI from 64 to 65 causes a case to be classified by different subtrees, and yet a difference as small as this could be due to unavoidable measurement error.

The same kind of weighting presented in the previous sections can be used to "soften" absolute thresholds. A simple scheme proposed by Carter and Catlett [1987] defines subsidiary cutpoints Z^- and Z^+ below and above each threshold Z. If a test on continuous attribute A is encountered while classifying a case whose value of A is V, the probability of the outcome $A \leq Z$ is determined as follows:

- If V is less than Z^-, the probability is 1.

- If V lies between Z^- and Z, interpolate between 1 and 0.5.

- If V lies between Z and Z^+, interpolate between 0.5 and 0.

- If V is greater than Z^+, the probability is 0.

This probability curve is drawn in Figure 8–2. The outcome $A > Z$ receives the complementary probability and the probabilities of the two outcomes are then used in the same manner as previously.

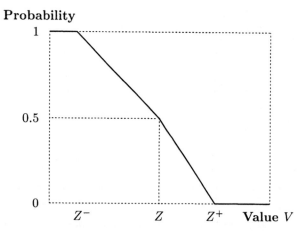

Figure 8–2. Probability of "$\leq$" outcome near threshold

The foregoing begs the question of how Z^- and Z^+ are to be determined. Carter and Catlett investigated a number of schemes which are apparently applicable only when there are exactly two classes. These attempt to find Z^- and Z^+ so that the probability of the outcome $A \leq Z$ defined above most closely approximates the probability that a training case is in one of the classes.

A more direct approach can be defined as follows. If the threshold Z were to be changed to a new value Z', the decision tree would classify some cases of the training set differently. The number of training cases misclassified by the tree can be determined for values of Z' in the neighborhood of Z. If E of the training cases T are misclassified when the threshold has its original value, the standard deviation of the number of errors can be estimated as

$$\sqrt{(E + 0.5) \times (|T| - E - 0.5)/|T|}.$$

Z^- and Z^+ are then chosen so that, if the threshold were set to either of them, the number of misclassified training cases associated with this test would be one standard deviation more than E. This approach allows for either sharp or vague threshold effects. In the former situation, errors increase rapidly as Z is changed so that Z^- and Z^+ are close to Z. In the latter situation, cases with values near the threshold might be expected to be classified equally well by the subtree associated with either outcome, so errors increase relatively slowly and the interval from Z^- to Z^+ is larger.

To illustrate this, we focus on the test of TT4 in the above tree. The threshold Z is 150 and the values determined for Z^- and Z^+ are approximately 146.6 and 151.5 respectively. (As this demonstrates, the interpolation ranges need not be symmetric—here, errors increase more rapidly as the threshold is increased above the chosen value than when it is reduced.) When the soft threshold option is invoked at the time the decision tree is constructed, the transcript changes to the following:

TSH: *8.8*
FTI: *75*
on thyroxine: *f*
TSH measured: *t*
thyroid surgery: *f*
TT4: *148*
TT4 measured: *t*

Decision:
    compensated hypothyroid CF = 0.79 [0.77 - 0.84]
    negative CF = 0.20 [0.16 - 0.23]
    primary hypothyroid CF = 0.01 [0.00 - 0.07]

(Without soft thresholds, the compensated hypothyroid class has the much higher certainty factor of 0.99.) Since the value of TT4 lies within the interpolation range, both outcomes are explored, with weights approximately 0.8 and 0.2 respectively. Even though the TT4 value does not exceed the threshold 150, the predicted class is influenced significantly by the branch of the tree for high TT4 values. Lowering the TT4 value further to 147 diminishes the influence of the other branch:

```
TSH: 8.8
FTI: 75
on thyroxine: f
TSH measured: t
thyroid surgery: f
TT4: 147
TT4 measured: t

Decision:
     compensated hypothyroid CF = 0.93 [ 0.92 - 0.95 ]
     negative CF = 0.06 [ 0.05 - 0.08 ]
     primary hypothyroid CF = 0.01 [ 0.00 - 0.04 ]
```

With these soft thresholds, attributes specified by a range rather than a value require a more complex interpolation scheme. Using the probability curve of Figure 8–2, the program computes the area under the curve lying between the lower and upper limits and compares this to the interval size to obtain the probability of the "$\leq$" outcome.

8.2 Production rule models

A second program, consultr, provides interactive interpretation of rule-based models derived from decision trees (Chapter 5). The program accepts the same forms of imprecise attribute value specification as above. The characterization of classification certainty is less elaborate, though— the program suggests only one class together with an estimated certainty factor.

The principal extension to the simple interpreter of Chapter 5 concerns the way imprecise values are handled. The left-hand side of a rule can contain conditions of three kinds:

- $A = V$, where V is a possible value of discrete attribute A.
  The probability that this condition is satisfied by a case is just the probability assigned to value V. This is either 0 or 1 when a precise value is specified, but may have any intermediate value if a series of values and probabilities is input.

- A in $\{V_1, V_2, \ldots\}$, where V_1, V_2, $\ldots$ are possible values of A; this form can arise when the value grouping option described in the previous chapter is invoked.
  Since the specified values are mutually exclusive, the probability that

the condition is satisfied is the sum of the probabilities specified for the individual values.

- $A \leq Z$ or $A > Z$, where A is a continuous attribute and Z is a threshold.

  The rule interpreter does not make use of the soft threshold information described in the previous section. The probability that $A \leq Z$ is satisfied is thus the proportion of the range given for the value of A that lies below Z, with an analogous expression for ">."

No matter what its form, a condition that involves attribute A is not satisfied if the value of A is unknown.

To assess the probability that the left-hand side of a rule is satisfied by a case, the interpreter makes the simplifying (but usually incorrect) assumption that the conditions are independent, and forms the product of the probabilities that the individual conditions are satisfied. If this product exceeds a parameter (set at 0.5 in the program), the rule is regarded as being satisfied.

As before, the consultr program scans the list of rules until one is satisfied and predicts that the case will belong to the class given in the rule's right-hand side. The final certainty factor attached to the classification is the product of the probability that the rule was satisfied and the estimated reliability of the rule. If no rule is satisfied, the case is assigned to the default class, but with no estimated certainty factor.

When the same information is provided as for the decision tree interpreter, consultr reaches the same conclusion in this case:

```
on thyroxine: f
thyroid surgery: f
TSH: 8.8
TT4: 148
FTI: 75

Decision:
     compensated hypothyroid CF = 0.99
```

using the first rule shown in Section 5.3. Suppose now that TT4 was specified only to lie somewhere in the range 130–151. The fraction of this interval that lies below the threshold of 150 is 20/21, so the corresponding condition is satisfied with 95% probability. All other conditions are still satisfied with certainty, so the probability that the rule is satisfied is also 95%. The confidence of the classification is reduced accordingly:

on thyroxine: f
thyroid surgery: f
TSH: *8.8*
TT4: *130-151*
FTI: *75*

Decision:
    compensated hypothyroid CF = 0.94

8.3 Caveat

The fact that imprecise information is handled differently in the decision tree and production rule interpreters should underline the warning given earlier about the ad hoc nature of the methods used by both. The certainty factors and ranges produced by the programs are not intended to be probabilities (hence their lack of exact specification). Rather, they provide a subjective indication of the degree of confidence with which the classification models' predictions can be accepted.

## CHAPTER 9

Guide to Using the System

We must finally descend to the level of nitty-gritty detail to discuss the way that C4.5 is used. The advice given by the *Hitch-Hikers' Guide* is relevant here: DON'T PANIC! Although there are numerous options that control how the system behaves, many of these need never concern the typical user.

In the following sections it is often necessary to denote parts of commands and file names that may or may not be present. We follow the usual convention of enclosing this optional material in brackets; remember that these brackets should be omitted when typing commands.

9.1 Files

9.1.1 Filestem

As mentioned in Chapter 1, every task needs a short name, referred to as its *filestem*, that identifies its files. All files read and written by the system are of the form *filestem.extension*, where *extension* characterizes the type of information involved. The filestem used in Chapter 1 was labor-neg; generally, a filestem can be any string of characters that is acceptable as a file name to your operating system. If your environment imposes restrictions on the length of file names, the filestem should be at least nine characters shorter than this limit to allow for the addition of extensions, and shorter still if you intend to use the cross-validation shell script.

9.1.2 Names file

The fundamental file for any task is the *names* file, called *filestem*.names, that provides names for classes, attributes, and attribute values. Each name consists of a string of characters of any length, with some restrictions:

- A name cannot be the single character "?."

- Although any character can appear in a name, the *special characters* comma (,), colon (:), vertical bar (|), and backslash (\) have particular meanings and must be *escaped* (preceded by a backslash character) if they appear in a name.

- A period may appear in a name provided it is not followed by a space.

- Embedded spaces are also permitted in a name, but multiple *white-space* characters (spaces and tabs) are replaced by a single space.

Otherwise, the form of a name is rather unconstrained—for example, numbers are perfectly acceptable as names.

The names file consists of a series of entries, each starting on a new line and ending with a period. Blank lines, spaces, and tabs may be used to make the file more readable and have no significance (except within a name). In addition, the vertical bar character (|) appearing anywhere on a line causes the rest of that line to be ignored, and can be used to incorporate comments in the file.

The first entry in the names file gives the class names, separated by commas (and don't forget the period at the end of the entry!). There must be at least two class names and their order is not important.

The rest of the file consists of a single entry for each attribute. An attribute entry begins with the attribute name followed by a colon, and then a specification of the values that the attribute can take. Four specifications are possible:

- ignore; causes the value of the attribute to be disregarded.

- continuous; indicates that the attribute has numeric values, either integer or floating point.

- discrete N, where N is a positive integer; specifies that the attribute has discrete values, and there are no more than N of them.

- A list of names separated by commas; also indicates that the attribute has discrete values and specifies them explicitly (preferred to discrete since it enables the data to be checked). As with class names, the order of attribute values is arbitrary.

Each entry is terminated with a period.

This will probably be clearer if you look again at the sample names file in Figure 1–1. The first line contains the class names and is followed by an optional blank line to improve readability. Next come 16 entries, 1 for every attribute. Each attribute name is followed by a colon and then either continuous (if it is a real-valued attribute) or a list of the possible values it can take if it is a discrete attribute. In these entries, tabs have been used to make the file more intelligible. Some attribute names such as wage increase first year, and some attribute values such as below average, contain embedded spaces, which are significant; all other spaces and tabs are ignored.

9.1.3 Data file

The data file *filestem*.data is used to describe the training cases from which decision trees and/or rulesets are to be constructed. Each line describes one case, providing the values for all the attributes and then the case's class, separated by commas and terminated by a period. The attribute values must appear in the same order that the attributes were given in the names file. The order of cases themselves does not matter.

Names used as attribute or class values obey the same restrictions as for the names file; in particular, embedded special characters must be escaped by preceding them with a backslash. If the value of an attribute, either discrete or continuous, is not known or is not relevant, that value is specified by a question mark. Values of continuous attributes may be given in integer, fixed-point, or floating-point form, so that all the following are acceptable:

$$1, \ 1.2, \ +1.2, \ -.2, \ -12\text{E}-3, \ 0.00012$$

In fact, any numeric value that is acceptable to your local C compiler will probably work.

The data file can also contain embedded comments. The appearance of the character | (unescaped) anywhere on a line causes the remainder of that line to be ignored. It is unwise to commence a comment in the middle of a name.

9.1.4 Test file

For some applications, you may decide to reserve part of the available data as a test set to evaluate the classifier you have produced. If there is one, the test set appears in the file *filestem*.test, in exactly the same format as the data file.

9.1.5 Files generated by the system

The programs C4.5 and C4.5RULES and the cross-validation script described later also generate files with the same filestem as above. As a user, you will not have to worry about these, other than to make sure that you do not delete or modify them while they are still relevant! The principal file extensions are:

- **unpruned**, containing the one or more unpruned trees generated by C4.5. Used by C4.5RULES.

- **tree**, the final pruned tree; if more than one tree is generated via windowing, this is the tree chosen as the best. Used by CONSULT.

- **rules**, the final ruleset generated by C4.5RULES. Used by CONSULTR.

- **to***i*[+*identifier*] and **ro***i*[+*identifier*], for $i = 0, 1, 2, \ldots$; output of the decision tree and rules programs on different sections of a cross-validation experiment that has an optional identifier.

- **tres**[+*identifier*] and **rres**[+*identifier*]; summary of results for trees and rules on the cross-validation.

9.1.6 Size restrictions

The software does not impose any (practical) limit on the number of classes, attributes, attribute values, or cases in the **data** and **test** files. The numbers of classes, attributes, and discrete values per attribute must all be representable by short integers; in most implementations of C, this allows more than 16,000 of each. The number of training and test cases are represented by full integers, normally permitting about 10^9 of each. However, your particular operating system may limit the amount of memory that can be allocated to any one process, affecting the size of problem that can be attempted.

If a large training set is processed on a machine with a small physical memory, the programs will run very slowly as a result of the need to swap pages in and out.

9.2 Running the programs

Each of the programs allows options to be invoked on the command line. Although some of them are rarely used, they are all given here for completeness, together with the default values that are used if the option is not invoked.

9.2.1 Decision tree induction

The command for invoking the program to build a decision tree is c4.5. The options that can be used with this command are:

-f *filestem* (Default: DF)
> This option is almost always used to specify the filestem of the task as above. If no filestem is given, the default filestem DF is assumed.

-u (Default: no test set)
> This option is invoked when a test file has been prepared.

-s (Default: no grouping)
> As described in Chapter 7, this option causes the values of discrete attributes to be grouped for tests. The default is no grouping, in which case tests on discrete attributes have a separate branch for every possible value of the attribute.

-m *weight* (Default: 2)
> Near-trivial tests in which almost all the training cases have the same outcome can lead to odd trees with little predictive power. To avoid this undesirable eventuality, C4.5 requires that any test used in the tree must have at least two outcomes with a minimum number of cases (or, to be more precise, the sum of the weights of the cases for at least two of the subsets T_i must attain some minimum). The default minimum is 2, but can be changed by this option; a higher value may be a good idea for tasks where there is a lot of noisy data.

-c *CF* (Default: 25%)
> The *CF* value affects decision tree pruning, discussed in Chapter 4. Small values cause more heavy pruning than large values, with a most pronounced effect on smaller data sets. The default value seems to work reasonably well for many tasks, but you might want to alter it to a lower value if you notice that the actual error rate of pruned trees on test cases is much higher than the estimated error rate (indicative of underpruning).

-v *level*   (Default: level 0)

The program contains embedded code to show what is going on during the execution of the algorithms. Level 0, the default, generates no expository output of this kind, level 1 a little, and so on. The levels 3 and above can generate an *enormous* amount of output which is meaningful only to people who have an intimate knowledge of the code. The maximum level is 5.

-t *trees*   (Default: 10)

This is one of the options that can be used to invoke windowing, discussed in Chapter 6, in which trees are grown iteratively. It specifies the number of trees to be grown in this manner before one is selected as the best. Unless one of the windowing options is specified, the program will grow a single tree in the standard way as described in Chapter 2.

-w *size*   (Default: determined by data file)

This option invokes windowing and specifies the number of cases to be included in the initial window. The default is the maximum of 20% of the training cases and twice the square root of the number of training cases.

-i *increment*   (Default: determined by window size)

This option activates windowing and gives the maximum number of cases that can be added to the window at each iteration. The default is 20% of the initial window size. Whatever the value of this option, however, at least half of the training cases misclassified by the current rule are added to the next window.

-g   (Default: gain ratio criterion)

The criterion used for assessing possible splits, described in Chapter 2, can be changed to the older gain criterion by this option.

-p   (Default: hard thresholds)

When this option is invoked, subsidiary cutpoints Z^+ and Z^- are determined for each test on a continuous attribute. The subsidiary cutpoints affect only the way cases are classified using the interactive decision tree interpreter as described in Chapter 8.

Options can appear in any order. For example, the command

c4.5 -c 10 -u -f mytask -s

would invoke the decision tree program on a task with filestem mytask (so with names file mytask.names and training cases in mytask.data). A single tree would be constructed with grouped-value tests for discrete attributes, pruned using a *CF* value of 10%, and tested on the unseen cases in mytask.test.

9.2.2 Rule induction

The rule induction program, invoked by the command c4.5rules, should only be used after running the decision tree program C4.5, since it reads the unpruned file containing the unpruned tree(s). Four of the six options have the same meaning as for the previous program, namely

-f *filestem* (Default: DF)

-u (Default: no test set)

-v *level* (Default: level 0)

-c *CF* (Default: 25%)

(where the *CF* value is used to prune rules rather than trees). The last two options are:

-F *confidence* (Default: no significance testing)
> If this option is used, the significance of each condition in the left-hand side of a rule is checked using Fisher's "exact" test; each condition must be judged significant at the specified confidence level. This will generally have the effect of producing shorter rules than the standard pruning method, with some risk of over-generalization for tasks with little data.

-r *redundancy* (Default: 1.0)
> The number of bits required to encode a set of rules, as presented in Chapter 5, can be increased substantially by the presence of irrelevant or redundant attributes. This

option can be used to specify an approximate redundancy factor when the user has reason to believe that there are many redundant attributes. A redundancy value of 2.5, for instance, implies that there are 2.5 times more attributes than are likely to be useful. The -r option is likely to be beneficial only when the user knows the data well and can estimate an appropriate value.

9.2.3 Interactive classification model interpreters

These programs, CONSULT for decision tree models and CONSULTR for production rule models, accept the same input and so can be dealt with together. Naturally enough, the programs should be used only after the appropriate models have been generated by the C4.5 and C4.5RULES programs, and are invoked respectively by

$$\text{consult } [\text{-f } \textit{filestem}] \ [\text{-t}]$$
$$\text{consultr } [\text{-f } \textit{filestem}] \ [\text{-t}]$$

where the -f option gives the filestem, as before. If the -t option appears, the decision tree or ruleset is printed at the start of the consultation session.

These programs request information from the user by prompting for the values of attributes. A prompt consists of an attribute name followed by a colon. If the attribute is discrete, the user can reply with

- "?" indicating the attribute value is not known;

- a single possible value; or

- a set of possible values of the form

$$V_1 : P_1, \ V_2 : P_2, \ \ldots, \ V_k : P_k$$

where the V_i's are possible values and the P_i's are corresponding value probabilities (see Chapter 8). If the V_i's do not cover all possible values and the sum of the P_i's is less than one, the unassigned probability is distributed equally over the remaining values.

Similarly, the user can reply to a query concerning a real-valued attribute with

- "?" indicating the attribute value is not known;

- a single number; or

- an interval consisting of two numbers separated by a hyphen (-). In this latter case, the value of the attribute is treated as being uniformly distributed in the interval.

Each reply must be followed by a carriage return. Any incorrect input will cause a brief error message to appear, after which the user will be prompted again for the same attribute value.

When the classification model has inquired after all relevant information, the conclusion is presented as described in the previous chapter. The interpreter then prompts the user with

Retry, new case or quit [r,n,q]:

The response to this prompt is one of the three characters indicated, with the following effects:

- q: The program exits.

- n: A new case is classified; the queries recommence as above.

- r: The same case is reexamined. At each query, the reply given last time appears in square brackets. This previous information can be left unchanged by simply pressing carriage return, or can be altered by providing new information in the same manner as before.

9.3 Conducting experiments

Up to this point, the method suggested for estimating the reliability of a classification model is to divide the data into a training and test set, build the model using only the training set, and examine its performance on the unseen test cases. This is quite satisfactory when there is plenty of data, but in the more common circumstance of having less data than we would like, two problems arise. First, in order to get a reasonably accurate fix on error rate, the test set must be large, so the training set is impoverished. Secondly, when the total amount of data is moderate (several hundred cases, say), different divisions of the data into training and test sets can produce surprisingly large variations in error rates on unseen cases.

A more robust estimate of accuracy on unseen cases can be obtained by *cross-validation*. In this procedure, the available data is divided into N blocks so as to make each block's number of cases and class distribution as uniform as possible. N different classification models are then built, in each of which one block is omitted from the training data, and the resulting model is tested on the cases in that omitted block. In this way, each case appears in exactly one test set. Provided that N is not too small—10 is a common number—the average error rate over the N unseen test sets is a good predictor of the error rate of a model built from all the data.[8]

Cross-validation may seem complex, but two small programs and the shell script that invokes them have been included to facilitate trials. The command to execute the script is

$$\text{xval.sh } \textit{filestem } N \textit{ [options] [+identifier]}$$

where

- *filestem* is the name of the task, as above. The script expects to find the corresponding **names** and **data** files and, if there is also a **test** file, the cases in the **data** and **test** files are merged before being divided into blocks.

- N is the number of blocks to be used, and so the number of train/test runs to be made. N should never exceed the number of cases available.

- *options*, if they appear, are any options that are to be applied to C4.5 and/or C4.5RULES, in any order.

- the optional *+identifier* is used to label and recognize the output from this particular cross-validation run. There should not be any spaces between the "+" and the identifier. Since this suffix will be attached to every file name generated, it should be short—two or three characters is recommended.

The script generates successive **data** and **test** files, builds a decision tree model and a production rule model from the training cases, and uses the models to classify the unseen test cases. The average figures for the two model types are written to the files *filestem*.**tres**[*+identifier*] and *filestem*.**rres**[*+identifier*]. Files with extension **to***i*[*+identifier*] and **ro***i*[*+identifier*] contain the output from C4.5 and C4.5RULES for the *i*th of the N runs.

---

8. This gives a slight overestimate of the error rate, since each of the N models is constructed from a subset of the data.

For example, suppose that we wished to carry out a ten-way cross-validation of mytask, grouping tests for the construction of trees and setting a redundancy factor of 2.5 when rules are produced. The command

xval.sh mytask 10 -s -r 2.5 +me

would invoke the cross-validation script as above. This would divide any data into ten blocks, numbered 0 through 9, and would produce the following output files:

- Output from individual runs from C4.5 in files mytask.to0+me to mytask.to9+me and a summary in mytask.tres+me.

- Similar output from the ten C4.5RULES runs in files mytask.ro0+me to mytask.ro9+me and a summary in mytask.rres+me.

The summary files are quite terse, giving the lines from each individual run that describe errors on the training and test sets, and similar lines that show the average errors on training and test. For instance, when a ten-way cross-validation was carried out on the labor-neg data from Chapter 1, the summary file for C4.5RULES (Figure 9–1) indicates that, on the first block, there were three errors on the training data and one on the test data, none on each for the second block, and so on. Averaged over the ten blocks, the rules had a 3.7% error rate on the training data and a 13.7% error rate on unseen test cases. This last figure would be the cross-validation estimate of the error rate of a ruleset built from all the data.

9.4 Using options: A credit approval example

We close this chapter with a small example that illustrates the use of some of the options above. The domain for this case study concerns approval of credit facilities using a dataset provided by a bank. The 690 cases are split 44% to 56% between two classes; the 15 attributes include 6 with numeric values and 9 discrete-valued attributes, the latter having from 2 to 14 possible values. This dataset is distributed with the system under the name crx, but the names of classes, attributes, and attribute values have been disguised by replacing them with symbols to protect the bank's interest in the data. (Such bowdlerization does not affect the learning task in any way but makes the resulting classification models rather uninformative.)

```
Tested 51, errors 3 (5.9%) <<
Tested 6, errors 1 (16.7%) <<
Tested 51, errors 0 (0.0%) <<
Tested 6, errors 0 (0.0%) <<
Tested 51, errors 2 (3.9%) <<
Tested 6, errors 2 (33.3%) <<
Tested 51, errors 1 (2.0%) <<
Tested 6, errors 0 (0.0%) <<
Tested 51, errors 3 (5.9%) <<
Tested 6, errors 3 (50.0%) <<
Tested 51, errors 1 (2.0%) <<
Tested 6, errors 0 (0.0%) <<
Tested 51, errors 3 (5.9%) <<
Tested 6, errors 1 (16.7%) <<
Tested 52, errors 1 (1.9%) <<
Tested 5, errors 1 (20.0%) <<
Tested 52, errors 2 (3.8%) <<
Tested 5, errors 0 (0.0%) <<
Tested 52, errors 3 (5.8%) <<
Tested 5, errors 0 (0.0%) <<

train:   Tested 51.3, errors 1.9 (3.7%) <<
test:    Tested 5.7, errors 0.8 (13.7%) <<
```

Figure 9–1. Summary file for rule models, labor-neg data

As a sighting shot, a ten-way cross-validation using all default options is carried out by the command

xval.sh crx 10

The key information extracted from the summary files crx.tres and crx.rres is given in the first line of Table 9–1. For this cross-validation, the average simplified decision tree of 58.8 nodes has an error rate of 17.5% on unseen cases whereas the pessimistic error rate predicted from the training data is 12.4%. The unseen error rate for production rules, 17.4%, is quite close to that for the trees.

Inspection of the simplified trees in files crx.to0 to crx.to9 reveals that the multivalued discrete attributes appear infrequently. This could be because they contain little information relevant to classification, or alternatively because they are not being treated equitably by the default gain ratio selection criterion. To explore this further, the cross-validation

Table 9–1. Results with selected options

Options	Decision Trees			Rules
	Size	Unseen Error Rate	Predicted Error Rate	Unseen Error Rate
default	58.8	17.5%	12.4%	17.4%
-s	69.5	17.4%	11.6%	15.2%
-m15	15.9	14.5%	14.4%	14.3%
-c10	39.1	15.8%	15.6%	16.1%
-m15 -c10	10.7	14.5%	16.6%	14.2%
-t10	67.1	17.1%	11.8%	16.8%
-t10 -m15	15.9	15.1%	14.1%	14.5%

is rerun with the -s option that enables the formation of value groups. As Table 9–1 shows, this appears to have little effect on the decision trees (in fact, their average size increases slightly), but results in a lower error rate for the rule-based classifiers. The lack of significant improvement for trees suggests that value grouping is not going to be helpful for this task.

The feature that stands out in the first default run is the disparity between the observed and estimated error rates for unseen cases. This sort of situation can arise when the attributes allow an almost "pure" partition of the training cases into single-class subsets, but where much of the structure induced by this partition has little predictive power. (Since a single continuous attribute can give rise to numerous possible divisions, the phenomenon often occurs when there are many independent continuous attributes.) There are two ways to address the problem: increasing the -m value so as to prevent overly fine-grained divisions of the training set, or reducing the -c option with the effect that more structure is pruned away. When the same cross-validation is repeated with -m15 and with -c10, Table 9–1 shows that the former is more effective here. The error rates on unseen cases obtained with -m15 are much smaller for both trees and rules; moreover, the predicted error rate for trees is almost exactly correct, indicating an appropriate level of pruning. If we try to gild the lily by using both options together, Table 9–1 shows that the error rate is still low but the simplified trees are smaller.

So far, we have reduced the error rate from 17.5% to 14.5% for pruned trees and from 17.4% to 14.2% for rules, an improvement of roughly 20%. Next, we investigate whether windowing would help in this domain. The -t10 option causes ten trees to be produced, one of which is selected as the best tree, but all of which are used when a ruleset is constructed. The windowing option slows down the cross-validation by a factor of 20 or so and has little apparent benefit, either on its own or when invoked with the -m15 option.

At this stage it seems sensible to call a halt to further trials and to recommend using the options -m15 and -c10. The values 15 and 10 were more or less plucked from the air, so we could perhaps see whether other values near these give noticeably better results; in my experience, such fine-tuning is not terribly productive because the system is relatively insensitive to small changes in parameter values. In an actual application we would now return to the dataset and generate a single tree or production rule classifier from all the available cases using these options.

CHAPTER 10

Limitations

This chapter, like the previous one, is concerned with pragmatic issues arising from using the software. Instead of looking at *how-to-use* matters such as commands and options, we turn to more intangible *when-to-use* issues: For what kinds of tasks are decision tree methods in general, and this system in particular, likely to be appropriate? Of course, it never hurts to try it and see. However, a better understanding of the relationship between tasks and methods can not only reduce wasted time, but can also suggest ways in which the task can be changed to make it more amenable to these methods.

10.1 Geometric interpretation

Early research in induction, such as that described in the classic reference *Learning Machines* [Nilsson, 1965], was based on a geometric model of the learning task in which objects (cases) are described by vectors of real numbers. If there are N attributes, such a vector corresponds to a point in an N-dimensional Euclidean *description space*. From this perspective, a classifier corresponds to a division of the description space into regions, each labelled with a class. An unseen case is classified by determining the region into which the corresponding point falls and assigning it to the class associated with that region. The induction task is then one of finding an appropriate partition of the description space or, equivalently, of describing the surfaces that bound each region.

This notion can easily be generalized to discrete attributes as well— such an attribute corresponds to an axis with only a fixed number of possible values. Ignoring the messy complication of unknown attribute values, it is clear that each case can still be represented as a point. The resulting description space is not generally Euclidean, however, because distances and distance relations can be altered by reordering the discrete values on such an axis or by spacing them differently. Consider the simple case of Figure 10–1 in which there is one continuous attribute, size, and a discrete attribute, shape. The order of values of shape has no intrinsic significance. In the left-hand layout the point A (corresponding to a

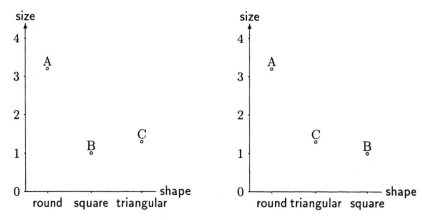

Figure 10–1. Two possible description spaces

case with size 3.2 and shape round) is closer to B than to C, but this relationship is reversed in the right-hand layout.

Like any classifier, a decision tree specifies how a description space is to be carved up into regions associated with the classes. In the labor-neg task of Chapter 1, for example, each case is described by 16 attributes. The corresponding 16-dimensional description space is divided into two regions by the first test of the decision tree in Figure 1–3. Each of these regions is differently subdivided by the relevant test at the second level, and two of the regions are further split by tests at the third level. There are seven regions in the final partition of the space, one corresponding to each leaf of the decision tree.

This point-and-region perspective holds many insights about induction tasks and the behavior of learning algorithms. Rendell and Cho [1990] discuss classes of tasks and characterize their difficulty in terms of metrics such as the number of regions and the density of points in them. Aha, Kibler, and Albert [1991] describe instance-based algorithms and prove theorems about their properties using this spatial interpretation. (The well-known *Explorations in Parallel Distributed Processing* [McClelland and Rumelhart, 1988] uses an analogous weight space to describe the performance of back propagation.) The geometric interpretation of classification tasks is used here to highlight some weaknesses inherent in divide-and-conquer methods and to discuss ways of detecting when they affect particular tasks.

10.2 Nonrectangular regions

Each of the divisions that results from the sort of test we have encountered so far corresponds to a special kind of surface in the description space, namely a hyperplane that is orthogonal to the axis of the tested attribute and parallel to all other axes. This observation is crucial because the regions produced by a decision tree that uses such tests are not arbitrary—they are all hyperrectangles.

When the task at hand is such that class regions are not hyperrectangles, the best that a decision tree can do is to approximate the regions by hyperrectangles. This is illustrated by the artificial task of Figure 10–2 in which 100 cases of two classes (represented by o and +) are described by two continuous attributes, X and Y. The intended division of the description space by an oblique line is shown on the left, while the right-hand side of the figure displays the approximation to this division that is found by C4.5. Rather surprisingly, the division of the description space into 4 rectangular regions misclassifies only 2 of the 100 training cases. It is a different story on unseen cases, however, for which the rectangular approximation has an error rate of 11%. As the number of training cases is increased, the approximation of the oblique division by a collection of rectangles becomes better and better, but at the expense of a substantial increase in the number of regions—the decision tree that results from 1,000 similar cases partitions the description space into 17 rectangular regions and has an error rate of 3% on unseen cases.

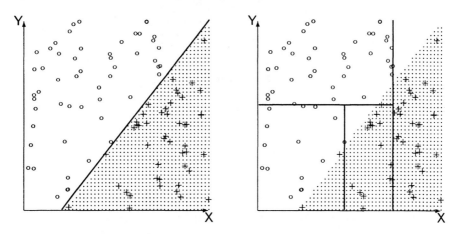

Figure 10–2. Real and approximate divisions for an artificial task

The unlimited growth of the decision tree as more training cases are used, coupled with a more or less constant error rate on the same training cases, serves as a kind of signature of this condition in which the surfaces bounding regions are not naturally orthogonal hyperplanes. The remedy is to look for some arithmetic combination of the attributes to be included as a new attribute. Some decision tree systems provide assistance in this direction by allowing tests that contain linear combinations of attributes. Instead of comparing one selected attribute against a threshold, these systems consider tests such as

$$\sum_i w_i \times A_i > Z$$

and find weights $\{w_i\}$ to maximize the worth of a split under the prevailing criterion—the CART system allows this as an option. In a similar vein, *linear machine* decision trees [Utgoff and Brodley, 1991] employ tests of this kind, but find the weights by hill-climbing. Moreover, the search for weights in the latter system is biased towards combinations of a few attributes, rather than all of them, with the idea of producing more comprehensible tests. These approaches can be useful, and would have circumvented the problem of Figure 10–2. However, broadening the range of possible tests in this way covers only one form of arithmetic combination of the attributes and does not address, for example, products of the attributes. To incorporate general arithmetic combinations would require the kind of extensive search carried out by programs like BACON [Langley, Bradshaw, and Simon, 1983] and MARS [Friedman, 1988], but even the limited generalization to linear combinations can slow down the process of building trees by an order of magnitude.

10.3 Poorly delineated regions

Decision trees are constructed by successive refinement, splitting existing regions of the description space with the aim of producing regions that contain points of a single class. Since the early divisions are decided on the basis of progress towards this goal, it is important that the goal itself be realistic. If the final regions are such that each contains a distinguishable cluster of points with a class distribution that differs markedly from at least one adjacent region, the goal can be seen to have been realized. In two situations, though, the goal has clearly not been attained:

- The density of points in some regions is low, so that there is a great deal of latitude in the positioning of the boundary surfaces.

- The classification task is essentially probabilistic, so that the target regions contain substantial numbers of points that do not belong to the majority class.

In either case, the indefinite nature of the final regions provides poor guidance for the initial divisions of the description space.

The second concern is well-illustrated in data constructed by Michael Walker of Stanford University. The left-hand side of Figure 10–3 shows 120 cases belonging to two classes (again labelled o and +) with two continuous attributes. Appropriate regions are not immediately obvious to the eye, but division of the description space into 4 quadrants reveals the underlying model used to generate this data. The northeast quadrant contains only + cases, the northwest and southeast quadrants contain a two-thirds majority of the same class, while the southwest quadrant contains a two-thirds majority of the other class. When this data is processed by C4.5, the system splits the description space into 16 regions rather than the 4 from which the cases were generated.

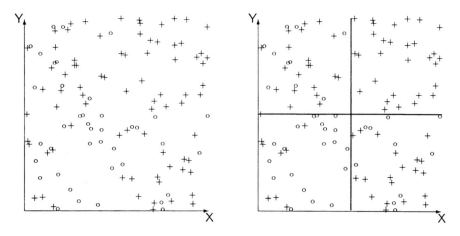

Figure 10–3. Description space and points for probabilistic classifier

The situation in which the "best" classifier is probabilistic in at least some regions of the description space is signalled by the occurrence, in the simplified decision tree, of leaves with a substantial number of training cases, but also a relatively large number of predicted errors. In these circumstances it is often worthwhile trying a larger value of the minimum weight parameter or a smaller value of the confidence parameter (the -m and -c options, Chapter 9), with the aim of preventing overly fine-grained divisions of the description space.

The above example raises another important question. Should the northeast quadrant be separated from the northwest quadrant, or from the southeast? All three quadrants have the same majority class, so C4.5 will merge them wherever possible. However, merging regions like these with dissimilar class distributions loses information on the reliability of classification that may be valuable when using the interactive consultation programs.

10.4 Fragmented regions

The geometric perspective of induction provides a clear picture of the sort of classifier that is easiest to learn. It should divide the description space into as few regions as possible, in each of which there is a high concentration of points, all of the same class. Consequently, there should be few classes and (especially) few regions per class, many cases relative to the volume of the regions, and no misclassification of the training cases. Most real tasks deviate from this ideal in one or more respects, but we focus here on tasks that have many regions, or that have low point densities in the regions.

Sometimes the proliferation of regions can be unexpected. Spackman [1988] notes that biomedical diagnostic tests commonly require m of a possible n conditions to be present to support a positive finding. If each of the n possible conditions refers to a different attribute, such a diagnostic rule would require at least $\binom{m}{n}$ regions labelled with the positive finding. He cites one rule in which any 4 of 11 conditions are sufficient to support a finding; such a rule would require 330 regions for the positive findings alone! Similarly, if it is always necessary to examine m or more attributes before deciding whether or not a case belongs to a particular class, the description space must be divided into at least 2^m regions. An example of this situation is the parity problem in which each case is described by m binary attributes and belongs to class **odd** if an odd number of attributes have the value 1. In both these examples, a class description that appears disarmingly simple translates to a classifier that requires numerous regions to specify.

The number of training cases needed to construct a classifier is clearly related to the number of regions needed to specify it—the more regions there are, the more data is required. Even when a concept seems to have a compact description, such as the m-of-n rules, it is the geometric representation of the concept in the description space and the language used to express theories that determine its real complexity.

Another cause of fragmented regions is not the concept itself, but the presence of irrelevant attributes. If these are numerous, the probability of choosing one of them at a decision node increases and each such split at least doubles the number of leaves for the relevant subtree. However, the divide-and-conquer paradigm itself suggests a simple means of detecting and eliminating at least some irrelevant attributes. A tree is first produced using all the attributes, then those that do not appear in the tree (or do not appear on the paths to the more populous leaves) are eliminated. Another tree is grown with the reduced set of attributes and the process is repeated until no further attributes can be discarded. Each time an irrelevant attribute is removed, the chance of using one of them in a tree is reduced, yielding fewer leaves. This can be illustrated with respect to the credit approval dataset described in Chapter 9. The credit data is fairly noisy and, on a cross-validation study with the default options, the error on unseen cases is 17.5% for decision trees and 17.4% for rules. However, the simplified tree produced from all the data uses only 9 of the 15 attributes. When the others are removed, the same cross-validation gives error rates of 16.2% for trees and 15.4% for rules, a substantial improvement.

Sometimes fragmentation of the description space can be avoided by introducing new attributes rather than removing old ones. As a simple example, suppose that we had cases described by nine logical attributes $\{A_1, A_2, \ldots, A_9\}$ and the target concept was specified by

$$(A_1 \lor A_2 \lor A_3) \land (A_4 \lor A_5 \lor A_6) \land (A_7 \lor A_8 \lor A_9).$$

Now, each leaf of a decision tree corresponds to a conjunction of conditions, as noted in Chapter 5. The above expression contains 27 terms when rewritten in conjunctive form, so a correct decision tree must have 27 leaves corresponding to instances of the concept. The number of leaves grows to about 50 when leaves for noninstances are included, so the concept requires the same number of regions in the description space. If new attributes are introduced for each of the three disjunctive terms (such as B_1 for $A_1 \lor A_2 \lor A_3$), it is possible to specify a correct decision tree with only 4 leaves, so the minimum number of regions is reduced from 50 to 4. This kind of simplification via *constructive induction*, or the development of new attributes, is described well in Pagallo and Haussler [1990]. Recent work by Murphy and Pazzani [1991] also addresses construction of new attributes, but, rather than forming conjunctions or disjunctions of existing attributes, the new attributes are expressed in m-of-n form discussed above.

Fragmentation, whether caused by irrelevant attributes or concept complexity, is a major obstacle in the induction of efficient and comprehensible classifiers. Any transformation of the description space, by the removal of attributes or the inclusion of appropriate logical or arithmetic combinations of attributes, that has the effect of reducing the number of regions needed to represent a classifier, is potentially of benefit. If no such transformations can be found, the only way to deal with fragmentation is to bring more data to bear on the problem.

10.5 A more cheerful note

The tone of this chapter has been rather negative, emphasising as it does the shortcomings of tree-based methods. To counter all this gloom, we should not lose sight of the fact that these methods also have substantial advantages. The divide-and-conquer paradigm itself is very fast, and, unlike many statistical approaches, it does not depend on assumptions about the distribution of attribute values or the independence of the attributes themselves.

Numerous authors have compared classifiers based on decision trees and production rules with other approaches that use the same data, notably statistical techniques and neural network classifiers. In one study, Breiman *et al.* [1984] addressed the problem of predicting long-term survival chances of patients admitted to intensive care after a heart attack. The decision tree produced by CART was almost trivial—three decision nodes and four leaves—yet the authors write:

> [The tree's] simplicity raises the suspicion that standard statistical methods may give classification rules that are more accurate. When these were tried, the rules produced were considerably more intricate, but less accurate.

Other comparison studies include those by Michalski and Chilausky [1980], Quinlan [1988a], Spackman [1988], Dieterich, Hild, and Bakiri [1989], Fisher and McKusick [1989], Weiss and Kapouleas [1989], Buntine [1991], Shavlik, Mooney, and Towell [1991], Weiss and Kulikowski [1991], and Quinlan [1993]. (As this list suggests, the interest in comparing the performance of learning systems has picked up recently.) Two general conclusions of such studies are:

- Tree-based symbolic methods and neural networks tend to be more robust across tasks than most other techniques.

- Tree-based and network classifiers usually have similar accuracy (but with networks slightly ahead). Networks, however, require orders of magnitude more computation to develop.

CHAPTER 11

Desirable Additions

There is always the temptation to go on adding knobs and whistles to a computer system so that it will have every imaginable capability and facility. While this may be a noble aspiration, it does slow down completion of the product! The first version of ID3 that I distributed consisted of 540 lines of Pascal. The C4.5 code published here comes to nearly 9,000 lines and still lacks many extensions that I would like to incorporate. This final chapter presents some of these missing but useful features, most of which have been implemented in at least one other system.

11.1 Continuous classes

One annoyance is C4.5's requirement that classes be discrete and unordered. (The discrete classes may actually be ordered, but C4.5 has no way of making use of this information.) Continuous classes are needed whenever the quantity to be predicted is numeric rather than categorical; training data relates the value of this dependent variable to the other variables and the task is to construct a model that will predict the value for unseen cases. In this light, building a model for data with continuous classes involves approximating an unknown function.

CART copes with continuous classes by installing a value rather than a class name at each leaf. Breiman *et al.* [1984] refer to such trees as *regression trees* rather than decision trees. The value predicted by such a tree can be expressed as

$$\sum_l V_l \times S_l$$

where, for each leaf l, V_l is the value stored at the leaf and S_l is a selector that is 1 if all the conditions on the path from the root to leaf l are satisfied by a case, and 0 otherwise. The predicted value is thus a weighted sum, where the weights are the values at the leaves and the basis functions are the selectors. Although function approximations of this form are clearly discontinuous, techniques akin to soft thresholds can be used to "smooth" the predicted values [Daryl Pregibon, private communication]. More recently, Friedman [1988] describes an improved method that uses continuous basis functions but also moves away from a tree-based structure.

I have implemented an experimental program similar to C4.5 for continuous classes [Quinlan, 1992]. This program also generates tree-based models, but allows leaves to hold general linear models instead of single values. The same sort of questions posed in the context of discrete classes arise here, too; for example:

- What is a good criterion for ranking possible tests at a decision node?

- When should a tree be pruned to avoid overfitting? When should a subtree be replaced by one of its branches or by a leaf, and when should the model at a leaf be simplified by eliminating some of the coefficients?

Unfortunately, the answers that appear to work best involve rather different heuristics than those that apply to discrete classes. This has persuaded me not to attempt to incorporate continuous classes in C4.5 by way of an option, but to keep the two systems separate.

11.2 Ordered discrete attributes

Attributes in C4.5 are either continuous, and hence ordered, or discrete, in which case they are presumed to be unordered. Many systems implement a third kind of attribute, *ordinal*, that has discrete, ordered values. Common uses of ordinal attributes are for qualitative descriptions, such as giving a reading as very low, low, medium, high, or very high. An attribute like this should often be treated similarly to a continuous attribute, with tests that divide the values into those below and those above a threshold value.

The only way to represent attributes of this kind in C4.5 is to map the discrete values onto integers (e.g., setting very low=1, low=2, and so on), and then to pretend that the attribute is continuous. This transformation does not lose any of the functionality of ordinal attributes, but does make the resulting classifier more difficult to understand.

11.3 Structured attributes

Another handy facility would permit discrete attributes to have a hierarchy of possible values rather than the current list. Consider an attribute like color that can be specified at different levels of detail. For some tests, it may be appropriate to use only the four primary colors, or the seven bands of the visible spectrum. Other tests in the same tree might require a finer gradation, such as subdividing blue into the dozens of blues used by artists. The values of an attribute like color really form a treelike hierarchy with each value at one level connected to several subvalues at the next, as suggested in Figure 11–1. A test could then use values at any level of the hierarchy, or even at a mixture of levels.

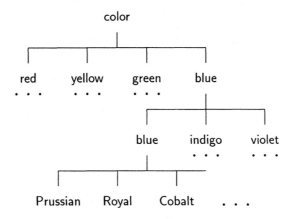

Figure 11–1. Value hierarchy for color

It is tempting to simply enumerate the values at the greatest level of detail in the hope that attribute value grouping methods (Chapter 7) will do the rest, dividing the fine values into appropriate subcollections. Another line of attack that I have found more reliable is to define several different attributes for color, one with values at the first level of the hierarchy, another with values at the second, and so on.

11.4 Structured induction

While it is possible to fudge the effects of ordinal attributes and attribute value hierarchies, the absence of facilities for structured induction is a fundamental limitation. Shapiro [1987] coined the term to refer to decision trees with tests on attributes whose values are themselves determined by decision trees. Recursion of this kind allows trees to be used to define new subconcepts that appear in the trees defining higher-level concepts. Shapiro demonstrated that the structured induction approach can yield much more compact trees while simultaneously reducing the number of training cases needed to construct an accurate classifier.

11.5 Incremental induction

The algorithms presented here proceed directly from training cases to classifier. There is no role in this scheme of things for a previous or partially completed classifier; even when windowing is invoked, each iteration discards the tree constructed in the previous cycle. There are two situations in which the inability to make use of an existing classifier is unsatisfactory.

The first of these concerns the availability of new data after a classifier has been constructed, a common occurrence in practical applications of machine learning where the continual collection of data is the norm. Of course, it may be that the existing classifier deals correctly with all the new data, so providing no reason to change the classifier under the maxim, "If it isn't broken, don't fix it." If we are not so fortunate, there are two alternatives:

- Ignore the new data (at least for the moment); or

- Discard the previous classifier, add the new data to the training set, and build a new classifier.

Neither of these alternatives is attractive if the classifier seems likely to benefit from new data, yet the computational cost of developing a classifier from scratch is high. Catlett [1991a] cites such a case involving fault detection for one component of the space shuttle in which the induced classifier is still improving in accuracy after hundreds of thousands of training cases, yet hours of computer time on a fast workstation are needed to construct a new classifier from all the accumulated data.

Some learning algorithms finesse this problem by modifying an existing theory in the light of new data; Mitchell's [1977] *version spaces* is an early and influential example. It is only recently that similarly incremental algorithms for constructing decision trees have been developed by Schlimmer and Fisher [1986] and Utgoff [1989]. These algorithms retain information at the nodes of the tree sufficient to permit its modification in the light of new data. Utgoff's ID5R has the interesting property that the modified tree produced in response to new data is always the same as the tree that would have been produced if all the training cases had been processed in one batch.

There is a second, less obvious situation that requires an iterative approach. Suppose that more computation time, rather than more data, becomes available after a classifier has been generated. The greedy algorithms used in C4.5 require a fixed amount of time to run; they cannot exploit more, and will produce nothing in less. An ideal **algorithm**, however, would produce some classifier quickly, then use any **additional** time available to it to improve the classifier, e.g., by exploring alternative subtrees in a search for a better tree. What is wanted is a resource-constrained algorithm that will do the best it can within a specified computational budget and can pick up the threads and continue if this budget is increased. This would make a challenging thesis topic!

11.6 Prospectus

Hunt, Marin, and Stone conclude their 1966 book with these words:

> Factor-analytic techniques have developed far beyond their original formulation. CLS techniques could be similarly developed. ...Our most optimistic view of CLS techniques would be exceeded if they turn out to be the complement to factor analysis for nominal data.

The tree-based approach that they pioneered has gone a long way towards achieving this goal. It is now widely recognized as a powerful nonparametric technique for extracting information from data—and not just nominal data!

It is my hope, in turn, that publication of the source code of a mature system for induction of decision tree and production-rule classifiers will make the technology more accessible and so increase its use. Further, having the source should permit adventurous souls to experiment with new algorithms by tweaking the code, without the overhead of having to assemble a working system beforehand.

Experimentation with variants of current learning algorithms, especially when it is directed towards probing their weaknesses, should lead to a better understanding of how methods relate to families of tasks. This is essential if we are to design a new generation of more robust and effective learning systems.

Appendix:
Program Listings

The appendix consists of four parts:

- A brief description of the files that contain routines and declarations.

- An overview of some data structures whose purpose and/or organization may be more obscure than usual.

- The program listings themselves.

- An alphabetic index of all routines.

Brief descriptions of the contents of the files

Notes on some important data structures

(a) General

For a concise summary of nonstandard types, see types.i. Many of the global data structures are documented briefly in the files defining external variables (extern.i, buildex.i and rulex.i).

(b) Names and cases

Names of attributes are found in AttName[1..MaxAtt]. If a is a discrete attribute, its possible values are in AttValName[a][1..MaxAttVal[a]]; MaxAttVal[a]=0 otherwise. Class names are kept in ClassName[0..MaxClass].

Cases are referenced through an array of pointers Item[0..MaxItem], where Item[i] points to the description of the ith case in the current ordering. Item is reordered frequently so that the cases of current interest appear in Item[Fp..Lp] for some bounds Fp and Lp. The description of a case is a vector; elements 0..MaxAtt contain the attribute values and element MaxAtt+1 contains the case's class. Each element is a union capable of holding either a discrete or continuous value, usually referenced through macros; for case Item[i], CVal(Item[i],a) or DVal(Item[i],a) reference the (continuous or discrete) value of attribute a, and Class(Item[i]) references the class of the case (always discrete). Unknown attribute values are recorded as 0 for a discrete attribute, or a defined value Unknown for a continuous attribute.

(c) Decision trees

During the construction of a decision tree, cases may be assigned fractionally to training subsets as a result of unknown values (Chapter 3). Weight[i] holds the relevant fraction of Item[i] in the current subset.

Trees are linked structures, the record for each node being of type TreeRec. Every node contains the local class distribution, the local majority class, various counts, and whether the node is a leaf (NodeType=0) or one of three types of test. If a node is not a leaf, the field Tested contains the attribute on which the test is based, with outcomes 1..Forks. If appropriate, other information about the test is also stored—the threshold Cut against which a continuous attribute is tested, or the groups of discrete values Subset[1..Forks] corresponding to each outcome. Pointers to the subtrees associated with each outcome are kept in Branch[1..Forks]. The simplified decision trees built by the program are kept in Pruned[0..TRIALS-1].

When potential tests are being evaluated, the class distribution that would be associated with each outcome is determined. Freq[x][c] is the (fractional) number of cases of class c that have outcome x, where x=0 signifies an unknown outcome. Similarly, ValFreq[x] is the number of cases with outcome x.

After all possible tests have been assessed, Gain[a] holds the information gain arising from a test on attribute a and Info[a] holds the corresponding split information (see Section 2.2). When a is a continuous attribute, Bar[a] gives the threshold value for the best split on a.

(d) Production rules

Many of the processes involved in generating and sifting sets of production rules are inherently time-consuming. Speeding them up has increased the complexity of some of the data structures.

As described in types.i, a set of rules is of type RuleSetRec. The field SRule[r] points to rule r and SRuleIndex[i] is the number of the ith rule in the set, $1 \leq i \leq$ SNRules. A single rule (type ProdRuleRec) has conditions Lhs[1..Size], consequent class Rhs, and some ancillary information on coding cost, error rate, etc. Each condition consists of a test and a designated outcome required by the condition. The test part itself is similar to the information stored at a node of a decision tree, with the addition of the current case's outcome of the test (when known). This latter is saved explicitly because the same test may appear several times in a ruleset; all references to the same test point to the same record.

When rules are being generalized in prunerule.c, the conditions on a path from the root of the tree to a leaf are kept in Cond[1..NCond]. Whether or not cases satisfy individual conditions is computed and saved; CondSatisfiedBy[d][i] is true if condition Cond[d] is satisfied by case Item[i]. Generalization itself is facilitated by information maintained in arrays Total, Errors, and Pessimistic:

- Total[0] is the number of cases that satisfy all current conditions;

- Errors[0] is the number of these cases that are misclassified by the rule;

- Pessimistic[0] is the predicted error rate for this rule (see Section 5.1); and

- Total[d], Errors[d] and Pessimistic[d] have similar meanings, but refer to hypothetical counts *if condition d were to be deleted.* (These are determined efficiently by routine FindTables using CondSatisfiedBy above.)

Deleted[d] is set to true when condition d has been eliminated from the current conditions.

Another bunch of local arrays is used in siftrules.c when a subset of the possible rules for each class is selected and the order of class rulesets is established. Rules initially appear in any order in Rule[1..NRules], with RuleIn[r] signalling whether rule r is currently included. For efficiency again, Match[r][i] shows whether case Item[i] satisfies all the conditions of rule r. Rules for each class are considered in turn as a group and, for each group, three key quantities are:

- Covered[i] is the number of currently included rules that match Item[i];

- For cases covered by a *single* currently-included rule r, Right[r] holds the number of them that are correctly classified by rule r; and

- Wrong[r] is the similar number of misclassified cases.

These variables allow the effect of adding or deleting a rule to be assessed quickly. Their values are adjusted every time a rule is added to, or deleted from, the current subset of active rules.

File Makefile

```
#*************************************************************************#
#*                                                                     *#
#*              Makefile for the C4.5 induction system                 *#
#*              ──────────────────────────────────────                 *#
#*                                                                     *#
#*************************************************************************#

#       Set CFLAGS for your C compiler, e.g.
#
#          * if you need to debug the programs (sorry about that!)
#              CFLAGS = -g
#            (You might also want to reactivate the lint commands that
#            have been commented out below.)
#
#          * if your C compiler supports higher optimization levels
#              CFLAGS = -O3 etc

CFLAGS = -O2

#       Definitions of file sets

core.ln = \
        getnames.ln getdata.ln trees.ln getopt.ln header.ln

trees.ln = \
        besttree.ln build.ln info.ln discr.ln contin.ln subset.ln\
        prune.ln stats.ln st-thresh.ln classify.ln confmat.ln\
        sort.ln $(core.ln)

rules.ln = \
        rules.ln genlogs.ln genrules.ln makerules.ln prunerule.ln\
        siftrules.ln testrules.ln stats.ln confmat.ln sort.ln $(core.ln)

core = \
        getnames.o getdata.o trees.o getopt.o header.o

trees = \
        besttree.o build.o info.o discr.o contin.o subset.o prune.o\
        stats.o st-thresh.o classify.o confmat.o sort.o $(core)

rules = \
        rules.o genlogs.o genrules.o makerules.o prunerule.o\
        siftrules.o testrules.o stats.o confmat.o sort.o $(core)

#   C4.5 decision tree generator

c4.5:   c4.5.o $(trees)
#           lint -x c4.5.ln $(trees.ln)  -lm
            cc -o c4.5 c4.5.o $(trees)  -lm

#           (Sample only: for compiler that supports global optimization,
#           e.g. DECstation 3100)
```

```
c4.5gt:
        cat     defns.i types.i\
                c4.5.c\
                besttree.c build.c info.c discr.c contin.c subset.c\
                prune.c stats.c st-thresh.c confmat.c sort.c\
                getnames.c getdata.c classify.c trees.c header.c\
                | egrep -v 'defns.i|types.i|extern.i|buildex.i' >c4.5gt.c
        cc -O4 -o c4.5gt c4.5gt.c -lm
        rm c4.5gt.c


#   C4.5 production rule generator

c4.5rules: c4.5rules.o $(rules)
#       lint -x c4.5rules.ln $(rules.ln) -lm
        cc -o c4.5rules c4.5rules.o $(rules) -lm


#   C4.5 decision tree interpreter

consult: consult.o userint.o $(core)
#       lint -x consult.ln userint.ln $(core.ln) -lm
        cc -o consult consult.o userint.o $(core) -lm


#   C4.5 production rule interpreter

consultr: consultr.o rules.o userint.o $(core)
#       lint -x consultr.ln rules.ln userint.ln $(core.ln) -lm
        cc -o consultr consultr.o rules.o userint.o $(core) -lm


.c.o:
#       lint -c $<
        cc $(CFLAGS) -c $<


#   Make everything

all:
        make c4.5
        make c4.5rules
        make consult
        make consultr
        cc -o xval-prep xval-prep.c -lm
        cc -o average average.c -lm

$(trees): defns.i types.i extern.i
$(rules): defns.i types.i extern.i
```

File defns.i

```
/**************************************************************************/
/*                                                                        */
/*                  Definitions used in C4.5                              */
/*                  ————————————————                                      */
/*                                                                        */
/*                                                                        */
/**************************************************************************/

#include <stdio.h>
#include <math.h>

#define    Eof                  EOF              /*char read on end of file*/
#define    Nil                  0                /*null pointer*/
#define    false                0
#define    true                 1
#define    None                 -1
#define    Epsilon              1E-3

long       random();
#define    Random               ((random()&2147483647) / 2147483648.0)

#define    Max(a,b)             ((a)>(b) ? a : b)
#define    Min(a,b)             ((a)<(b) ? a : b)
#define    Round(x)             ((int) (x+0.5))
#define    Log2                 0.69314718055994530942
#define    Log(x)               ((x) <= 0 ? 0.0 : log(x) / Log2)

#define    Bit(b)               (1 << (b))
#define    In(b,s)              ((s[(b) >> 3]) & Bit((b) & 07))
#define    ClearBits(n,s)       memset(s,0,n)
#define    CopyBits(n,f,t)      memcpy(t,f,n)
#define    SetBit(b,s)          (s[(b) >> 3] |= Bit((b) & 07))

#define    ForEach(v,f,l)       for(v=f ; v<=l ; ++v)

#define    Verbosity(d)         if(VERBOSITY >= d)
```

File types.i

```
/*************************************************************************/
/*                                                                     */
/*              Type definitions for C4.5                              */
/*              ---------------------------                            */
/*                                                                     */
/*                                                                     */
/*************************************************************************/


typedef  char     Boolean, *String, *Set;

typedef  int      ItemNo;              /* data item number */
typedef  float    ItemCount;           /* count of (partial) items */

typedef  short    ClassNo,             /* class number, 0..MaxClass */
                  DiscrValue;          /* discrete attribute value (0 = ?)   */
typedef  short    Attribute;           /* attribute number, 0..MaxAtt */

typedef  union  _attribute_value
         {
             DiscrValue   _discr_val;
             float        _cont_val;
         }
                  AttValue, *Description;

#define  CVal(Case,Attribute)    Case[Attribute]._cont_val
#define  DVal(Case,Attribute)    Case[Attribute]._discr_val
#define  Class(Case)             Case[MaxAtt+1]._discr_val

#define  Unknown  -999           /* unknown value for continuous attribute */

#define  BrDiscr        1        /* node types:  branch */
#define  ThreshContin   2        /*              threshold cut */
#define  BrSubset       3        /*              subset test */

typedef  struct _tree_record *Tree;
typedef  struct _tree_record
         {
             short        NodeType;      /* 0=leaf 1=branch 2=cut 3=subset */
             ClassNo      Leaf;          /* most frequent class at this node */
             ItemCount    Items,         /* no of items at this node */
                          *ClassDist,    /* class distribution of items */
                          Errors;        /* no of errors at this node */
             Attribute    Tested;        /* attribute referenced in test */
             short        Forks;         /* number of branches at this node */
             float        Cut,           /* threshold for continuous attribute */
                          Lower,         /* lower limit of soft threshhold */
                          Upper;         /* upper limit ditto */
             Set          *Subset;       /* subsets of discrete values   */
             Tree         *Branch;       /* Branch[x] = (sub)tree for outcome x */
         }
                  TreeRec;
```

```
#define   IGNORE       1          /* special attribute status: do not use */
#define   DISCRETE     2          /* ditto: collect values as data read */

typedef short    RuleNo;                      /* rule number */

typedef struct TestRec *Test;

struct TestRec
      {
          short         NodeType;       /* test type (see tree nodes) */
          Attribute     Tested;         /* attribute tested */
          short         Forks;          /* possible branches */
          float         Cut;            /* threshold (if relevant) */
          Set           *Subset;        /* subset (if relevant) */
          char          Outcome;        /* result of test on current item */
      };

typedef struct CondRec *Condition;

struct CondRec
      {
          Test          CondTest;       /* test part of condition */
          short         TestValue;      /* specified outcome of test */
      };

typedef struct ProdRuleRec PR;

struct ProdRuleRec
      {
          short         Size;           /* number of conditions */
          Condition     *Lhs;           /* conditions themselves */
          ClassNo       Rhs;            /* class given by rule */
          float         Error,          /* estimated error rate */
                        Bits;           /* bits to encode rule */
          ItemNo        Used,           /* times rule used */
                        Incorrect;      /* times rule incorrect */
      };

typedef struct RuleSetRec RuleSet;

struct RuleSetRec
      {
          PR            *SRule;         /* rules */
          RuleNo        SNRules,        /* number of rules */
                        *SRuleIndex;    /* ranking of rules */
          ClassNo       SDefaultClass;  /* default class for this ruleset */
   };
```

File extern.i

```
/************************************************************************/
/*                                                                    */
/*              Global data for C4.5                                  */
/*              ─────────────────                                     */
/*                                                                    */
/************************************************************************/

extern   short          MaxAtt,         /* max att number */
                        MaxClass,       /* max class number */
                        MaxDiscrVal;    /* max discrete values for any att */

extern   ItemNo         MaxItem;        /* max data item number */

extern   Description    *Item;          /* data items */

extern   DiscrValue     *MaxAttVal;     /* number of values for each att */

extern   char           *SpecialStatus; /* special att treatment */

extern   String         *ClassName,     /* class names */
                        *AttName,       /* att names */
                        **AttValName,   /* att value names */
                        FileName;       /* family name of files */

extern   Boolean        AllKnown;       /* true if there have been no splits
                                           on atts with missing values above
                                           the current position in the tree */


/************************************************************************/
/*                                                                    */
/*              Global parameters for C4.5                            */
/*              ──────────────────────                                */
/*                                                                    */
/************************************************************************/

extern   short          VERBOSITY,      /* verbosity level (0 = none) */
                        TRIALS;         /* number of trees to be grown */

extern   Boolean        GAINRATIO,      /* true=gain ratio, false=gain */
                        SUBSET,         /* true if subset tests allowed */
                        BATCH,          /* true if windowing turned off */
                        UNSEENS,        /* true if to evaluate on test data */
                        PROBTHRESH;     /* true if to use soft thresholds */

extern   ItemNo         MINOBJS,        /* minimum items each side of a cut */
                        WINDOW,         /* initial window size */
                        INCREMENT;      /* max window increment each iteration */

extern   float          CF;             /* confidence limit for tree pruning */
```

File buildex.i

```
/**********************************************************************/
/*                                                                  */
/*          Global data for C4.5 used for building decision trees   */
/*          ─────────────────────────────────────────────          */
/*                                                                  */
/**********************************************************************/

#include "defns.i"
#include "types.i"
#include "extern.i"


extern ItemCount
        *Weight,        /* Weight[i]   = current fraction of item i */
        **Freq,         /* Freq[x][c]  = no. items of class c with outcome x */
        *ValFreq;       /* ValFreq[x]  = no. items with att value v */

extern float
        *Gain,          /* Gain[a]  = info gain by split on att a */
        *Info,          /* Info[a]  = potential info from split on att a */
        *Bar,           /* Bar[a]   = best threshold for contin att a */
        *UnknownRate;   /* UnknownRate[a]  = current unknown rate for att a */

extern char
        *Tested;        /* Tested[a]  = true if att a already tested */
```

File c4.5.c

```
/*********************************************************************/
/*                                                                 */
/*       Main routine, c4.5                                        */
/*       ─────────────────────                                     */
/*                                                                 */
/*                                                                 */
/*********************************************************************/


#include "defns.i"
#include "types.i"


        /*  External data, described in extern.i  */

short           MaxAtt, MaxClass, MaxDiscrVal = 2;

ItemNo          MaxItem;

Description      *Item;

DiscrValue      *MaxAttVal;

char            *SpecialStatus;

String          *ClassName,
                *AttName,
                **AttValName,
                FileName = "DF";

short           VERBOSITY = 0,
                TRIALS   = 10;

Boolean         GAINRATIO  = true,
                SUBSET    = false,
                BATCH     = true,
                UNSEENS   = false,
                PROBTHRESH = false;

ItemNo          MINOBJS = 2,
                WINDOW = 0,
                INCREMENT = 0;

float           CF = 0.25;

Tree            *Pruned;

Boolean         AllKnown = true;
```

```
      main(Argc, Argv)
/*    ———— */
      int Argc;
      char *Argv[];
{
      int o;
      extern char *optarg;
      extern int optind;
      Boolean FirstTime=true;
      short Best, BestTree();

      PrintHeader("decision tree generator");

      /*  Process options  */

      while ( (o = getopt(Argc, Argv, "f:bupv:t:w:i:gsm:c:")) != EOF )
      {
          if ( FirstTime )
          {
              printf("\n    Options:\n");
              FirstTime = false;
          }

          switch (o)
          {
          case 'f':    FileName = optarg;
                       printf("\tFile stem <%s>\n", FileName);
                       break;
          case 'b':    BATCH = true;
                       printf("\tWindowing disabled (now the default)\n");
                       break;
          case 'u':    UNSEENS = true;
                       printf("\tTrees evaluated on unseen cases\n");
                       break;
          case 'p':    PROBTHRESH = true;
                       printf("\tProbability thresholds used\n");
                       break;
          case 'v':    VERBOSITY = atoi(optarg);
                       printf("\tVerbosity level %d\n", VERBOSITY);
                       break;
          case 't':    TRIALS = atoi(optarg);
                       printf("\tWindowing enabled with %d trials\n", TRIALS);
                       BATCH = false;
                       break;
          case 'w':    WINDOW = atoi(optarg);
                       printf("\tInitial window size of %d items\n", WINDOW);
                       BATCH = false;
                       break;
          case 'i':    INCREMENT = atoi(optarg);
                       printf("\tMaximum window increment of %d items\n",
                               INCREMENT);
                       BATCH = false;
                       break;
```

```
        case 'g':   GAINRATIO = false;
                    printf("\tGain criterion used\n");
                    break;
        case 's':   SUBSET = true;
                    printf("\tTests on discrete attribute groups\n");
                    break;
        case 'm':   MINOBJS = atoi(optarg);
                    printf("\tSensible test requires 2 branches with >=%d cases\n",
                            MINOBJS);
                    break;
        case 'c':   CF = atof(optarg);
                    printf("\tPruning confidence level %g%%\n", CF);
                    CF /= 100;
                    break;
        case '?':   printf("unrecognised option\n");
                    exit(1);
        }
    }

    /*  Initialise  */

    GetNames();
    GetData(".data");
    printf("\nRead %d cases (%d attributes) from %s.data\n",
            MaxItem+1, MaxAtt+1, FileName);

    /*  Build decision trees  */

    if ( BATCH )
    {
        TRIALS = 1;
        OneTree();
        Best = 0;
    }
    else
    {
        Best = BestTree();
    }

    /*  Soften thresholds in best tree  */

    if ( PROBTHRESH )
    {
        printf("Softening thresholds");
        if ( ! BATCH ) printf(" for best tree from trial %d", Best);
        printf("\n");
        SoftenThresh(Pruned[Best]);
        printf("\n");
        PrintTree(Pruned[Best]);
    }
```

```
    /*   Save best tree  */
    if ( BATCH || TRIALS == 1 )
    {
        printf("\nTree saved\n");
    }
    else
    {
        printf("\nBest tree from trial %d saved\n", Best);
    }
    SaveTree(Pruned[Best], ".tree");

    /*   Evaluation  */

    printf("\n\nEvaluation on training data (%d items):\n", MaxItem+1);
    Evaluate(false, Best);

    if ( UNSEENS )
    {
        GetData(".test");
        printf("\nEvaluation on test data (%d items):\n", MaxItem+1);
        Evaluate(true, Best);
    }
}
```

File besttree.c

```
/***********************************************************************/
/*                                                                     */
/*        Routines to manage tree growth, pruning, and evaluation      */
/*        ───────────────────────────────────────────────────         */
/*                                                                     */
/***********************************************************************/

#include "defns.i"
#include "types.i"
#include "extern.i"

ItemNo          *TargetClassFreq;
Tree            *Raw;
extern Tree     *Pruned;


/***********************************************************************/
/*                                                                     */
/*        Grow and prune a single tree from all data                   */
/*                                                                     */
/***********************************************************************/

    OneTree()
/*  ─────────  */
{
    Tree FormTree(), CopyTree();
    Boolean Prune();

    InitialiseTreeData();
    InitialiseWeights();

    Raw = (Tree *) calloc(1, sizeof(Tree));
    Pruned = (Tree *) calloc(1, sizeof(Tree));

    AllKnown = true;
    Raw[0] = FormTree(0, MaxItem);
    printf("\n");
    PrintTree(Raw[0]);

    SaveTree(Raw[0], ".unpruned");

    Pruned[0] = CopyTree(Raw[0]);
    if ( Prune(Pruned[0]) )
    {
        printf("\nSimplified ");
        PrintTree(Pruned[0]);
    }
}
```

```
/***************************************************************************/
/*                                                                         */
/*        Grow and prune TRIALS trees and select the best of them          */
/*                                                                         */
/***************************************************************************/


short BestTree()
/*    ———————  */
{
    Tree CopyTree(), Iterate();
    Boolean Prune();
    short t, Best=0;

    InitialiseTreeData();

    TargetClassFreq = (ItemNo *) calloc(MaxClass+1, sizeof(ItemNo));

    Raw    = (Tree *) calloc(TRIALS, sizeof(Tree));
    Pruned = (Tree *) calloc(TRIALS, sizeof(Tree));

    /*  If necessary, set initial size of window to 20% (or twice
        the sqrt, if this is larger) of the number of data items,
        and the maximum number of items that can be added to the
        window at each iteration to 20% of the initial window size  */

    if ( ! WINDOW )
    {
        WINDOW = Max(2 * sqrt(MaxItem+1.0), (MaxItem+1) / 5);
    }

    if ( ! INCREMENT )
    {
        INCREMENT = Max(WINDOW / 5, 1);
    }

    FormTarget(WINDOW);

    /*  Form set of trees by iteration and prune  */

    ForEach(t, 0, TRIALS-1 )
    {
        FormInitialWindow();

        printf("\n--------\nTrial %d\n--------\n\n", t);

        Raw[t]  = Iterate(WINDOW, INCREMENT);
        printf("\n");
        PrintTree(Raw[t]);

        SaveTree(Raw[t], ".unpruned");

        Pruned[t]  = CopyTree(Raw[t]);
        if ( Prune(Pruned[t]) )
        {
            printf("\nSimplified ");
            PrintTree(Pruned[t]);
        }
```

```
        if ( Pruned[t]->Errors < Pruned[Best]->Errors )
        {
            Best = t;
        }
    }
    printf("\n--------\n");

    return Best;
}


/*************************************************************************/
/*                                                                     */
/*  The windowing approach seems to work best when the class           */
/*  distribution of the initial window is as close to uniform as       */
/*  possible.  FormTarget generates this initial target distribution,  */
/*  setting up a TargetClassFreq value for each class.                 */
/*                                                                     */
/*************************************************************************/


    FormTarget(Size)
/*  ------------  */
    ItemNo Size;
{
    ItemNo i, *ClassFreq;
    ClassNo c, Smallest, ClassesLeft=0;

    ClassFreq = (ItemNo *) calloc(MaxClass+1, sizeof(ItemNo));

    /*  Generate the class frequency distribution  */

    ForEach(i, 0, MaxItem)
    {
        ClassFreq[ Class(Item[i]) ]++;
    }

    /*  Calculate the no. of classes of which there are items  */

    ForEach(c, 0, MaxClass)
    {
        if ( ClassFreq[c]  )
        {
            ClassesLeft++;
        }
        else
        {
            TargetClassFreq[c]  = 0;
        }
    }

    while ( ClassesLeft )
    {
        /*  Find least common class of which there are some items  */

        Smallest = -1;
```

```
        ForEach(c, 0, MaxClass)
        {
            if ( ClassFreq [c]  &&
                 ( Smallest < 0 || ClassFreq [c] < ClassFreq [Smallest] ) )
            {
                Smallest = c;
            }
        }

        /*  Allocate the no. of items of this class to use in the window  */

        TargetClassFreq [Smallest] = Min (ClassFreq [Smallest], Round (Size/ClassesLeft));

        ClassFreq [Smallest] = 0;

        Size -= TargetClassFreq [Smallest];
        ClassesLeft--;
    }

    cfree (ClassFreq);
}


/*************************************************************************/
/*                                                                     */
/*  Form initial window, attempting to obtain the target class profile  */
/*  in TargetClassFreq.   This is done by placing the targeted number   */
/*  of items of each class at the beginning of the set of data items.   */
/*                                                                     */
/*************************************************************************/


        FormInitialWindow()
/*      ———————————————  */
{
    ItemNo i, Start=0, More;
    ClassNo c;
    void Swap();

    Shuffle();

    ForEach(c, 0, MaxClass)
    {
        More = TargetClassFreq [c];

        for ( i = Start ; More ; i++ )
        {
            if ( Class (Item [i]) == c )
            {
                Swap(Start, i);
                Start++;
                More--;
            }
        }
    }
}
```

```
/**************************************************************************/
/*                                                                        */
/*                   Shuffle the data items randomly                      */
/*                                                                        */
/**************************************************************************/

    Shuffle()
/*  ———— */
{
    ItemNo This, Alt, Left;
    Description Hold;

    This = 0;
    for( Left = MaxItem+1 ; Left ; )
    {
        Alt = This + (Left--) * Random;
        Hold = Item[This];
        Item[This++] = Item[Alt];
        Item[Alt] = Hold;
    }
}


/**************************************************************************/
/*                                                                        */
/*  Grow a tree iteratively with initial window size Window and           */
/*  initial window increment IncExceptions.                               */
/*                                                                        */
/*  Construct a classifier tree using the data items in the               */
/*  window, then test for the successful classification of other          */
/*  data items by this tree.  If there are misclassified items,           */
/*  put them immediately after the items in the window, increase          */
/*  the size of the window and build another classifier tree and          */
/*  so on until we have a tree which successfully classifies all          */
/*  of the test items or no improvement is apparent.                      */
/*                                                                        */
/*  On completion, return the tree which produced the least errors.       */
/*                                                                        */
/**************************************************************************/

Tree Iterate(Window, IncExceptions)
/*     ———— */
    ItemNo Window, IncExceptions;
{
    Tree Classifier, BestClassifier=Nil, FormTree();
    ItemNo i, Errors, TotalErrors, BestTotalErrors=MaxItem+1,
           Exceptions, Additions;
    ClassNo Assigned, Category();
    short Cycle=0;
    void Swap();

    printf("Cycle    Tree    -----Cases----");
    printf("      ----------------Errors----------------\n");
```

```c
printf("           size    window   other");
printf("      window  rate   other   rate    total  rate\n");
printf("-----    ----   ------  ------");
printf("       ------  ----  ------  ----  ------   ----\n");

do
{
    /*  Build a classifier tree with the first Window items  */

    InitialiseWeights();
    AllKnown = true;
    Classifier = FormTree(0, Window-1);

    /*  Error analysis  */

    Errors = Round(Classifier->Errors);

    /*  Move all items that are incorrectly classified by the
        classifier tree to immediately after the items in the
        current window.  */

    Exceptions = Window;
    ForEach(i, Window, MaxItem)
    {
        Assigned = Category(Item[i], Classifier);
        if ( Assigned != Class(Item[i]) )
        {
            Swap(Exceptions, i);
            Exceptions++;
        }
    }
    Exceptions -= Window;
    TotalErrors = Errors + Exceptions;

    /*  Print error analysis  */

    printf("%3d  %7d  %8d  %6d  %8d%5.1f%%  %6d%5.1f%%  %6d%5.1f%%\n",
            ++Cycle, TreeSize(Classifier), Window, MaxItem-Window+1,
            Errors, 100*(float)Errors/Window,
            Exceptions, 100*Exceptions/(MaxItem-Window+1.001),
            TotalErrors, 100*TotalErrors/(MaxItem+1.0));

    /*  Keep track of the most successful classifier tree so far  */

    if ( ! BestClassifier || TotalErrors < BestTotalErrors )
    {
        if ( BestClassifier ) ReleaseTree(BestClassifier);
        BestClassifier = Classifier;
        BestTotalErrors = TotalErrors;
    }
    else
    {
        ReleaseTree(Classifier);
    }
```

```
        /*  Increment window size  */

        Additions = Min(Exceptions, IncExceptions);
        Window = Min(Window + Max(Additions, Exceptions / 2), MaxItem + 1);
    }
    while ( Exceptions );

    return BestClassifier;
}


/**************************************************************************/
/*                                                                        */
/*      Print report of errors for each of the trials                     */
/*                                                                        */
/**************************************************************************/

    Evaluate(CMInfo, Saved)
/*  ————  */
    Boolean CMInfo;
    short Saved;
{
    ClassNo RealClass, PrunedClass, Category();
    short t;
    ItemNo *ConfusionMat, i, RawErrors, PrunedErrors;

    if ( CMInfo )
    {
        ConfusionMat = (ItemNo *) calloc((MaxClass+1)*(MaxClass+1), sizeof(ItemNo));
    }

    printf("\n");

    if ( TRIALS > 1 )
    {
        printf("Trial\t Before Pruning            After Pruning\n");
        printf("-----\t-------------------------------------------\n");
    }
    else
    {
        printf("\t Before Pruning          After Pruning\n");
        printf("\t--------------- ---------------------------\n");
    }
    printf("\tSize      Errors    Size      Errors    Estimate\n\n");

    ForEach(t, 0, TRIALS-1)
    {
        RawErrors = PrunedErrors = 0;

        ForEach(i, 0, MaxItem)
        {
            RealClass = Class(Item[i]);

            if ( Category(Item[i], Raw[t]) != RealClass ) RawErrors++;

            PrunedClass = Category(Item[i], Pruned[t]);
```

```
        if ( PrunedClass != RealClass ) PrunedErrors++;

        if ( CMInfo && t == Saved )
        {
            ConfusionMat[RealClass*(MaxClass+1)+PrunedClass]++;
        }
    }

    if ( TRIALS > 1 )
    {
        printf("%4d", t);
    }

    printf("\t%4d  %3d(%4.1f%%)  %4d  %3d(%4.1f%%)   (%4.1f%%)%s\n",
            TreeSize(Raw[t]), RawErrors, 100.0*RawErrors / (MaxItem+1.0),
            TreeSize(Pruned[t]), PrunedErrors, 100.0*PrunedErrors / (MaxItem+1.0),
            100 * Pruned[t]->Errors / Pruned[t]->Items,
            ( t == Saved ? "   <<" : "" ));
}

if ( CMInfo )
{
    PrintConfusionMatrix(ConfusionMat);
    free(ConfusionMat);
}
}
```

File build.c

```
/*************************************************************************/
/*                                                                       */
/*      Central tree-forming algorithm incorporating all criteria        */
/*      ────────────────────────────────────────────────                 */
/*                                                                       */
/*************************************************************************/


#include "defns.i"
#include "types.i"
#include "extern.i"

ItemCount
        *Weight,        /* Weight[i]   = current fraction of item i */
        **Freq,         /* Freq[x][c]  = no. items of class c with outcome x */
        *ValFreq,       /* ValFreq[x]  = no. items with outcome x */
        *ClassFreq;     /* ClassFreq[c] = no. items of class c */

float
        *Gain,          /* Gain[a] = info gain by split on att a */
        *Info,          /* Info[a] = potential info of split on att a */
        *Bar,           /* Bar[a]  = best threshold for contin att a */
        *UnknownRate;   /* UnknownRate[a] = current unknown rate for att a */

char
        *Tested;        /* Tested[a]  set if att a has already been tested */


        /*   External variables initialised here   */

extern float
        *SplitGain,     /* SplitGain[i] = gain with att value of item i as threshold */
        *SplitInfo;     /* SplitInfo[i] = potential info ditto */

extern ItemCount
        *Slice1,        /* Slice1[c]   = saved values of Freq[x][c]  in subset.c */
        *Slice2;        /* Slice2[c]   = saved values of Freq[y][c]  */

extern Set
        **Subset;       /* Subset[a][s] = subset s for att a */

extern short
        *Subsets;       /* Subsets[a] = no. subsets for att a */
```

```
/**************************************************************************/
/*                                                                      */
/*                  Allocate space for tree tables                      */
/*                                                                      */
/**************************************************************************/


        InitialiseTreeData()
/*      ——————————  */
{
        DiscrValue v;
        Attribute a;

        Tested      = (char *) calloc(MaxAtt+1, sizeof(char));

        Gain        = (float *) calloc(MaxAtt+1, sizeof(float));
        Info        = (float *) calloc(MaxAtt+1, sizeof(float));
        Bar         = (float *) calloc(MaxAtt+1, sizeof(float));

        Subset = (Set **) calloc(MaxAtt+1, sizeof(Set *));
        ForEach(a, 0, MaxAtt)
        {
            if ( MaxAttVal[a] )
            {
                Subset[a]   = (Set *) calloc(MaxDiscrVal+1, sizeof(Set));
                ForEach(v, 0, MaxAttVal[a])
                {
                    Subset[a][v] = (Set) malloc((MaxAttVal[a]>>3) + 1);
                }
            }
        }
        Subsets = (short *) calloc(MaxAtt+1, sizeof(short));

        SplitGain = (float *) calloc(MaxItem+1, sizeof(float));
        SplitInfo = (float *) calloc(MaxItem+1, sizeof(float));

        Weight = (ItemCount *) calloc(MaxItem+1, sizeof(ItemCount));

        Freq  = (ItemCount **) calloc(MaxDiscrVal+1, sizeof(ItemCount *));
        ForEach(v, 0, MaxDiscrVal)
        {
            Freq[v]   = (ItemCount *) calloc(MaxClass+1, sizeof(ItemCount));
        }

        ValFreq = (ItemCount *) calloc(MaxDiscrVal+1, sizeof(ItemCount));
        ClassFreq = (ItemCount *) calloc(MaxClass+1, sizeof(ItemCount));

        Slice1 = (ItemCount *) calloc(MaxClass+2, sizeof(ItemCount));
        Slice2 = (ItemCount *) calloc(MaxClass+2, sizeof(ItemCount));

        UnknownRate = (float *) calloc(MaxAtt+1, sizeof(float));
}
```

```
/*************************************************************************/
/*                                                                     */
/*              Initialise the weight of each item                     */
/*                                                                     */
/*************************************************************************/


    InitialiseWeights()
/*  ───────────────  */
{
    ItemNo i;

    ForEach(i, 0, MaxItem)
    {
        Weight[i] = 1.0;
    }
}



/*************************************************************************/
/*                                                                     */
/*  Build a decision tree for the cases Fp through Lp:                 */
/*                                                                     */
/*  - if all cases are of the same class, the tree is a leaf and so    */
/*         the leaf is returned labelled with this class               */
/*                                                                     */
/*  - for each attribute, calculate the potential information provided */
/*         by a test on the attribute (based on the probabilities of each */
/*         case having a particular value for the attribute)  and the gain */
/*         in information that would result from a test on the attribute */
/*         (based on the probabilities of each case with a particular  */
/*         value for the attribute being of a particular class)        */
/*                                                                     */
/*  - on the basis of these figures, and depending on the current      */
/*         selection criterion, find the best attribute to branch on.  */
/*         Note:  this version will not allow a split on an attribute   */
/*         unless two or more subsets have at least MINOBJS items.     */
/*                                                                     */
/*  - try branching and test whether better than forming a leaf        */
/*                                                                     */
/*************************************************************************/


Tree FormTree(Fp, Lp)
/*  ─────────  */
    ItemNo Fp, Lp;
{
    ItemNo i, Kp, Ep, Group();
    ItemCount Cases, NoBestClass, KnownCases, CountItems();
    float Factor, BestVal, Val, AvGain=0, Worth();
    Attribute Att, BestAtt, Possible=0;
    ClassNo c, BestClass;
    Tree Node, Leaf();
    DiscrValue v;
    Boolean PrevAllKnown;
```

```
Cases = CountItems(Fp, Lp);

/*   Generate the class frequency distribution   */

ForEach(c, 0, MaxClass)
{
    ClassFreq[c]  =  0;
}
ForEach(i, Fp, Lp)
{
    ClassFreq[ Class(Item[i]) ]  +=  Weight[i];
}

/*   Find the most frequent class   */

BestClass = 0;
ForEach(c, 0, MaxClass)
{
    if ( ClassFreq[c]  >  ClassFreq[BestClass]  )
    {
        BestClass = c;
    }
}
NoBestClass = ClassFreq[BestClass];

Node = Leaf(ClassFreq, BestClass, Cases, Cases - NoBestClass);

/*   If all cases are of the same class or there are not enough
     cases to divide, the tree is a leaf   */

if ( NoBestClass == Cases  ||  Cases < 2 * MINOBJS )
{
    return Node;
}

Verbosity(1)
    printf("\n%d items, total weight %.1f\n", Lp - Fp + 1, Cases);

/*   For each available attribute, find the information and gain   */

ForEach(Att, 0, MaxAtt)
{
    Gain[Att]  =  -Epsilon;

    if ( SpecialStatus[Att]  ==  IGNORE ) continue;

    if ( MaxAttVal[Att]  )
    {
        /*   discrete valued attribute   */

        if ( SUBSET && MaxAttVal[Att] > 2 )
        {
            EvalSubset(Att, Fp, Lp, Cases);
        }
        else
```

```
            if ( ! Tested[Att] )
            {
                EvalDiscreteAtt(Att, Fp, Lp, Cases);
            }
        }
        else
        {
            /*  continuous attribute  */

            EvalContinuousAtt(Att, Fp, Lp);
        }

        /*  Update average gain, excluding attributes with very many values  */

        if ( Gain[Att] >= 0 && ( SUBSET || MaxAttVal[Att] < 0.3 * MaxItem ) )
        {
            Possible++;
            AvGain += Gain[Att];
        }
    }

    /*  Find the best attribute according to the given criterion  */

    BestVal = -Epsilon;
    BestAtt = None;
    AvGain  = ( Possible ? AvGain / Possible : 1E6 );

    Verbosity(2) printf("\taverage gain %.3f\n", AvGain);

    ForEach(Att, 0, MaxAtt)
    {
        if ( Gain[Att] >= 0 )
        {
            Val = Worth(Info[Att], Gain[Att], AvGain);
            if ( Val > BestVal )
            {
                BestAtt = Att;
                BestVal = Val;
            }
        }
    }

    /*  Decide whether to branch or not  */

    if ( BestAtt != None )
    {
        Verbosity(1)
        {
            printf("\tbest attribute %s", AttName[BestAtt]);
            if ( ! MaxAttVal[BestAtt] )
            {
                printf(" cut %.3f", Bar[BestAtt]);
            }
            printf(" inf %.3f gain %.3f val %.3f\n",
                    Info[BestAtt], Gain[BestAtt], BestVal);
        }
```

```
/*    Build a node of the selected test   */

if ( MaxAttVal[BestAtt]  )
{
    /*    Discrete valued attribute   */

    if ( SUBSET && MaxAttVal[BestAtt] > 2 )
    {
        SubsetTest(Node, BestAtt);
    }
    else
    {
        DiscreteTest(Node, BestAtt);
    }
}
else
{
    /*    Continuous attribute   */

    ContinTest(Node, BestAtt);
}

/*    Remove unknown attribute values   */

PrevAllKnown = AllKnown;

Kp = Group(0, Fp, Lp, Node)  + 1;
if ( Kp != Fp ) AllKnown = false;
KnownCases = Cases - CountItems(Fp, Kp-1);
UnknownRate[BestAtt]  =  (Cases - KnownCases) / (Cases + 0.001);

Verbosity(1)
    printf("\tunknown rate for %s = %.3f\n",
            AttName[BestAtt], UnknownRate[BestAtt]);

/*    Recursive divide and conquer   */

++Tested[BestAtt];

Ep = Kp - 1;
Node->Errors = 0;

ForEach(v, 1, Node->Forks)
{
    Ep = Group(v, Kp, Lp, Node);

    if ( Kp <= Ep )
    {
        Factor = CountItems(Kp, Ep)  /  KnownCases;

        ForEach(i, Fp, Kp-1)
        {
            Weight[i]  *=  Factor;
        }

        Node->Branch[v]  =  FormTree(Fp, Ep);
        Node->Errors +=  Node->Branch[v]->Errors;
```

```
            Group(0, Fp, Ep, Node);
            ForEach(i, Fp, Kp-1)
            {
                Weight[i]  /=  Factor;
            }
        }
        else
        {
            Node->Branch[v]  =  Leaf(Node->ClassDist, BestClass, 0.0, 0.0);
        }
    }

    --Tested[BestAtt];
    AllKnown = PrevAllKnown;

    /*   See whether we would have been no worse off with a leaf   */

    if ( Node->Errors >= Cases - NoBestClass - Epsilon )
    {
        Verbosity(1)
            printf("Collapse tree for %d items to leaf %s\n",
                    Lp - Fp + 1, ClassName[BestClass]);

        Node->NodeType = 0;
    }
}
else
{
    Verbosity(1)
        printf("\tno sensible splits  %.1f/%.1f\n",
                Cases, Cases - NoBestClass);
}

return Node;
}
```

```
/****************************************************************************/
/*                                                                        */
/*   Group together the items corresponding to branch V of a test         */
/*   and return the index of the last such                                */
/*                                                                        */
/*   Note: if V equals zero, group the unknown values                     */
/*                                                                        */
/****************************************************************************/


ItemNo Group(V, Fp, Lp, TestNode)
/*     ————  */
    DiscrValue V;
    ItemNo Fp, Lp;
    Tree TestNode;
{
    ItemNo i;
    Attribute Att;
    float Thresh;
    Set SS;
    void Swap();

    Att = TestNode->Tested;

    if ( V )
    {
        /*   Group items on the value of attribute Att, and depending
             on the type of branch   */

        switch ( TestNode->NodeType )
        {
            case BrDiscr:

                ForEach(i, Fp, Lp)
                {
                    if ( DVal(Item[i], Att) == V ) Swap(Fp++, i);
                }
                break;

            case ThreshContin:

                Thresh = TestNode->Cut;
                ForEach(i, Fp, Lp)
                {
                    if ( (CVal(Item[i], Att) <= Thresh) == (V == 1) ) Swap(Fp++, i);
                }
                break;

            case BrSubset:

                SS = TestNode->Subset[V];
                ForEach(i, Fp, Lp)
                {
                    if ( In(DVal(Item[i], Att), SS) ) Swap(Fp++, i);
                }
                break;
        }
```

```
        }
        else
        {
            /*  Group together unknown values  */

            switch ( TestNode->NodeType )
            {
                case BrDiscr:
                case BrSubset:

                    ForEach(i, Fp, Lp)
                    {
                        if ( ! DVal(Item[i], Att) ) Swap(Fp++, i);
                    }
                    break;

                case ThreshContin:

                    ForEach(i, Fp, Lp)
                    {
                        if ( CVal(Item[i], Att) == Unknown ) Swap(Fp++, i);
                    }
                    break;
            }
        }

        return Fp - 1;
}


/*************************************************************************/
/*                                                                       */
/*        Return the total weight of items from Fp to Lp                 */
/*                                                                       */
/*************************************************************************/

ItemCount CountItems(Fp, Lp)
/*        ----------        */
    ItemNo Fp, Lp;
{
    register ItemCount Sum=0.0, *Wt, *LWt;

    if ( AllKnown ) return Lp - Fp + 1;

    for ( Wt = Weight + Fp, LWt = Weight + Lp ; Wt <= LWt ; )
    {
        Sum += *Wt++;
    }

    return Sum;
}
```

```
/******************************************************************/
/*                                                                */
/*                Exchange items at a and b                       */
/*                                                                */
/******************************************************************/

void Swap(a,b)
/*   ─────  */
    ItemNo a, b;
{
    register Description Hold;
    register ItemCount HoldW;

    Hold = Item[a];
    Item[a]  = Item[b];
    Item[b]  = Hold;

    HoldW = Weight[a];
    Weight[a] = Weight[b];
    Weight[b] = HoldW;
}
```

File contin.c

```
/***********************************************************************/
/*                                                                     */
/*        Evaluation of a test on a continuous valued attribute        */
/*        ─────────────────────────────────────────────────────        */
/*                                                                     */
/***********************************************************************/

#include "buildex.i"

float
        *SplitGain,        /* SplitGain[i]  =  gain with att value of item i as threshold */
        *SplitInfo;        /* SplitInfo[i]  =  potential info ditto */


/***********************************************************************/
/*                                                                     */
/*  Continuous attributes are treated as if they have possible values  */
/*        0 (unknown), 1 (less than cut), 2 (greater than cut)         */
/*  This routine finds the best cut for items Fp through Lp and sets    */
/*  Info[], Gain[] and Bar[]                                           */
/*                                                                     */
/***********************************************************************/

        EvalContinuousAtt(Att, Fp, Lp)
/*      ───────────────────  */
        Attribute Att;
        ItemNo Fp, Lp;
{
        ItemNo i, BestI, Xp, Tries=0;
        ItemCount Items, KnownItems, LowItems, MinSplit, CountItems();
        ClassNo c;
        float AvGain=0, Val, BestVal, BaseInfo, ComputeGain(), TotalInfo(), Worth();
        void Swap();

        Verbosity(2) printf("\tAtt %s", AttName[Att]);
        Verbosity(3) printf("\n");

        ResetFreq(2);

        /* Omit and count unknown values */

        Items = CountItems(Fp, Lp);
        Xp = Fp;
        ForEach(i, Fp, Lp)
        {
            if ( CVal(Item[i],Att)  ==  Unknown )
            {
                Freq[ 0 ][ Class(Item[i]) ]  +=  Weight[i];
                Swap(Xp, i);
                Xp++;
```

```
        }
}
ValFreq[0] = 0;
ForEach(c, 0, MaxClass)
{
    ValFreq[0] += Freq[0][c];
}
KnownItems = Items - ValFreq[0];
UnknownRate[Att] = 1.0 - KnownItems / Items;

/*  Special case when very few known values  */

if ( KnownItems < 2 * MINOBJS )
{
    Verbosity(2) printf("\tinsufficient cases with known values\n");

    Gain[Att] = -Epsilon;
    Info[Att] = 0.0;
    return;
}

Quicksort(Xp, Lp, Att, Swap);

/*  Count base values and determine base information  */

ForEach(i, Xp, Lp)
{
    Freq[ 2 ][ Class(Item[i]) ] += Weight[i];
    SplitGain[i] = -Epsilon;
    SplitInfo[i] = 0;
}

BaseInfo = TotalInfo(Freq[2], 0, MaxClass) / KnownItems;

/*  Try possible cuts between items i and i+1, and determine the
    information and gain of the split in each case.  We have to be wary
    of splitting a small number of items off one end, as we can always
    split off a single item, but this has little predictive power.  */

MinSplit = 0.10 * KnownItems / (MaxClass + 1);
if ( MinSplit <= MINOBJS ) MinSplit = MINOBJS;
else
if ( MinSplit > 25 ) MinSplit = 25;

LowItems = 0;
ForEach(i, Xp, Lp - 1)
{
    c = Class(Item[i]);
    LowItems  += Weight[i];
    Freq[1][c] += Weight[i];
    Freq[2][c] -= Weight[i];

    if ( LowItems < MinSplit ) continue;
    else
    if ( LowItems > KnownItems - MinSplit ) break;
```

```
        if ( CVal(Item[i],Att) < CVal(Item[i+1],Att) - 1E-5 )
        {
            ValFreq[1]  = LowItems;
            ValFreq[2]  = KnownItems - LowItems;
            SplitGain[i] = ComputeGain(BaseInfo, UnknownRate[Att], 2, KnownItems);
            SplitInfo[i] = TotalInfo(ValFreq, 0, 2) / Items;
            AvGain += SplitGain[i];
            Tries++;

            Verbosity(3)
            {   printf("\t\tCut at %.3f   (gain %.3f, val %.3f):",
                        ( CVal(Item[i],Att) + CVal(Item[i+1],Att) ) / 2,
                        SplitGain[i],
                        Worth(SplitInfo[i], SplitGain[i], Epsilon));
                PrintDistribution(Att, 2, true);
            }
        }
    }
}

/*  Find the best attribute according to the given criterion  */

BestVal = -Epsilon;
BestI   = None;
AvGain  = ( Tries ? AvGain / Tries : 1E6 );
ForEach(i, Xp, Lp - 1)
{
    Val = Worth(SplitInfo[i], SplitGain[i], AvGain);
    if ( SplitGain[i] >= 0 && Val >= BestVal )
    {
        BestI   = i;
        BestVal = Val;
    }
}

/*  If a test on the attribute is able to make a gain,
    set the best break point, gain, and information  */

if ( BestI == None )
{
    Gain[Att] = -Epsilon;
    Info[Att] = 0.0;

    Verbosity(2) printf("\tno gain\n");
}
else
{
    Bar[Att]  = (CVal(Item[BestI],Att) + CVal(Item[BestI+1],Att)) / 2;
    Gain[Att] = SplitGain[BestI];
    Info[Att] = SplitInfo[BestI];

    Verbosity(2)
        printf("\tcut=%.3f, inf %.3f, gain %.3f\n",
                Bar[Att], Info[Att], Gain[Att]);
}
}
```

```
/**************************************************************************/
/*                                                                        */
/*   Change a leaf into a test on a continuous attribute                  */
/*                                                                        */
/**************************************************************************/

        ContinTest(Node, Att)
/*      ───────────   */
        Tree Node;
        Attribute Att;
{
        float Thresh, GreatestValueBelow();
        ItemCount CountItems();

        Sprout(Node, 2);

        Thresh = GreatestValueBelow(Att, Bar[Att]);

        Node->NodeType      = ThreshContin;
        Node->Tested        = Att;
        Node->Cut           =
        Node->Lower         =
        Node->Upper         = Thresh;
        Node->Errors        = 0;
}



/**************************************************************************/
/*                                                                        */
/*   Return the greatest value of attribute Att below threshold t         */
/*                                                                        */
/**************************************************************************/

float GreatestValueBelow(Att, t)
/*    ───────────────────   */
        Attribute Att;
        float t;
{
        ItemNo i;
        float v, Best;

        Best = -1E20;

        ForEach(i, 0, MaxItem)
        {
            v = CVal(Item[i], Att);
            if ( v != Unknown && v <= t && v > Best ) Best = v;
        }

        return Best;
}
```

File discr.c

```
/**************************************************************************/
/*                                                                      */
/*        Evaluation of a test on a discrete valued attribute           */
/*        ─────────────────────────────────────────────                 */
/*                                                                      */
/**************************************************************************/

#include "buildex.i"

/**************************************************************************/
/*                                                                      */
/*  Set Info[] and Gain[] for discrete partition of items Fp to Lp      */
/*                                                                      */
/**************************************************************************/

    EvalDiscreteAtt(Att, Fp, Lp, Items)
/*  ───────────────  */
    Attribute Att;
    ItemNo Fp, Lp;
    ItemCount Items;
{
    ItemCount KnownItems;
    float DiscrKnownBaseInfo(), ComputeGain(), TotalInfo();

    ComputeFrequencies(Att, Fp, Lp);

    KnownItems = Items - ValFreq[0];

    /*  Special case when no known values of the attribute  */

    if ( Items <= ValFreq[0] )
    {
        Verbosity(2) printf("\tAtt %s: no known values\n", AttName[Att]);

        Gain[Att] = -Epsilon;
        Info[Att] = 0.0;
        return;
    }

    Gain[Att] = ComputeGain(DiscrKnownBaseInfo(KnownItems, MaxAttVal[Att]),
                        UnknownRate[Att], MaxAttVal[Att], KnownItems);
    Info[Att] = TotalInfo(ValFreq, 0, MaxAttVal[Att]) / Items;

    Verbosity(2)
    {
        printf("\tAtt %s", AttName[Att]);
        Verbosity(3) PrintDistribution(Att, MaxAttVal[Att], true);
        printf("\tinf %.3f, gain %.3f\n", Info[Att], Gain[Att]);
    }

}
```

```
/*************************************************************************/
/*                                                                     */
/*   Compute frequency tables Freq[][] and ValFreq[] for attribute     */
/*   Att from items Fp to Lp, and set the UnknownRate for Att          */
/*                                                                     */
/*************************************************************************/


      ComputeFrequencies(Att, Fp, Lp)
/*    ————————————————   */
      Attribute Att;
      ItemNo Fp, Lp;
{
      Description Case;
      ClassNo c;
      DiscrValue v;
      ItemCount CountItems();
      ItemNo p;

      ResetFreq(MaxAttVal[Att]);

      /*   Determine the frequency of each class amongst cases
           with each possible value for the given attribute   */

      ForEach(p, Fp, Lp)
      {
          Case = Item[p];
          Freq[ DVal(Case,Att) ][ Class(Case) ] += Weight[p];
      }

      /*   Determine the frequency of each possible value for the
           given attribute   */

      ForEach(v, 0, MaxAttVal[Att])
      {
          ForEach(c, 0, MaxClass)
          {
              ValFreq[v]  += Freq[v][c];
          }
      }

      /*   Set the rate of unknown values of the attribute   */

      UnknownRate[Att]  =  ValFreq[0]  /  CountItems(Fp, Lp);
}
```

```
/*************************************************************************/
/*                                                                       */
/*   Return the base info for items with known values of a discrete      */
/*   attribute, using the frequency table Freq[] []                      */
/*                                                                       */
/*************************************************************************/


float DiscrKnownBaseInfo(KnownItems, MaxVal)
/*    ——————————    */
    DiscrValue MaxVal;
    ItemCount KnownItems;
{
    ClassNo c;
    ItemCount ClassCount;
    double Sum=0;
    DiscrValue v;

    ForEach(c, 0, MaxClass)
    {
        ClassCount = 0;
        ForEach(v, 1, MaxVal)
        {
            ClassCount += Freq[v] [c];
        }
        Sum += ClassCount * Log(ClassCount);
    }

    return (KnownItems * Log(KnownItems) - Sum) / KnownItems;
}



/*************************************************************************/
/*                                                                       */
/*   Construct and return a node for a test on a discrete attribute      */
/*                                                                       */
/*************************************************************************/


    DiscreteTest(Node, Att)
/*    ————————    */
    Tree Node;
    Attribute Att;
{
    ItemCount CountItems();

    Sprout(Node, MaxAttVal[Att]);

    Node->NodeType    = BrDiscr;
    Node->Tested      = Att;
    Node->Errors      = 0;
}
```

File info.c

```
/**************************************************************************/
/*                                                                        */
/*          Calculate information, information gain, and print dists      */
/*          ───────────────────────────────────────────────              */
/*                                                                        */
/**************************************************************************/

#include "buildex.i"

/**************************************************************************/
/*                                                                        */
/*   Determine the worth of a particular split according to the           */
/*   operative criterion                                                  */
/*                                                                        */
/*           Parameters:                                                  */
/*                SplitInfo:           potential info of the split        */
/*                SplitGain:           gain in info of the split          */
/*                MinGain:             gain above which the Gain Ratio     */
/*                                     may be used                        */
/*                                                                        */
/*   If the Gain criterion is being used, the information gain of         */
/*   the split is returned, but if the Gain Ratio criterion is           */
/*   being used, the ratio of the information gain of the split to        */
/*   its potential information is returned.                               */
/*                                                                        */
/**************************************************************************/

float Worth(ThisInfo, ThisGain, MinGain)
/*    ─────   */
    float ThisInfo, ThisGain, MinGain;
{
    if ( GAINRATIO )
    {
        if ( ThisGain >= MinGain - Epsilon && ThisInfo > Epsilon )
        {
            return ThisGain / ThisInfo;
        }
        else
        {
            return -Epsilon;
        }
    }
    else
    {
        return ThisInfo > 0 && ThisGain > 0 ? ThisGain : - Epsilon;
    }
}
```

```
/***********************************************************************/
/*                                                                     */
/*   Zero the frequency tables Freq[][]  and ValFreq[]  up to MaxVal   */
/*                                                                     */
/***********************************************************************/


      ResetFreq(MaxVal)
/*    ————————   */
      DiscrValue MaxVal;
  {
      DiscrValue v;
      ClassNo c;

      ForEach(v, 0, MaxVal)
        {
          ForEach(c, 0, MaxClass)
            {
              Freq[v][c] = 0;
            }
          ValFreq[v] = 0;
        }
  }



/***********************************************************************/
/*                                                                     */
/*   Given tables Freq[][]  and ValFreq[], compute the information gain.*/
/*                                                                     */
/*          Parameters:                                                */
/*              BaseInfo:            average information for all items with */
/*                                   known values of the test attribute */
/*              UnknownRate:         fraction of items with unknown ditto */
/*              MaxVal:              number of forks                    */
/*              TotalItems:          number of items with known values of */
/*                                   test att                          */
/*                                                                     */
/*   where Freq[x][y]  contains the no. of cases with value x for a    */
/*   particular attribute that are members of class y,                 */
/*   and ValFreq[x]  contains the no. of cases with value x for a      */
/*   particular attribute                                              */
/*                                                                     */
/***********************************************************************/

float ComputeGain(BaseInfo, UnknFrac, MaxVal, TotalItems)
/*    ——————————   */
      float BaseInfo, UnknFrac;
      DiscrValue MaxVal;
      ItemCount TotalItems;
  {
      DiscrValue v;
      float ThisInfo=0.0, ThisGain, TotalInfo();
      short ReasonableSubsets=0;
```

```
    /*  Check whether all values are unknown or the same  */

    if ( ! TotalItems )  return -Epsilon;

    /*  There must be at least two subsets with MINOBJS items  */

    ForEach(v, 1, MaxVal)
    {
        if ( ValFreq[v] >= MINOBJS )  ReasonableSubsets++;
    }
    if ( ReasonableSubsets < 2 )  return -Epsilon;

    /*  Compute total info after split, by summing the
        info of each of the subsets formed by the test  */

    ForEach(v, 1, MaxVal)
    {
        ThisInfo += TotalInfo(Freq[v], 0, MaxClass);
    }

    /*  Set the gain in information for all items, adjusted for unknowns  */

    ThisGain = (1 - UnknFrac) * (BaseInfo - ThisInfo / TotalItems);

    Verbosity(5)
        printf("ComputeThisGain: items %.1f info %.3f base %.3f unkn %.3f result %.3f\n",
                TotalItems + ValFreq[0], ThisInfo, BaseInfo, UnknFrac, ThisGain);

    return ThisGain;
}


/*************************************************************************/
/*                                                                       */
/*  Compute the total information in V[ MinVal..MaxVal ]                  */
/*                                                                       */
/*************************************************************************/

float TotalInfo(V, MinVal, MaxVal)
/*    ————————    */
    ItemCount V[];
    DiscrValue MinVal, MaxVal;
{
    DiscrValue v;
    float Sum=0.0;
    ItemCount N, TotalItems=0;

    ForEach(v, MinVal, MaxVal)
    {
        N = V[v];

        Sum += N * Log(N);
        TotalItems += N;
    }

    return TotalItems * Log(TotalItems) - Sum;
}
```

```
/*************************************************************************/
/*                                                                     */
/*        Print distribution table for given attribute                 */
/*                                                                     */
/*************************************************************************/

    PrintDistribution(Att, MaxVal, ShowNames)
/*  ──────────────  */
    Attribute Att;
    DiscrValue MaxVal;
    Boolean ShowNames;
{
    DiscrValue v;
    ClassNo c;
    String Val;

    printf("\n\t\t\t ");
    ForEach(c, 0, MaxClass)
    {
        printf("%7.6s", ClassName[c]);
    }
    printf("\n");

    ForEach(v, 0, MaxVal)
    {
        if ( ShowNames )
        {
            Val = ( !v ? "unknown" :
                    MaxAttVal[Att] ? AttValName[Att][v] :
                    v == 1 ? "below" : "above" );
            printf("\t\t[%-7.7s:", Val);
        }
        else
        {
            printf("\t\t[%-7d:", v);
        }

        ForEach(c, 0, MaxClass)
        {
            printf(" %6.1f", Freq[v][c]);
        }

        printf("]\n");
    }
}
```

File classify.c

```
/**********************************************************************/
/*                                                                  */
/*  Determine the class of a case description from a decision tree   */
/*  _____          */
/*                                                                  */
/**********************************************************************/

#include "defns.i"
#include "types.i"
#include "extern.i"

float     *ClassSum=Nil;          /* ClassSum[c] = total weight of class c */


/**********************************************************************/
/*                                                                  */
/*  Categorize a case description using the given decision tree      */
/*                                                                  */
/**********************************************************************/

ClassNo Category(CaseDesc, DecisionTree)
/*      _____  */
    Description CaseDesc;
    Tree DecisionTree;
{
    ClassNo c, BestClass;

    if ( ! ClassSum )
    {
        ClassSum = (float *) malloc((MaxClass+1) * sizeof(float));
    }

    ForEach(c, 0, MaxClass)
    {
        ClassSum[c] = 0;
    }

    Classify(CaseDesc, DecisionTree, 1.0);

    BestClass = 0;
    ForEach(c, 0, MaxClass)
    {
        Verbosity(5) printf("class %s weight %.2f\n", ClassName[c], ClassSum[c]);

        if ( ClassSum[c] > ClassSum[BestClass] ) BestClass = c;
    }

    return BestClass;
}
```

```
/**************************************************************************/
/*                                                                        */
/*   Classify a case description using the given subtree by adjusting     */
/*   the value ClassSum for each class                                    */
/*                                                                        */
/**************************************************************************/

    Classify(CaseDesc, T, Weight)
/*  ———— */
    Description CaseDesc;
    Tree T;
    float Weight;
{
    DiscrValue v, dv;
    float Cv;
    Attribute a;
    ClassNo c;

    switch ( T->NodeType )
    {
        case 0:  /* leaf */

            if ( T->Items > 0 )
            {
                /*  Update from ALL classes  */

                ForEach(c, 0, MaxClass)
                {
                    if ( T->ClassDist[c]  )
                    {
                        ClassSum[c]  += Weight * T->ClassDist[c]  / T->Items;
                    }
                }
            }
            else
            {
                ClassSum[T->Leaf]  += Weight;
            }

            return;

        case BrDiscr:  /*  test of discrete attribute */

            a = T->Tested;
            v = DVal(CaseDesc, a);

            if ( v && v <= T->Forks )   /*  Make sure not new discrete value  */
            {
                Classify(CaseDesc, T->Branch[v], Weight);
            }
            else
            {
                ForEach(v, 1, T->Forks)
                {
```

```
                    Classify(CaseDesc, T->Branch[v],
                            (Weight * T->Branch[v]->Items) / T->Items);
                }
            }

        return;

case ThreshContin:   /* test of continuous attribute */

        a = T->Tested;
        Cv = CVal(CaseDesc, a);

        if ( Cv == Unknown )
        {
            ForEach(v, 1, 2)
            {
                Classify(CaseDesc, T->Branch[v],
                        (Weight * T->Branch[v]->Items) / T->Items);
            }
        }
        else
        {
            v = ( Cv <= T->Cut ? 1 : 2 );
            Classify(CaseDesc, T->Branch[v], Weight);
        }

        return;

case BrSubset:   /* subset test on discrete attribute   */

        a = T->Tested;
        dv = DVal(CaseDesc, a);

        if ( dv )
        {
            ForEach(v, 1, T->Forks)
            {
                if ( In(dv, T->Subset[v]) )
                {
                    Classify(CaseDesc, T->Branch[v], Weight);

                    return;
                }
            }
        }

        /*  Value unknown or not found in any of the subsets  */

        ForEach(v, 1, T->Forks)
        {
            Classify(CaseDesc, T->Branch[v],
                    (Weight * T->Branch[v]->Items) / T->Items);
        }

        return;
    }
}
```

File prune.c

```
/*************************************************************************/
/*                                                                       */
/*          Prune a decision tree and predict its error rate             */
/*          ---------------------------------------------                */
/*                                                                       */
/*************************************************************************/


#include "defns.i"
#include "types.i"
#include "extern.i"

extern   ItemCount        *Weight;

Set       *PossibleValues=Nil;
Boolean Changed;

#define  LocalVerbosity(x)         if (Sh >= 0 && VERBOSITY >= x)
#define  Intab(x)                  Indent(x, "|  ")


/*************************************************************************/
/*                                                                       */
/*  Prune tree T, returning true if tree has been modified               */
/*                                                                       */
/*************************************************************************/

Boolean Prune(T)
/*      -----  */
    Tree T;
{
    ItemNo i;
    float EstimateErrors();
    Attribute a;

    InitialiseWeights();
    AllKnown = true;

    Verbosity(1) printf("\n");

    Changed = false;

    EstimateErrors(T, 0, MaxItem, 0, true);

    if ( SUBSET )
    {
        if ( ! PossibleValues )
        {
            PossibleValues = (Set *) calloc(MaxAtt+1, sizeof(Set));
        }
```

```
        ForEach(a, 0, MaxAtt)
        {
            if ( MaxAttVal[a] )
            {
                PossibleValues[a] = (Set) malloc((MaxAttVal[a]>>3) + 1);
                ClearBits((MaxAttVal[a]>>3) + 1, PossibleValues[a]);
                ForEach(i, 1, MaxAttVal[a])
                {
                    SetBit(i, PossibleValues[a]);
                }
            }
        }

        CheckPossibleValues(T);
    }

    return Changed;
}



/*************************************************************************/
/*                                                                       */
/*      Estimate the errors in a given subtree                           */
/*                                                                       */
/*************************************************************************/


float EstimateErrors(T, Fp, Lp, Sh, UpdateTree)
/*    ─────────────    */
    Tree T;
    ItemNo Fp, Lp;
    short Sh;
    Boolean UpdateTree;
{
    ItemNo i, Kp, Ep, Group();
    ItemCount Cases, KnownCases, *LocalClassDist, TreeErrors, LeafErrors,
        ExtraLeafErrors, BranchErrors, CountItems(), Factor, MaxFactor, AddErrs();
    DiscrValue v, MaxBr;
    ClassNo c, BestClass;
    Boolean PrevAllKnown;

    /*  Generate the class frequency distribution  */

    Cases = CountItems(Fp, Lp);
    LocalClassDist = (ItemCount *) calloc(MaxClass+1, sizeof(ItemCount));

    ForEach(i, Fp, Lp)
    {
        LocalClassDist[ Class(Item[i]) ] += Weight[i];
    }
```

```
/*  Find the most frequent class and update the tree  */

BestClass = T->Leaf;
ForEach(c, 0, MaxClass)
{
    if ( LocalClassDist[c] > LocalClassDist[BestClass] )
    {
        BestClass = c;
    }
}
LeafErrors = Cases - LocalClassDist[BestClass];
ExtraLeafErrors = AddErrs(Cases, LeafErrors);

if ( UpdateTree )
{
    T->Items = Cases;
    T->Leaf  = BestClass;
    memcpy(T->ClassDist, LocalClassDist, (MaxClass + 1) * sizeof(ItemCount));
}

if ( ! T->NodeType )        /*  leaf  */
{
    TreeErrors = LeafErrors + ExtraLeafErrors;

    if ( UpdateTree )
    {
        T->Errors = TreeErrors;

        LocalVerbosity(1)
        {
            Intab(Sh);
            printf("%s  (%.2f:%.2f/%.2f)\n", ClassName[T->Leaf],
                    T->Items, LeafErrors, T->Errors);
        }
    }

    free(LocalClassDist);

    return TreeErrors;
}

/*  Estimate errors for each branch  */

Kp = Group(0, Fp, Lp, T) + 1;
KnownCases = CountItems(Kp, Lp);

PrevAllKnown = AllKnown;
if ( Kp != Fp ) AllKnown = false;

TreeErrors = MaxFactor = 0;

ForEach(v, 1, T->Forks)
{
    Ep = Group(v, Kp, Lp, T);
```

```
        if ( Kp <= Ep )
        {
            Factor = CountItems(Kp, Ep) / KnownCases;

             if ( Factor >= MaxFactor )
             {
                 MaxBr = v;
                 MaxFactor = Factor;
             }
            ForEach(i, Fp, Kp-1)
            {
                 Weight[i] *= Factor;
            }
            TreeErrors += EstimateErrors(T->Branch[v], Fp, Ep, Sh+1, UpdateTree);

            Group(0, Fp, Ep, T);
            ForEach(i, Fp, Kp-1)
            {
                 Weight[i] /= Factor;
            }
        }
    }

    AllKnown = PrevAllKnown;

    if ( ! UpdateTree )
    {
        free(LocalClassDist);

        return TreeErrors;
    }

    /*  See how the largest branch would fare  */

    BranchErrors = EstimateErrors(T->Branch[MaxBr], Fp, Lp, -1000, false);

    LocalVerbosity(1)
    {
        Intab(Sh);
        printf("%s:    [%d%%  N=%.2f  tree=%.2f  leaf=%.2f+%.2f   br[%d]=%.2f]\n",
               AttName[T->Tested],
               (int)  ((TreeErrors * 100) / (T->Items + 0.001)),
               T->Items, TreeErrors, LeafErrors, ExtraLeafErrors,
               MaxBr, BranchErrors);
    }

    /*  See whether tree should be replaced with leaf or largest branch  */

    if ( LeafErrors + ExtraLeafErrors <= BranchErrors + 0.1 &&
         LeafErrors + ExtraLeafErrors <= TreeErrors + 0.1 )
    {
        LocalVerbosity(1)
        {
            Intab(Sh);
            printf("Replaced with leaf %s\n", ClassName[T->Leaf]);
```

```
        }
        T->NodeType = 0;
        T->Errors = LeafErrors + ExtraLeafErrors;
        Changed = true;
    }
    else
    if ( BranchErrors <= TreeErrors + 0.1 )
    {
        LocalVerbosity(1)
        {
            Intab(Sh);
            printf("Replaced with branch %d\n", MaxBr);
        }

        AllKnown = PrevAllKnown;
        EstimateErrors(T->Branch[MaxBr], Fp, Lp, Sh, true);
        memcpy((char *) T, (char *) T->Branch[MaxBr], sizeof(TreeRec));
        Changed = true;
    }
    else
    {
        T->Errors = TreeErrors;
    }

    AllKnown = PrevAllKnown;
    free(LocalClassDist);

    return T->Errors;
}


/*************************************************************************/
/*                                                                       */
/*        Remove unnecessary subset tests on missing values             */
/*                                                                       */
/*************************************************************************/


    CheckPossibleValues(T)
/*  ─────────────────  */
    Tree T;
{
    Set HoldValues;
    int v, Bytes, b;
    Attribute A;
    char Any=0;

    if ( T->NodeType == BrSubset )
    {
        A = T->Tested;

        Bytes = (MaxAttVal[A]>>3) + 1;
        HoldValues = (Set) malloc(Bytes);
```

```
    /*  See if last (default) branch can be simplified or omitted  */

    ForEach(b, 0, Bytes-1)
    {
        T->Subset[T->Forks][b]  &=  PossibleValues[A][b];
        Any |=  T->Subset[T->Forks][b];
    }

    if ( ! Any )
    {
        T->Forks--;
    }

    /*  Process each subtree, leaving only values in branch subset  */

    CopyBits(Bytes, PossibleValues[A], HoldValues);

    ForEach(v, 1, T->Forks)
    {
        CopyBits(Bytes, T->Subset[v], PossibleValues[A]);

        CheckPossibleValues(T->Branch[v]);
    }

    CopyBits(Bytes, HoldValues, PossibleValues[A]);

    free(HoldValues);
    }
    else
    if ( T->NodeType )
    {
        ForEach(v, 1, T->Forks)
        {
            CheckPossibleValues(T->Branch[v]);
        }
    }
}
```

File subset.c

```
/**********************************************************************/
/*                                                                  */
/*          Evaluation of the subsetting of a discrete attribute    */
/*          ──────────────────────────────────────────────────      */
/*                                                                  */
/**********************************************************************/


#include "buildex.i"

ItemCount
        *Slice1,        /* Slice1 [c]    = saved values of Freq [x] [c]  in subset.c */
        *Slice2;        /* Slice2 [c]    = saved values of Freq [y] [c] */

Set
        **Subset;       /* Subset [a] [s] = subset s for att a */

short
        *Subsets;       /* Subsets [a]  = no. subsets for att a */


/**********************************************************************/
/*                                                                  */
/*  Evaluate subsetting a discrete attribute and form the chosen     */
/*  subsets Subset [Att] [], setting Subsets [Att]  to the number of  */
/*  subsets, and the Info [] and Gain [] of a test on the attribute   */
/*                                                                  */
/**********************************************************************/


        EvalSubset (Att, Fp, Lp, Items)
/*      ─────────  */
        Attribute Att;
        ItemNo Fp, Lp;
        ItemCount Items;
{
        DiscrValue V1, V2, BestV1, BestV2, Barred;
        ItemCount KnownItems;
        ClassNo c;
        float BaseInfo, MinGain, ThisGain, ThisInfo,
            Val, BestVal, BestGain, BestInfo,
            PrevVal, PrevGain, PrevInfo,
            DiscrKnownBaseInfo (), Worth (), ComputeGain (), TotalInfo ();
        short Blocks=0, MissingValues=0, ReasonableSubsets, Bytes, b;
        Boolean MergedSubsets = false;
        int SaveMINOBJS;

        SaveMINOBJS = MINOBJS;
        MINOBJS = 1;
```

```
/*  First compute Freq[][], ValFreq[], base info, and the gain
    and total info of a split on discrete attribute Att  */

ComputeFrequencies(Att, Fp, Lp);

KnownItems = Items - ValFreq[0];

BaseInfo = DiscrKnownBaseInfo(KnownItems, MaxAttVal[Att]);

PrevGain = ComputeGain(BaseInfo, UnknownRate[Att], MaxAttVal[Att],KnownItems);
PrevInfo = TotalInfo(ValFreq, 0, MaxAttVal[Att]) / Items;
PrevVal = Worth(PrevInfo, PrevGain, Epsilon);

Verbosity(2)
{
    printf("\tAtt %s", AttName[Att]);

    Verbosity(3)  PrintDistribution(Att, MaxAttVal[Att], true);

    printf("\tinf %.3f, gain %.3f, val=%.3f\n",
            PrevInfo, PrevGain, PrevVal);
}

/*  Eliminate unrepresented attribute values from Freq[] and ValFreq[]
    and form a separate subset for each represented attribute value  */

Bytes = (MaxAttVal[Att]>>3) + 1;
ClearBits(Bytes, Subset[Att][0]);

ForEach(V1, 1, MaxAttVal[Att])
{
    if ( ValFreq[V1] > 0.5 )
    {
        if ( ++Blocks < V1 )
        {
            ValFreq[Blocks] = ValFreq[V1];
            ForEach(c, 0, MaxClass)
            {
                Freq[Blocks][c] = Freq[V1][c];
            }
        }
        ClearBits(Bytes, Subset[Att][Blocks]);
        SetBit(V1, Subset[Att][Blocks]);
    }
    else
    {
        SetBit(V1, Subset[Att][0]);
        MissingValues++;
    }
}
```

```
/*  Merge any single-class subsets with others of the same class  */
/*  Note: have ValFreq[V] > 0 for all V  */

ForEach(V1, 1, Blocks-1)
{
    for ( c = 0 ; Freq[V1][c] < 0.1 ; c++ )
        ;

    if ( Freq[V1][c] < ValFreq[V1] - 0.1 ) continue;

    /*  Now have a single class -- look for others  */

    for ( V2 = V1+1 ; V2 <= Blocks ; )
    {
        if ( Freq[V2][c] < ValFreq[V2] - 0.1 )
        {
            V2++;
        }
        else
        {
            /*  Merge these subsets  */

            Combine(V1, V2, Blocks);

            ForEach(b, 0, Bytes-1)
            {
                Subset[Att][V1][b]  |= Subset[Att][V2][b];
                Subset[Att][V2][b]  = Subset[Att][Blocks][b];
            }

            Blocks--;
            MergedSubsets = true;
        }
    }
}

if ( MergedSubsets )
{
    PrevGain = ComputeGain(BaseInfo, UnknownRate[Att], Blocks, KnownItems);
    PrevInfo = TotalInfo(ValFreq, 0, Blocks) / Items;
    PrevVal = Worth(PrevInfo, PrevGain, Epsilon);

    Verbosity(2)
    {
        printf("\tAfter merging single-class subsets:");

        Verbosity(3) PrintDistribution(Att, Blocks, false);

        printf("\tinf %.3f, gain %.3f, val=%.3f\n",
                PrevInfo, PrevGain, PrevVal);
    }
}
```

```
/*  Examine possible pair mergers and hill-climb  */

MinGain = PrevGain / 2;

while ( Blocks > 2 )
{
    BestVal = BestV1 = 0;
    BestGain = -Epsilon;

    /*  Check reasonable subsets; if less than 3, bar mergers
        involving the largest block  */

    ReasonableSubsets = 0;
    Barred = 1;

    ForEach(V1, 1, Blocks)
    {
        if ( ValFreq[V1] >= SaveMINOBJS ) ReasonableSubsets++;

        if ( ValFreq[V1] > ValFreq[Barred] ) Barred = V1;
    }

    if ( ReasonableSubsets >= 3 ) Barred = 0;

    /*  For each possible pair of values, calculate the gain and
        total info of a split in which they are treated as one.
        Keep track of the pair with the best gain.  */

    ForEach(V1, 1, Blocks-1)
    {
        ForEach(V2, V1+1, Blocks)
        {
            if ( V1 == Barred || V2 == Barred ) continue;

            Combine(V1, V2, Blocks);

            ThisGain = ComputeGain(BaseInfo, UnknownRate[Att],
                                   Blocks-1, KnownItems);
            ThisInfo = TotalInfo(ValFreq, 0, Blocks-1) / Items;
            Val      = Worth(ThisInfo, ThisGain, Epsilon);

            Verbosity(4)
            {
                printf("\tcombine %d %d info %.3f gain %.3f val %.3f",
                       V1, V2, ThisInfo, ThisGain, Val);
                PrintDistribution(Att, Blocks-1, false);
            }

            /*  Force a split if
                    less than two reasonable subsets, or
                    using GAIN criterion
                Prefer this split to the previous one if
                    gain >= MinGain (and previous < MinGain), or
                    val >= previous best val  */

            if ( ThisGain >= MinGain && BestGain < MinGain ||
                 Val >= BestVal ||
                 ! BestV1 && ( ! GAINRATIO || ReasonableSubsets < 2 ) )
```

```
                    {
                        BestVal  = Val;
                        BestGain = ThisGain;
                        BestInfo = ThisInfo;
                        BestV1   = V1;
                        BestV2   = V2;
                    }

                    Uncombine(V1, V2);
                }
            }

            if ( GAINRATIO &&
                 ReasonableSubsets >= 2 &&
                 ( ! BestV1 ||
                   BestVal < PrevVal + 1E-5 ||
                   BestVal == PrevVal && BestGain < PrevGain ) ) break;

            PrevGain = BestGain;
            PrevInfo = BestInfo;
            PrevVal = BestVal;

            Combine(BestV1, BestV2, Blocks);

            ForEach(b, 0, Bytes-1)
            {
                Subset[Att][BestV1][b] |= Subset[Att][BestV2][b];
                Subset[Att][BestV2][b]  = Subset[Att][Blocks][b];
            }

            Blocks--;

            Verbosity(2)
            {
                printf("\t\tform subset ");
                PrintSubset(Att, Subset[Att][BestV1]);
                printf(": %d subsets, inf %.3f, gain %.3f, val %.3f\n",
                        Blocks, BestInfo, BestGain, BestVal);
                Verbosity(3)
                {
                    printf("\t\tcombine %d, %d", BestV1, BestV2);
                    PrintDistribution(Att, Blocks, false);
                }
            }
        }

    MINOBJS = SaveMINOBJS;

    if ( PrevVal <= 0 )
    {
        Gain[Att] = -Epsilon;
        Info[Att] = 0;
    }
    else
    {
        Gain[Att] = ComputeGain(BaseInfo, UnknownRate[Att], Blocks, KnownItems);
```

```
        Info[Att]  =  PrevInfo;

        if ( MissingValues )
        {
            Blocks++;
            CopyBits(Bytes, Subset[Att][0], Subset[Att][Blocks]);
        }

        Subsets[Att]  =  Blocks;

        Verbosity(2)  printf("\tFinal subsets:");
        Verbosity(3)  PrintDistribution(Att, Blocks, false);
        Verbosity(2)
            printf("\tinf %.3f gain %.3f val %.3f\n",
                    Info[Att], Gain[Att], Worth(Info[Att], Gain[Att], Epsilon));
    }
}


/*************************************************************************/
/*                                                                       */
/*  Combine the distribution figures of discrete attribute values        */
/*  x and y, putting the combined figures in Freq[x][]  and              */
/*  ValFreq[x][], and saving old values in Slice1 and Slice2             */
/*                                                                       */
/*************************************************************************/


    Combine(x, y, Last)
/*  ———————  */
    DiscrValue x, y, Last;
{
    ClassNo c;

    ForEach(c, 0, MaxClass)
    {
        Slice1[c]  =  Freq[x][c];
        Slice2[c]  =  Freq[y][c];

        Freq[x][c]  +=  Freq[y][c];
        Freq[y][c]  =  Freq[Last][c];
    }

    Slice1[MaxClass+1]  =  ValFreq[x];
    Slice2[MaxClass+1]  =  ValFreq[y];

    ValFreq[x]  +=  ValFreq[y];
    ValFreq[y]  =  ValFreq[Last];
}
```

```
/************************************************************************/
/*                                                                      */
/*   Restore old class distribution figures of discrete attribute       */
/*   values x and y from Slice1 and Slice2                              */
/*                                                                      */
/************************************************************************/


        Uncombine(x, y)
/*      ───────────  */
        DiscrValue x, y;
{
        ClassNo c;

        ForEach(c, 0, MaxClass)
        {
            Freq[x][c]  = Slice1[c];
            Freq[y][c]  = Slice2[c];
        }

        ValFreq[x]  = Slice1[MaxClass+1];
        ValFreq[y]  = Slice2[MaxClass+1];
}



/************************************************************************/
/*                                                                      */
/*   Print the values of attribute Att which are in the subset Ss       */
/*                                                                      */
/************************************************************************/


        PrintSubset(Att, Ss)
/*      ───────────  */
        Attribute Att;
        Set Ss;
{
        DiscrValue V1;
        Boolean First=true;

        ForEach(V1, 1, MaxAttVal[Att])
        {
            if ( In(V1, Ss) )
            {
                if ( First )
                {
                    First = false;
                }
                else
                {
                    printf(", ");
                }
                printf("%s", AttValName[Att][V1]);
            }
        }
}
```

```
/*************************************************************************/
/*                                                                     */
/*   Construct and return a node for a test on a subset of values      */
/*                                                                     */
/*************************************************************************/


        SubsetTest(Node, Att)
/*      ——————————  */
        Tree Node;
        Attribute Att;
{
        ItemCount CountItems();
        short S, Bytes;

        Sprout(Node, Subsets[Att]);

        Node->NodeType    = BrSubset;
        Node->Tested      = Att;
        Node->Errors      = 0;

        Bytes = (MaxAttVal[Att]>>3) + 1;
        Node->Subset = (Set *) calloc(Subsets[Att] + 1, sizeof(Set));
        ForEach(S, 1, Node->Forks)
        {
            Node->Subset[S] = (Set) malloc(Bytes);
            CopyBits(Bytes, Subset[Att][S], Node->Subset[S]);
        }
}
```

File st-thresh.c

```
/**********************************************************************/
/*                                                                  */
/*       Soften thresholds for continuous attributes                */
/*       _____                */
/*                                                                  */
/**********************************************************************/


#include "defns.i"
#include "types.i"
#include "extern.i"

Boolean *LHSErr,        /*  Does a misclassification occur with this value of an att  */
        *RHSErr;        /*  if the below or above threshold branches are taken  */

ItemNo *ThreshErrs;     /*  ThreshErrs[i] is the no. of misclassifications if thresh is i  */

float   *CVals;         /*  All values of a continuous attribute  */

#define  Below(v,t)     (v <= t + 1E-6)


/**********************************************************************/
/*                                                                  */
/*  Soften all thresholds for continuous attributes in tree T       */
/*                                                                  */
/**********************************************************************/

        SoftenThresh(T)
/*      _____  */
        Tree T;
{
        CVals = (float *) calloc(MaxItem+1, sizeof(float));
        LHSErr = (Boolean *) calloc(MaxItem+1, sizeof(Boolean));
        RHSErr = (Boolean *) calloc(MaxItem+1, sizeof(Boolean));
        ThreshErrs = (ItemNo *) calloc(MaxItem+1, sizeof(ItemNo));

        InitialiseWeights();

        ScanTree(T, 0, MaxItem);

        cfree(ThreshErrs);
        cfree(RHSErr);
        cfree(LHSErr);
        cfree(CVals);
}
```

```
/*************************************************************************/
/*                                                                       */
/*   Calculate upper and lower bounds for each test on a continuous      */
/*   attribute in tree T, using data items from Fp to Lp                 */
/*                                                                       */
/*************************************************************************/


	ScanTree(T, Fp, Lp)
/*      ————————  */
	Tree T;
	ItemNo Fp, Lp;
{
	short v;
	float Val, Se, Limit, Lower, Upper, GreatestValueBelow();
	ItemNo i, Kp, Ep, LastI, Errors, BaseErrors;
	ClassNo CaseClass, Class1, Class2, Category();
	Boolean LeftThresh=false;
	Description CaseDesc;
	Attribute Att;
	void Swap();

	/*  Stop when get to a leaf  */

	if ( ! T->NodeType )  return;

	/*  Group the unknowns together  */

	Kp = Group(0, Fp, Lp, T);

	/*  Soften a threshold for a continuous attribute  */

	Att = T->Tested;

	if ( T->NodeType == ThreshContin )
	{
		printf("\nTest %s <> %g\n", AttName[Att], T->Cut);

		Quicksort(Kp+1, Lp, Att, Swap);

		ForEach(i, Kp+1, Lp)
		{
			/*  See how this item would be classified if its
			    value were on each side of the threshold  */

			CaseDesc = Item[i];
			CaseClass = Class(CaseDesc);
			Val = CVal(CaseDesc, Att);

			Class1 = Category(CaseDesc, T->Branch[1]);
			Class2 = Category(CaseDesc, T->Branch[2]);

			CVals[i] = Val;
			LHSErr[i] = (Class1 != CaseClass ? 1 : 0);
			RHSErr[i] = (Class2 != CaseClass ? 1 : 0);
		}
```

```
/*  Set Errors to total errors if take above thresh branch,
    and BaseErrors to errors if threshold has original value  */

Errors = BaseErrors = 0;
ForEach(i, Kp+1, Lp)
{
    Errors += RHSErr[i];

    if ( Below(CVals[i], T->Cut) )
    {
        BaseErrors += LHSErr[i];
    }
    else
    {
        BaseErrors += RHSErr[i];
    }
}

/*  Calculate standard deviation of the number of errors  */

Se = sqrt( (BaseErrors+0.5) * (Lp-Kp-BaseErrors+0.5) / (Lp-Kp+1) );
Limit = BaseErrors + Se;

Verbosity(1)
{
    printf("\t\t\tBase errors %d, items %d, se=%.1f\n",
            BaseErrors, Lp-Kp, Se);
    printf("\n\tVal <=    Errors\t\t+Errors\n");
    printf("\t             %6d\n", Errors);
}

/*  Set ThreshErrs[i] to the no. of errors if the threshold were i  */

ForEach(i, Kp+1, Lp)
{
    ThreshErrs[i] = Errors = Errors + LHSErr[i] - RHSErr[i];

    if ( i == Lp || CVals[i] != CVals[i+1] )
    {
        Verbosity(1)
            printf("\t%6g    %6d\t\t%7d\n",
                CVals[i], Errors, Errors - BaseErrors);
    }
}

/*  Choose Lower and Upper so that if threshold were set to
    either, the number of items misclassified would be one
    standard deviation above BaseErrors  */

LastI = Kp+1;
Lower = Min(T->Cut, CVals[LastI]);
Upper = Max(T->Cut, CVals[Lp]);
while ( CVals[LastI+1] == CVals[LastI] ) LastI++;
```

```
    while ( LastI < Lp )
    {
        i = LastI + 1;
        while ( i < Lp && CVals[i+1] == CVals[i] ) i++;

        if ( ! LeftThresh &&
             ThreshErrs[LastI] > Limit &&
             ThreshErrs[i] <= Limit &&
             Below(CVals[i], T->Cut) )
        {
            Lower = CVals[i] -
                    (CVals[i] - CVals[LastI]) * (Limit - ThreshErrs[i]) /
                    (ThreshErrs[LastI] - ThreshErrs[i]);
            LeftThresh = true;
        }
        else
        if ( ThreshErrs[LastI] <= Limit &&
             ThreshErrs[i] > Limit &&
             ! Below(CVals[i], T->Cut) )
        {
            Upper = CVals[LastI] +
                    (CVals[i] - CVals[LastI]) * (Limit - ThreshErrs[LastI]) /
                    (ThreshErrs[i] - ThreshErrs[LastI]);
            if ( Upper < T->Cut ) Upper = T->Cut;
        }

        LastI = i;
    }

    T->Lower = Lower;
    T->Upper = Upper;

    Verbosity(1) printf("\n");

    printf("\tLower = %g, Upper = %g\n", T->Lower, T->Upper);
}
/*  Recursively scan each branch  */

ForEach(v, 1, T->Forks)
{
    Ep = Group(v, Kp+1, Lp, T);

    if ( Kp < Ep )
    {
        ScanTree(T->Branch[v], Kp+1, Ep);
        Kp = Ep;
    }
}
}
```

File rulex.i

```
/**********************************************************************/
/*                                                                  */
/*        Global data for constructing and applying rules           */
/*        _____          */
/*                                                                  */
/**********************************************************************/

extern PR        *Rule;            /* production rules */

extern RuleNo     NRules,          /* number of production rules */
                 *RuleIndex;       /* index to production rules */

extern short      RuleSpace;       /* space currently allocated for rules */

extern RuleSet   *PRSet;           /* set of rulesets */

extern ClassNo    DefaultClass;    /* default class associated with ruleset */

extern Boolean    SIGTEST;         /* use Fisher's test in rule pruning */

extern float      SIGTHRESH,       /* sig level used in rule pruning */
                  REDUNDANCY,      /* factor governing encoding tradeoff
                                      between rules and exceptions */
                  AttTestBits,     /* average bits to encode tested attribute */
                 *BranchBits;      /* ditto attribute value */

extern float     *LogItemNo;       /* LogItemNo[i] = log2(i) */
extern double    *LogFact;         /* LogFact[i] = log2(i!)  */
```

File c4.5rules.c

```
/**************************************************************************/
/*                                                                        */
/*   Main routine for constructing sets of production rules from trees     */
/*   _____          */
/*                                                                        */
/*                                                                        */
/**************************************************************************/
```

```
#include "defns.i"
#include "types.i"
```

/*   External data.   Note: uncommented variables have the same meaning
     as for decision trees (see extern.i)   */

short	MaxAtt, MaxClass, MaxDiscrVal;
ItemNo	MaxItem;
Description	*Item;
DiscrValue	*MaxAttVal;
char	*SpecialStatus;
String	*ClassName, *AttName, **AttValName, FileName = "DF";
short	VERBOSITY = 0, TRIALS;
Boolean	UNSEENS= false; SIGTEST = false; /* use significance test in rule pruning */

float	SIGTHRESH= 0.05,
	CF = 0.25,
	REDUNDANCY = 1.0; /* factor that guesstimates the
	                                amount of redundancy and
	                                irrelevance in the attributes */

PR	*Rule; /* current rules */
RuleNo	NRules = 0, /* number of current rules */ *RuleIndex; /* rule index */
short	RuleSpace = 0; /* space allocated for rules */
ClassNo	DefaultClass; /* current default class */
RuleSet	*PRSet; /* sets of rulesets */
float	AttTestBits, /* bits to encode tested att */ *BranchBits; /* ditto attribute value */

```
        main(Argc, Argv)
/*      ——————  */
        int Argc;
        char *Argv[];
{
        int o;
        extern char *optarg;
        extern int optind;
        Boolean FirstTime=true;

        PrintHeader("rule generator");

        /*  Process options  */

        while (  (o = getopt(Argc, Argv, "f:uv:c:r:F:")) != EOF )
        {
            if ( FirstTime )
            {
                printf("\n      Options:\n");
                FirstTime = false;
            }

            switch (o)
            {
                case 'f':   FileName = optarg;
                            printf("\tFile stem <%s>\n", FileName);
                            break;
                case 'u':   UNSEENS = true;
                            printf("\tRulesets evaluated on unseen cases\n");
                            break;
                case 'v':   VERBOSITY = atoi(optarg);
                            printf("\tVerbosity level %d\n", VERBOSITY);
                            break;
                case 'c':   CF = atof(optarg);
                            printf("\tPruning confidence level %g%%\n", CF);
                            CF /= 100;
                            break;
                case 'r':   REDUNDANCY = atof(optarg);
                            printf("\tRedundancy factor %g\n", REDUNDANCY);
                            break;
                case 'F':   SIGTHRESH = atof(optarg);
                            printf("\tSignificance test in rule pruning, ");
                            printf("threshold %g%%\n", SIGTHRESH);
                            SIGTHRESH /= 100;
                            SIGTEST = true;
                            break;
                case '?':   printf("unrecognised option\n");
                            exit(1);
            }
        }
```

```
/*  Initialise  */

GetNames();
GetData(".data");
printf("\nRead %d cases (%d attributes) from %s\n",
        MaxItem+1, MaxAtt+1, FileName);

GenerateLogs();

/*  Construct rules  */

GenerateRules();

/*  Save current ruleset  */

SaveRules();

/*  Evaluations  */

printf("\n\nEvaluation on training data (%d items):\n", MaxItem+1);
EvaluateRulesets(true);

if ( UNSEENS )
{
    GetData(".test");
    printf("\nEvaluation on test data (%d items):\n", MaxItem+1);
    EvaluateRulesets(false);
}
}
```

File genrules.c

```
/**********************************************************************/
/*                                                                  */
/*        Generate all rulesets from the decision trees             */
/*        ───────────────────────────────────────────              */
/*                                                                  */
/**********************************************************************/


#include "defns.i"
#include "types.i"
#include "extern.i"
#include "rulex.i"


/**********************************************************************/
/*                                                                  */
/*  For each tree, form a set of rules and process them, then form a */
/*  composite set of rules from all of these sets.                   */
/*  If there is only one tree, then no composite set is formed.      */
/*                                                                  */
/*  Rulesets are stored in PRSet[0] to PRSet[TRIALS], where          */
/*  PRSet[TRIALS] contains the composite ruleset.                    */
/*                                                                  */
/*  On completion, the current ruleset is the composite ruleset (if one */
/*  has been made), otherwise the ruleset from the single tree.      */
/*                                                                  */
/**********************************************************************/


    GenerateRules()
/*  ─────────────  */
{
    Tree DecisionTree, GetTree();
    short t=0, RuleSetSpace=0, r;

    /*  Find bits to encode attributes and branches  */

    FindTestCodes();

    /*  Now process each decision tree  */

    while ( DecisionTree = GetTree(".unpruned") )
    {
        printf("\n-----------------\n");
        printf("Processing tree %d\n", t);

        /*  Form a set of rules from the next tree  */

        FormRules(DecisionTree);
```

```
/*  Process the set of rules for this trial  */

ConstructRuleset();

printf("\nFinal rules from tree %d:\n", t);
PrintIndexedRules();

/*  Make sure there is enough room for the new ruleset  */

if ( t + 1 >= RuleSetSpace )
{
    RuleSetSpace += 10;

    if ( RuleSetSpace > 10 )
    {
        PRSet = (RuleSet *) realloc(PRSet, RuleSetSpace * sizeof(RuleSet));
    }
    else
    {
        PRSet = (RuleSet *) malloc(RuleSetSpace * sizeof(RuleSet));
    }

}

PRSet[t].SNRules = NRules;
PRSet[t].SRule = Rule;
PRSet[t].SRuleIndex = RuleIndex;
PRSet[t].SDefaultClass = DefaultClass;

++t;
}

if ( ! t )
{
    printf("\nERROR:  can't find any decision trees\n");
    exit(1);
}

TRIALS = t;

/*  If there is more than one tree in the trees file,
    make a composite ruleset of the rules from all trees  */

if ( TRIALS > 1 )
{
    CompositeRuleset();
}
}
```

```
/*************************************************************************/
/*                                                                     */
/*        Determine code lengths for attributes and branches           */
/*                                                                     */
/*************************************************************************/


        FindTestCodes()
/*      ─────────────  */
{
        Attribute Att;
        DiscrValue v, V;
        ItemNo i, *ValFreq;
        int PossibleCuts;
        float Sum, SumBranches=0, p;
        void SwapUnweighted();

        BranchBits  = (float *) malloc((MaxAtt+1) * sizeof(float));

        ForEach(Att, 0, MaxAtt)
        {
            if ( (V = MaxAttVal[Att]) )
            {
                ValFreq = (ItemNo *) calloc(V+1, sizeof(ItemNo));

                ForEach(i, 0, MaxItem)
                {
                    ValFreq[DVal(Item[i],Att)]++;
                }

                Sum = 0;
                ForEach(v, 1, V)
                {
                    if ( ValFreq[v] )
                    {
                        Sum += (ValFreq[v] / (MaxItem+1.0)) *
                               (LogItemNo[MaxItem+1] - LogItemNo[ValFreq[v]]);
                    }
                }
                free(ValFreq);

                BranchBits[Att] = Sum;
            }
            else
            {
                Quicksort(0, MaxItem, Att, SwapUnweighted);

                PossibleCuts = 1;
                ForEach(i, 1, MaxItem)
                {
                    if ( CVal(Item[i],Att) > CVal(Item[i-1],Att) )
                    {
                        PossibleCuts++;
                    }
                }
```

```
                BranchBits[Att]  = PossibleCuts > 1 ?
                                   1 + LogItemNo[PossibleCuts]  / 2 : 0 ;
            }

            SumBranches += BranchBits[Att];
        }

        AttTestBits = 0;
        ForEach(Att, 0, MaxAtt)
        {
            if ( (p = BranchBits[Att] / SumBranches) > 0 )
            {
                AttTestBits -= p * log(p) / log(2.0);
            }
        }
    }
}


/****************************************************************************/
/*                                                                        */
/*  Exchange items at a and b.  Note:  unlike the similar routine in      */
/*  buildtree, this does not assume that items have a Weight to be        */
/*  swapped as well!                                                      */
/*                                                                        */
/****************************************************************************/

void SwapUnweighted(a, b)
/*   ———————————   */
    ItemNo a, b;
{
    Description Hold;

    Hold = Item[a];
    Item[a]  = Item[b];
    Item[b]  = Hold;
}
```

```
/**************************************************************************/
/*                                                                        */
/*        Form composite ruleset for all trials                           */
/*                                                                        */
/**************************************************************************/

    CompositeRuleset()
/*  ——————————  */
{
    RuleNo r;
    short t, ri;
    Boolean NewRule();

    InitialiseRules();

    /*  Lump together all the rules from each ruleset   */

    ForEach(t, 0, TRIALS-1)
    {
        ForEach(ri, 1, PRSet[t].SNRules)
        {
            r = PRSet[t].SRuleIndex[ri];
            NewRule(PRSet[t].SRule[r].Lhs, PRSet[t].SRule[r].Size,
                    PRSet[t].SRule[r].Rhs, PRSet[t].SRule[r].Error);
        }
    }

    /*   ... and select a subset in the usual way   */

    ConstructRuleset();

    printf("\nComposite ruleset:\n");
    PrintIndexedRules();

    PRSet[TRIALS].SNRules = NRules;
    PRSet[TRIALS].SRule    = Rule;
    PRSet[TRIALS].SRuleIndex = RuleIndex;
    PRSet[TRIALS].SDefaultClass = DefaultClass;
}
```

File makerules.c

```
/**********************************************************************/
/*                                                                    */
/*        Form a set of rules from a decision tree                    */
/*        _____                    */
/*                                                                    */
/**********************************************************************/


#include "defns.i"
#include "types.i"
#include "extern.i"
#include "rulex.i"


ItemNo  *TargetClassFreq,        /* [Boolean]  */
        *Errors,                 /* [Condition]  */
        *Total;                  /* [Condition]  */

float   *Pessimistic,            /* [Condition]  */
        *Actual,                 /* [Condition]  */
        *CondSigLevel;           /* [Condition]  */

Boolean **CondSatisfiedBy,       /* [Condition] [ItemNo]  */
        *Deleted;                /* [Condition]  */

DiscrValue *SingleValue;         /* [Attribute]  */

Condition *Stack;

short   MaxDisjuncts,
        MaxDepth;



/**********************************************************************/
/*                                                                    */
/*        Form a ruleset from decision tree t                         */
/*                                                                    */
/**********************************************************************/


    FormRules(t)
/*  _____  */
    Tree t;
{
    short i;

    /*  Find essential parameters and allocate storage  */

    MaxDepth = 0;
    MaxDisjuncts = 0;

    TreeParameters(t, 0);

    Actual = (float *) calloc(MaxDepth+2, sizeof(float));
    Total = (ItemNo *) calloc(MaxDepth+2, sizeof(ItemNo));
```

```
Errors = (ItemNo *) calloc(MaxDepth+2, sizeof(ItemNo));
Pessimistic = (float *) calloc(MaxDepth+2, sizeof(float));

CondSigLevel = (float *) calloc(MaxDepth+2, sizeof(float));

TargetClassFreq = (ItemNo *) calloc(2, sizeof(ItemNo));

Deleted = (Boolean *) calloc(MaxDepth+2, sizeof(Boolean));
CondSatisfiedBy = (char **) calloc(MaxDepth+2, sizeof(char *));
Stack = (Condition *) calloc(MaxDepth+2, sizeof(Condition));

ForEach(i, 0, MaxDepth+1)
{
    CondSatisfiedBy[i] = (char *) calloc(MaxItem+1, sizeof(char));
    Stack[i] = (Condition) malloc(sizeof(struct CondRec));
}

SingleValue = (DiscrValue *) calloc(MaxAtt+1, sizeof(DiscrValue));

InitialiseRules();

/*  Extract and prune disjuncts  */

Scan(t, 0);

/*  Deallocate storage  */

ForEach(i, 0, MaxDepth+1)
{
    cfree(CondSatisfiedBy[i]);
    cfree(Stack[i]);
}
cfree(Deleted);
cfree(CondSatisfiedBy);
cfree(Stack);

cfree(Actual);
cfree(Total);
cfree(Errors);
cfree(Pessimistic);

cfree(CondSigLevel);

cfree(TargetClassFreq);
}
```

```
/***************************************************************************/
/*                                                                         */
/*   Find the maximum depth and the number of leaves in tree t             */
/*   with initial depth d                                                  */
/*                                                                         */
/***************************************************************************/


    TreeParameters(t, d)
/*  ───────────────  */
    Tree t;
    short d;
{
    DiscrValue v;

    if ( t->NodeType )
    {
        ForEach(v, 1, t->Forks)
        {
            TreeParameters(t->Branch[v], d+1);
        }
    }
    else
    {
        /*  This is a leaf  */

        if ( d > MaxDepth ) MaxDepth = d;
        MaxDisjuncts++;
    }
}



/***************************************************************************/
/*                                                                         */
/*   Extract disjuncts from tree t at depth d, and process them            */
/*                                                                         */
/***************************************************************************/


    Scan(t, d)
/*  ────  */
    Tree t;
    short d;
{
    DiscrValue v;
    short i;
    Condition *Term;
    Test x, FindTest();

    if ( t->NodeType )
    {
        d++;

        x = (Test) malloc(sizeof(struct TestRec));
        x->NodeType = t->NodeType;
        x->Tested = t->Tested;
        x->Forks = t->Forks;
```

```
    x->Cut = ( t->NodeType == ThreshContin ? t->Cut : 0 );
    if ( t->NodeType == BrSubset )
    {
        x->Subset = (Set *) calloc(t->Forks + 1, sizeof(Set));
        ForEach(v, 1, t->Forks)
        {
            x->Subset[v] = t->Subset[v];
        }
    }

    Stack[d]->CondTest = FindTest(x);

    ForEach(v, 1, t->Forks)
    {
        Stack[d]->TestValue = v;
        Scan(t->Branch[v], d);
    }
}
else
{
    /*  Leaf of decision tree - construct the set of
        conditions associated with this leaf and prune  */

    Term = (Condition *) calloc(d+1, sizeof(Condition));
    ForEach(i, 1, d)
    {
        Term[i] = (Condition) malloc(sizeof(struct CondRec));
        Term[i]->CondTest = Stack[i]->CondTest;
        Term[i]->TestValue = Stack[i]->TestValue;
    }

    PruneRule(Term, d, t->Leaf);

    cfree(Term);
}
}
```

File prunerule.c

```
/**************************************************************************/
/*                                                                      */
/*          Pruning single rules                                        */
/*          ─────────────────                                           */
/*                                                                      */
/*                                                                      */
/**************************************************************************/

#include "defns.i"
#include "types.i"
#include "extern.i"
#include "rulex.i"

/*   External data structures used in building rules   */

extern ItemNo    *TargetClassFreq,        /* [Boolean] */
                 *Errors,                  /* [Condition] */
                 *Total;                   /* [Condition] */

extern float     *Pessimistic,            /* [Condition] */
                 *Actual,                  /* [Condition] */
                 *CondSigLevel;            /* [Condition] */

extern Boolean   **CondSatisfiedBy,       /* [Condition] [ItemNo] */
                 *Deleted;

#define Before(n1,n2)   (n1->Tested < n2->Tested ||\
                         n1->NodeType < n2->NodeType ||\
                         n1->Tested == n2->Tested && n1->Cut < n2->Cut)

#define IsTarget(case)  (Class(case) == TargetClass ? 1 : 0)


/**************************************************************************/
/*                                                                      */
/*   Prune the rule given by the conditions Cond, and the number of     */
/*   conditions NCond, and add the resulting rule to the current        */
/*   ruleset if it is sufficiently accurate                             */
/*                                                                      */
/**************************************************************************/

    PruneRule(Cond, NCond, TargetClass)
/*  ─────────  */
    Condition Cond[];
    short NCond;
    ClassNo TargetClass;
{
    short d, dd, id, Bestd, Bestid, Remaining=NCond;
    float DefaultError, Extra, AddErrs(), TableProb();
    Boolean Alter, Satisfies(), NewRule(), Redundant();
    Condition Hold;
    ItemNo i;
```

```
Verbosity(1)  printf("\n   pruning rule");

ForEach(d, 0, NCond)
{
    Deleted[d]  = false;
}

/*  Evaluate the satisfaction matrix  */

TargetClassFreq[0]  =  TargetClassFreq[1]  =  0;

ForEach(i, 0, MaxItem)
{
    ClearOutcomes();
    ForEach(d, 1, NCond)
    {
        CondSatisfiedBy[d][i]  =  Satisfies(Item[i], Cond[d]);
    }
    TargetClassFreq[IsTarget(Item[i])]++;
}

DefaultError = 1.0 - (TargetClassFreq[true]  + 1.0) / (MaxItem + 3.0);

/*  Find conditions to delete  */

do
{
    Alter = false;

    FindTables(NCond, TargetClass);

    /*  Find the condition, deleting which would most improve
        the accuracy of the rule.
        Notes: The pessimistic error rate, and not the actual
               error rate, is currently used.
               When d is 0, we are dealing with all conditions.  */

    Bestd = id = 0;

    Verbosity(1)
        printf("\n        Err Used    Pess\tAbsent condition\n");

    ForEach(d, 0, NCond)
    {
        if ( Deleted[d]  ) continue;

        if ( Total[d]  )
        {
            Actual[d]  = Errors[d]  /  (float) Total[d];
            Extra = AddErrs((float) Total[d], (float) Errors[d]);
            Pessimistic[d]  =  (Errors[d]  + Extra)  / Total[d];
        }
        else
        {
            Actual[d]  =  0;
            Pessimistic[d]  =  DefaultError;
        }
```

```
Verbosity(1)
    printf("    %5d%5d   %4.1f%%",
            Errors[d], Total[d], 100 * Pessimistic[d]);

if ( ! d )
{
    Verbosity(1) printf("\t<base rule>\n");
}
else
{
    id++;

    /*  If significance testing option used, invoke Fisher's
        exact test here to assess probability that division
        by d arises from chance.  */

    if ( SIGTEST )
    {
        CondSigLevel[d]  =
            TableProb(Errors[0],
                        Errors[d]-Errors[0],
                        Total[0]-Errors[0],
                        Total[d]-Total[0]-Errors[d]+Errors[0]);

        Verbosity(1) printf("   Sig=%.3f", CondSigLevel[d]);
    }

    Verbosity(1) PrintCondition(Cond[d]);

    /*  Bestd identifies the condition with lowest pessimistic
        error estimate  */

    if ( ! Bestd || Pessimistic[d] <= Pessimistic[Bestd] )
    {
        Bestd = d;
        Bestid = id;
    }

    /*  Alter is set true if we are going to drop a condition
        (either because we get lower pessimistic est, or
        because one of the conditions fails a significance test)  */

    if ( Pessimistic[d] <= Pessimistic[0] ||
         Actual[d] <= Actual[0] ||
         SIGTEST && CondSigLevel[d] > SIGTHRESH )
    {
        Alter = true;
    }
}
}
```

```
    if ( Alter )
    {
        Verbosity(1) printf("\teliminate test %d\n", Bestid);

        Deleted[Bestd] = true;
        Remaining--;
    }
} while ( Alter && Remaining );
if ( ! Remaining || ! Total[0] )
{
    return;
}
if ( Pessimistic[0] >= DefaultError )
{
    Verbosity(1) printf("\ttoo inaccurate\n");
    return;
}
/*  Sort the conditions  */
ForEach(d, 1, Remaining)
{
    dd = 0;
    ForEach(id, d, NCond)
    {
        if ( ! Deleted[id] &&
             ( ! dd ||
               Before(Cond[id]->CondTest, Cond[dd]->CondTest) ) )
        {
            dd = id;
        }
    }
    if ( dd != d )
    {
        Hold    = Cond[d];
        Cond[d] = Cond[dd];
        Cond[dd] = Hold;
        Deleted[dd] = Deleted[d];
    }
    Deleted[d] = true;
}

NewRule(Cond, Remaining, TargetClass, Pessimistic[0]);
}
```

```
/***********************************************************************/
/*                                                                     */
/*   See whether condition R is redundant                              */
/*                                                                     */
/***********************************************************************/


Boolean Redundant(R, Cond, NCond)
/*      ————————  */
    Condition Cond[];
    short R, NCond;
{
    short d, v, vv;
    Test t, Rt;
    Boolean IsSubset();

    Rt = Cond[R]->CondTest;
    v =  Cond[R]->TestValue;

    ForEach(d, 1, NCond)
    {
        if ( Deleted[d] || d == R ) continue;

        t = Cond[d]->CondTest;
        vv = Cond[d]->TestValue;

        if ( t->Tested != Rt->Tested ) continue;

        switch ( t->NodeType )
        {
            case BrDiscr:  /* test of discrete attribute */

                return false;

            case ThreshContin:  /* test of continuous attribute */

                if ( vv == v &&
                     ( v == 1 ? t->Cut < Rt->Cut : t->Cut > Rt->Cut ) )
                {
                    return true;
                }

                break;

            case BrSubset:  /* subset test on discrete attribute  */

                if ( IsSubset(t->Subset[vv], Rt->Subset[v], Rt->Tested) )
                {
                    return true;
                }
        }
    }

    return false;
}
```

```
/**************************************************************************/
/*                                                                        */
/*    Decide whether subset S1 of values is contained in subset S2        */
/*                                                                        */
/**************************************************************************/


Boolean IsSubset(S1, S2, Att)
/*      ————————  */
    Set S1, S2;
    Attribute Att;
{
    DiscrValue v;

    ForEach(v, 1, MaxAttVal[Att])
    {
        if ( In(v, S1) && ! In(v, S2) ) return false;
    }

    return true;
}




/**************************************************************************/
/*                                                                        */
/*    Find the frequency distribution tables for the current conditions:  */
/*                                                                        */
/*        Total[0]  = items matching all conditions                       */
/*        Total[d]  = items matching all except condition d               */
/*                                                                        */
/*        Errors[0] = wrong-class items matching all conditions           */
/*        Errors[d] = wrong-class items matching all but cond d           */
/*                                                                        */
/*    This routine is critical to the efficiency of rule pruning. It      */
/*    computes the information above in one pass through the data,         */
/*    looking at cases that fail to satisfy at most one of the            */
/*    nondeleted conditions                                               */
/*                                                                        */
/**************************************************************************/


    FindTables(NCond, TargetClass)
/*      ————————  */
    short NCond;
    ClassNo TargetClass;
{
    ItemNo i;
    short Misses, Missed[2], d;
    Boolean CorrectClass, First=true;
    Attribute Att;

    /*  Clear distributions  */

    ForEach(d, 0, NCond)
    {
        Total[d] = Errors[d] = 0;
    }
```

```
    /*   Set distributions   */

    ForEach(i, 0, MaxItem)
    {
        Misses = 0;
        CorrectClass = IsTarget(Item[i]);

        for ( d = 1 ; d <= NCond && Misses <= 1 ; d++ )
        {
            if ( ! Deleted[d]  && ! CondSatisfiedBy[d][i]  )
            {
                Missed[Misses++] = d;
            }
        }

        if ( ! Misses )
        {
            UpdateCount(Total, Errors, 0, CorrectClass);
        }
        else
        if ( Misses == 1 )
        {
            UpdateCount(Total, Errors, Missed[0], CorrectClass);
        }
    }

    /*   Adjust counts to reflect cases that met all conditions   */

    ForEach(d, 1, NCond)
    {
        if ( ! Deleted[d]  )
        {
            Total[d]  += Total[0];
            Errors[d]  += Errors[0];
        }
    }
}


/*************************************************************************/
/*                                                                       */
/*   Increment the counts Total[d]  and Errors[d]                        */
/*                                                                       */
/*************************************************************************/

    UpdateCount(T, E, d, OK)
/*  ————————  */
    ItemNo T[], E[];
    short d;
    Boolean OK;
{
    T[d]++;
    if ( ! OK ) E[d]++;
}
```

```
/**************************************************************************/
/*                                                                        */
/*    Determine whether the given case description satisfies the given    */
/*    condition. To save time, the outcome of every test on every item    */
/*    is set the first time it is needed and retained for later use.      */
/*                                                                        */
/**************************************************************************/


Boolean Satisfies(CaseDesc, OneCond)
/*              _____   */
    Description CaseDesc;
    Condition OneCond;
{
    DiscrValue v;
    float cv;
    Test t;
    short s;

    t = OneCond->CondTest;

    if ( ! t->Outcome )
    {
        /*  Determine the outcome of this test on this item  */

        switch ( t->NodeType )
        {
            case BrDiscr:  /* test of discrete attribute */

                v = DVal(CaseDesc, t->Tested);
                t->Outcome = ( v == 0 ? -1 : v );
                break;

            case ThreshContin:  /* test of continuous attribute */

                cv = CVal(CaseDesc, t->Tested);
                t->Outcome = ( cv == Unknown ? -1 : cv <= t->Cut ? 1 : 2 );
                break;

            case BrSubset:  /* subset test on discrete attribute  */

                v = DVal(CaseDesc, t->Tested);
                ForEach(s, 1, t->Forks)
                {
                    if ( In(v, t->Subset[s]) )
                    {
                        t->Outcome = s;
                        break;
                    }
                }
                t->Outcome = -1;
        }
    }

    return ( t->Outcome == OneCond->TestValue );
}
```

```
/************************************************************************/
/*                                                                      */
/*   Hypergeometric distribution (uses tabulated log factorials)        */
/*                                                                      */
/************************************************************************/

double Hypergeom(a, r, A, B)
/*          ———————  */
    int a, r, A, B;
{
    return exp( LogFact[A] + LogFact[B] + LogFact[r] + LogFact[A+B-r] -
              ( LogFact[a] + LogFact[r-a] + LogFact[A-a]
                + LogFact[B-(r-a)] + LogFact[A+B]) );
}



/************************************************************************/
/*                                                                      */
/*   TableProb examines the 2x2 contingency table t and computes the    */
/*   probability that a random division could have produced a split at  */
/*   least as extreme as this.  Also known as "Fisher's Exact Test,"    */
/*   after its inventor, R. A. Fisher.                                  */
/*                                                                      */
/************************************************************************/

float TableProb(t11, t12, t21, t22)
/*          ———————  */
    int t11, t12, t21, t22;
{
    double Sum=0.0;
    int A, B, r, a, k, a0;

    /*  First, rearrange the rows and columns of the table to get it into
        canonical form  */

    if ( t11 + t12 > t21 + t22 )
    {
        A = t11 + t12;
        B = t21 + t22;

        if ( t11 * (t21 + t22) > t21 * (t11 + t12) )
        {
            a0 = t11;
            r  = t11 + t21;
        }
        else
        {
            a0 = t12;
            r  = t12 + t22;
        }
    }
    else
    {
```

```
        A = t21 + t22;
        B = t11 + t12;
        if ( t21 * (t11 + t12) > t11 * (t21 + t22) )
        {
            a0 = t21;
            r  = t21 + t11;
        }
        else
        {
            a0 = t22;
            r  = t22 + t12;
        }
    }

    /*  Now compute the probability  */

    k = Min(r, A);
    ForEach(a, a0, k)
    {
        Sum += Hypergeom(a, r, A, B);
    }

    return Sum;
}
```

File siftrules.c

```
/**************************************************************************/
/*                                                                      */
/*        Process sets of rules                                         */
/*        _____                                           */
/*                                                                      */
/*                                                                      */
/**************************************************************************/


#include "defns.i"
#include "types.i"
#include "extern.i"
#include "rulex.i"


ItemNo  *ClassFreq,        /* ClassFreq[c] = no. items of class c  */
        *Covered,          /* Covered[i]  = no. included rules that cover item i */
        *FalsePos,         /* FalsePos[c] = no. false positives from rules
                                           selected for class c */
        *NoRule,           /* NoRule[c]  = no. items covered by no selected rule */

        *Right,            /* Right[r]   = no. correct rule firings */
        *Wrong;            /* Wrong[r]   = no. incorrect rule firings */

float   *Value,            /* Value[r]   = advantage attributable to rule r or
                                           realisable if rule r included */
        SubsetValue,       /* value of best class subset so far */
        CodeWeight;        /* multiplying factor for rule encodings */

Boolean *RuleIn,           /* RuleIn[r]    = true if rule r included */
        *Subset,           /* best class subset so far */
        **Match;           /* Match[r][i] = true if rule r fires on item i */

RuleNo  *ClassRules;       /* list of all rules for current target class */


/**************************************************************************/
/*                                                                      */
/*   Construct an ordered subset (indexed by RuleIndex) of the current  */
/*   set of rules                                                       */
/*                                                                      */
/**************************************************************************/


        ConstructRuleset()
/*      _____      */
{
    RuleNo r, OldNRules = NRules;
    ItemNo i;
    ClassNo c;

    /*  Allocate tables  */

    Right = (ItemNo *) calloc(NRules+1, sizeof(ItemNo));
    Wrong = (ItemNo *) calloc(NRules+1, sizeof(ItemNo));
```

```
Value = (float *) calloc(NRules+1, sizeof(float));

RuleIn = (Boolean *) calloc(NRules+1, sizeof(Boolean));
Subset = (Boolean *) malloc((NRules+1) * sizeof(Boolean));

ClassRules = (RuleNo *) malloc((NRules+1) * sizeof(RuleNo));

ClassFreq = (ItemNo *) calloc(MaxClass+1, sizeof(ItemNo));

Covered = (ItemNo *) calloc(MaxItem+1, sizeof(ItemNo));

Match = (Boolean **) calloc(NRules+1, sizeof(Boolean *));

FalsePos = (ItemNo *) calloc(MaxClass+1, sizeof(ItemNo));

NoRule = (ItemNo *) calloc(MaxClass+1, sizeof(ItemNo));

ForEach(r, 1, NRules)
{
    Match[r] = (Boolean *) calloc(MaxItem+1, sizeof(Boolean));
}

/*  Cover each class, then order the classes to give an index of rules  */

InitialiseTables();

FindRuleCodes();
CodeWeight = 0.5;

ForEach(c, 0, MaxClass)
{
    CoverClass(c);
}

MakeIndex();
FindDefault();

/*  Clear  */

cfree(Value);
cfree(RuleIn);
cfree(ClassRules);
cfree(Subset);
cfree(Covered);
cfree(FalsePos);
cfree(NoRule);
ForEach(r, 1, OldNRules)
    cfree(Match[r]);
cfree(Match);
}
```

```
/*************************************************************************/
/*                                                                     */
/*                  Initialise all tables used in sifting              */
/*                                                                     */
/*************************************************************************/


        InitialiseTables()
/*      ———————————  */
{
        ItemNo i;
        RuleNo r;
        ClassNo c;
        float Strength();

        ForEach(r, 1, NRules)
        {
            RuleIn[r]  = false;
            Rule[r].Used = Rule[r].Incorrect = 0;
        }

        ForEach(c, 0, MaxClass)
        {
            ClassFreq[c] = 0;
        }

        ForEach(i, 0, MaxItem)
        {
            ClassFreq[Class(Item[i])]++;

            ClearOutcomes();

            ForEach(r, 1, NRules)
            {
                Match[r][i] = Strength(Rule[r], Item[i]) > 0.3;

                if ( Match[r][i] )
                {
                    Rule[r].Used++;
                    if ( Class(Item[i]) != Rule[r].Rhs ) Rule[r].Incorrect++;
                }
            }
        }
}
```

```
/**************************************************************************/
/*                                                                        */
/*          Select a subset of the rules for class FocusClass             */
/*                                                                        */
/**************************************************************************/

    CoverClass(FocusClass)
/*  ──────────  */
    ClassNo FocusClass;
{
    RuleNo r, RuleCount=0;
    ItemNo i;

    Verbosity(1)
        printf("\nClass %s\n-----\nAction   Change   Value",
                ClassName[FocusClass]);

    ForEach(i, 0, MaxItem)
    {
        Covered[i] = 0;
    }

    ForEach(r, 1, NRules)
    {
        if ( Rule[r].Rhs == FocusClass )
        {
            RuleCount++;
            ClassRules[RuleCount] = r;
        }
    }
    if ( ! RuleCount )
    {
        return;
    }

    SubsetValue = 1E10;

    if ( RuleCount <= 10 )
    {
        AllCombinations(RuleCount, FocusClass);
    }
    else
    {
        SimAnneal(RuleCount, FocusClass);
    }

    memcpy(RuleIn, Subset, NRules+1);
    Verbosity(1) printf("\n\tBest value %.1f\n", SubsetValue);
}
```

```
/*************************************************************************/
/*                                                                       */
/*      Try all combinations of rules to find best value                 */
/*                                                                       */
/*************************************************************************/


        AllCombinations(NR, FocusClass)
/*      ——————————      */
        RuleNo NR;
        ClassNo FocusClass;
{
        float ThisValue, CalculateValue();
        RuleNo r;

        if ( ! NR )
        {
            ThisValue = CalculateValue(FocusClass);
            if ( ThisValue < SubsetValue )
            {
                SubsetValue = ThisValue;
                memcpy(Subset, RuleIn, NRules+1);
            }
        }
        else
        {
            r = ClassRules[NR];

            AllCombinations(NR-1, FocusClass);

            AddRule(r);
            AllCombinations(NR-1, FocusClass);

            DeleteRule(r);
            Verbosity(1) printf("\n");
        }
}



/*************************************************************************/
/*                                                                       */
/*  Find a good subset by simulated annealing                            */
/*                                                                       */
/*************************************************************************/


        SimAnneal(RuleCount, FocusClass)
/*      ————————      */
        RuleNo RuleCount;
        ClassNo FocusClass;
{
        RuleNo r, OutCount;
        ItemNo i;
        short ri, Tries;
        float Temp, Delta, ThisValue, CalculateValue();
        Boolean Changed;
```

```
/*   Keep dropping and adding rules until can't improve   */

for ( Temp = 1000 ; Temp > 0.001 ; Temp *= 0.95 )
{
    ThisValue = CalculateValue(FocusClass);
    if ( ThisValue < SubsetValue )
    {
        SubsetValue = ThisValue;
        memcpy(Subset, RuleIn, NRules+1);
    }

    Verbosity(2)
    {
        OutCount = 0;

        ForEach(ri, 1, RuleCount)
        {
            r = ClassRules[ri];

            if ( ! RuleIn[r]  )
            {
                if ( ! (OutCount++ % 3)  )  printf("\n\t\t");
                printf("%d<%d|%d=%.1f> ", r, Right[r], Wrong[r], Value[r]);
            }
        }

        printf("\n\n");
    }

    Changed = false;

    for ( Tries = 100 ; ! Changed && Tries > 0 ; Tries-- )
    {
        /*   Choose a rule to add or delete   */

        ri = RuleCount * Random + 1;

        r = ClassRules[ri];

        Delta = ( RuleIn[r]  ? -Value[r]  : Value[r]  );

        if ( Delta > 0 || Random < exp(Delta / Temp) )
        {
            if ( RuleIn[r]  )
            {
                DeleteRule(r);
            }
            else
            {
                AddRule(r);
            }

            Changed = true;
        }
    }
}
```

```
            if ( ! Changed ) break;
        }
}


/***************************************************************************/
/*                                                                       */
/*   Find the number of correct and incorrect rule firings for rules     */
/*   for class FocusClass and hence determine the Value of the rules     */
/*                                                                       */
/***************************************************************************/


float CalculateValue(FocusClass)
/*    ——————————    */
    ClassNo FocusClass;
{
    RuleNo r, Selected=0, InCount;
    ItemNo i, Times, FPos=0, FNeg=0, SumUsed=0, SumCover=0;
    float SumErrors=0, BaseBits, RuleBits=0, NewBits, ExceptionBits();
    ClassNo ThisClass;

    /*   Initialise Right and Wrong   */

    ForEach(r, 1, NRules)
    {
        if ( Rule[r].Rhs == FocusClass )
        {
            Right[r]  = Wrong[r]  = 0;

            if ( RuleIn[r]  )
            {
                SumUsed += Rule[r].Used;
                SumErrors += Rule[r].Error * Rule[r].Used;
                RuleBits += Rule[r].Bits;
                Selected++;
            }
        }
    }

    RuleBits -= LogFact[Selected];        /* allow for reordering of rules */

    /*   For each rule for the FocusClass, set Right to the number
         of items that correctly fire the rule and aren't covered by
         any other included rules, and Wrong to the number of items
         that incorrectly do so.   */

    ForEach(i, 0, MaxItem)
    {
        ThisClass = Class(Item[i]);

        if ( Times = Covered[i]  )
        {
            SumCover++;
            if( ThisClass != FocusClass ) FPos++;
        }
```

```
        else
        if ( ThisClass == FocusClass )
        {
            FNeg++;
        }

        ForEach(r, 1, NRules)
        {
            if ( Rule[r].Rhs == FocusClass &&
                 Match[r][i] &&
                 ( ! Times || Times == 1 && RuleIn[r] ) )
            {
                if ( ThisClass == FocusClass )
                {
                    Right[r]++;
                }
                else
                {
                    Wrong[r]++;
                }
            }
        }
    }

    BaseBits = CodeWeight * RuleBits + ExceptionBits(SumCover, FPos, FNeg);

    /*  From the Right and Wrong of each rule, calculate its Value  */

    Verbosity(1)
    {
        printf("\t");
        InCount = -1;
    }

    ForEach(r, 1, NRules)
    {
        if ( Rule[r].Rhs == FocusClass )
        {
            if ( RuleIn[r] )
            {
                NewBits = ExceptionBits(SumCover-Right[r]-Wrong[r],
                                FPos-Wrong[r], FNeg+Right[r]) +
                        CodeWeight *
                            (RuleBits - Rule[r].Bits + LogItemNo[Selected]);
                Value[r] = NewBits - BaseBits;
            }
            else
            {
                NewBits = ExceptionBits(SumCover+Right[r]+Wrong[r],
                                FPos+Wrong[r], FNeg-Right[r]) +
                        CodeWeight *
                            (RuleBits + Rule[r].Bits - LogItemNo[Selected+1]);
                Value[r] = BaseBits - NewBits;
            }
```

```
            Verbosity(1)
            {
                if ( RuleIn[r] )
                {
                    if ( ++InCount && ! (InCount % 3) ) printf("\n\t\t");
                    printf("%d [%d|%d=%.1f]  ", r, Right[r], Wrong[r], Value[r]);
                }
            }

        }
    }

    Verbosity(1)
    {
        printf("\n\t\t%d rules, %d firings: F+=%d, F-=%d, %.1f bits (rules=%.1f)\n",
               Selected, SumCover, FPos, FNeg, BaseBits, RuleBits);
    }

    return BaseBits;
}


/****************************************************************************/
/*                                                                         */
/*   Add rule r to the set of included rules and increase the number of    */
/*   rules covering each of the items that fire the rule                   */
/*                                                                         */
/****************************************************************************/


    AddRule(r)
/*  ———————  */
    RuleNo r;
{
    ItemNo i;

    RuleIn[r] = true;

    ForEach(i, 0, MaxItem)
    {
        if ( Match[r][i] )
        {
            Covered[i]++;
        }
    }

    Verbosity(1) printf("%5d+  %6.1f", r, Value[r]);
}
```

```
/*************************************************************************/
/*                                                                     */
/*   Delete rule r from the included rules and decrease the number of  */
/*   rules covering each of the items covered by the rule              */
/*                                                                     */
/*************************************************************************/


    DeleteRule(r)
/*  ─────────  */
    RuleNo r;
{
    ItemNo i;

    RuleIn[r]  = false;

    ForEach(i, 0, MaxItem)
    {
        if ( Match[r] [i]  )
        {
            Covered[i] --;
        }
    }

    Verbosity(1)  printf("%5d-   %6.1f", r, -Value[r]);
}



/*************************************************************************/
/*                                                                     */
/*   Make an index of included rules in RuleIndex.   Select first those */
/*   classes whose rules have the fewest false positives.   Within a    */
/*   class, put rules with higher accuracy ahead.                      */
/*                                                                     */
/*************************************************************************/


    MakeIndex()
/*  ─────────  */
{
    ClassNo c, BestC, Pass;
    RuleNo r, BestR, NewNRules = 0;
    ItemNo i;
    Boolean *Included;

    Included = (Boolean *) calloc(MaxClass+1, sizeof(Boolean));
    RuleIndex = (RuleNo *) calloc(NRules+1, sizeof(RuleNo));

    Verbosity(1)  printf("\nFalsePos   Class\n");

    ForEach(i, 0, MaxItem)
    {
        Covered[i]  = 0;
    }
```

```
/*  Select the best class to put next  */
ForEach(Pass, 0, MaxClass)
{
    ForEach(c, 0, MaxClass)
    {
        if ( Included[c] ) continue;

        FalsePos[c] = 0;

        ForEach(i, 0, MaxItem)
        {
            if ( Covered[i] || Class(Item[i]) == c ) continue;

            ForEach(r, 1, NRules)
            {
                if ( Rule[r].Rhs == c && RuleIn[r] && Match[r][i] )
                {
                    FalsePos[c]++;
                    break;
                }
            }
        }
    }

    BestC = -1;
    ForEach(c, 0, MaxClass)
    {
        if ( ! Included[c] &&
             ( BestC < 0 || FalsePos[c] < FalsePos[BestC] ) )
        {
            BestC = c;
        }
    }
    Included[BestC] = true;

    Verbosity(1)
        printf("%5d        %s\n", FalsePos[BestC], ClassName[BestC]);

    /*  Now grab the rules for this class  */

    do
    {
        BestR = 0;

        /*  Find the best rule to put next  */

        ForEach(r, 1, NRules)
        {
            if ( RuleIn[r] && Rule[r].Rhs == BestC &&
                 ( ! BestR || Rule[r].Error < Rule[BestR].Error ) )
            {
                BestR = r;
            }
        }
```

```
            if ( BestR )
            {
                RuleIndex[++NewNRules] = BestR;
                RuleIn[BestR] = false;

                ForEach(i, 0, MaxItem)
                {
                    Covered[i] |= Match[BestR][i];
                }
            }
        } while ( BestR );
    }

    NRules = NewNRules;
    cfree(Included);
}


/*************************************************************************/
/*                                                                       */
/*  Find the default class as the one with most items not covered by     */
/*  any rule.  Resolve ties in favour of more frequent classes.          */
/*  (Note: Covered has been set by MakeIndex.)                           */
/*                                                                       */
/*************************************************************************/


    FindDefault()
/*  ————————  */
{
    ClassNo c;
    ItemNo i;
    RuleNo r;

    /*  Determine uncovered items  */

    ForEach(c, 0, MaxClass)
    {
        NoRule[c] = 0;
    }

    ForEach(i, 0, MaxItem)
    {
        if ( ! Covered[i]  )
        {
            NoRule[Class(Item[i])]++;
        }
    }

    Verbosity(1)
    {
        printf("\nItems: Uncovered    Class\n");
        ForEach(c, 0, MaxClass)
        {
            printf("%5d %7d        %s\n", ClassFreq[c], NoRule[c], ClassName[c]);
        }
```

```
        printf("\n");
    }

    DefaultClass = 0;
    ForEach(c, 1, MaxClass)
    {
        if ( NoRule[c]  >  NoRule[DefaultClass]  ||
                NoRule[c]  ==  NoRule[DefaultClass]  &&
                ClassFreq[c]  >  ClassFreq[DefaultClass]  )
        {
            DefaultClass = c;
        }
    }
}


/***************************************************************************/
/*                                                                       */
/*   Given a rule and a case (ClearOutcomes performed), determine        */
/*   the strength with which we can conclude that the case belongs       */
/*   to the class specified by the rule's right-hand side.               */
/*                                                                       */
/*   If the case doesn't satisfy all the conditions of the rule,         */
/*   then this is 0.                                                     */
/*                                                                       */
/***************************************************************************/


float Strength(ThisRule, Case)
/*    ————  */
    PR ThisRule;
    Description Case;
{
    short d;
    Boolean Satisfies();

    if ( ThisRule.Error > 0.7 ) return 0.0;

    ForEach(d, 1, ThisRule.Size)
    {
        if ( ! Satisfies(Case, ThisRule.Lhs[d]) )
        {
            return 0.0;
        }
    }

    return ( 1 - ThisRule.Error );
}
```

```
/**************************************************************************/
/*                                                                      */
/*   Determine the number of bits to encode exceptions: FP false positives  */
/*   out of Fires firings, and FN false negatives in the remaining items    */
/*                                                                      */
/**************************************************************************/

#define nCrBits(E,N)  (LogFact[N] - (LogFact[E] + LogFact[N-(E)]))

float ExceptionBits(Fires, FP, FN)
/*   ——————— */
    int Fires, FP, FN;
{
    return nCrBits(FP, Fires) + nCrBits(FN, MaxItem+1-Fires);
}


/**************************************************************************/
/*                                                                      */
/*   Find encoding lengths for all rules                                */
/*                                                                      */
/**************************************************************************/

    FindRuleCodes()
/*   ——————— */
{
    RuleNo r;
    short d, NCond;
    float Bits, CondBits();

    ForEach(r, 1, NRules)
    {
        NCond = Rule[r].Size;
        Bits = 0;

        ForEach(d, 1, NCond)
        {
            Bits += CondBits(Rule[r].Lhs[d]);
        }

        /*  Must encode the number of conditions, but credit the total
            encoding by the ways conditions can be reordered   */

        Rule[r].Bits = Bits + LogItemNo[NCond] - LogFact[NCond];
    }
}
```

```
/**********************************************************************/
/*                                                                    */
/*   Determine the number of bits required to encode a condition      */
/*                                                                    */
/**********************************************************************/


float CondBits(C)
/*    ————— */
    Condition C;
{
    Test t;
    Attribute a;

    t = C->CondTest;
    a = t->Tested;

    switch ( t->NodeType )
    {
        case BrDiscr:           /* test of discrete attribute */
        case ThreshContin:      /* test of continuous attribute */

            return AttTestBits/REDUNDANCY + BranchBits[a];

        case BrSubset:          /* subset test on discrete attribute  */

            return AttTestBits/REDUNDANCY + MaxAttVal[a];
    }
}
```

File testrules.c

```
/****************************************************************************/
/*                                                                        */
/*          Evaluatation of rulesets                                      */
/*          ────────────────────────                                      */
/*                                                                        */
/****************************************************************************/

#include "defns.i"
#include "types.i"
#include "extern.i"
#include "rulex.i"


/****************************************************************************/
/*                                                                        */
/*          Evaluate all rulesets                                         */
/*                                                                        */
/****************************************************************************/


    EvaluateRulesets(DeleteRules)
/*  ─────────────────  */
    Boolean DeleteRules;
{
    short t;
    ItemNo i, *Errors, Interpret();
    float AvSize=0, AvErrs=0;
    Boolean Final;

    if ( TRIALS == 1 )
    {
        /*  Evaluate current ruleset as there is no composite ruleset  */

        Interpret(0, MaxItem, DeleteRules, true, true);
        return;
    }

    Errors = (ItemNo *) malloc((TRIALS+1) * sizeof(ItemNo));

    ForEach(t, 0, TRIALS)
    {
        NRules     = PRSet[t].SNRules;
        Rule       = PRSet[t].SRule;
        RuleIndex  = PRSet[t].SRuleIndex;
        DefaultClass = PRSet[t].SDefaultClass;
```

```
        if ( t < TRIALS )
        {
            printf("\nRuleset %d:\n", t);
        }
        else
        {
            printf("\nComposite ruleset:\n");
        }

        Final = (t == TRIALS);
        Errors[t] = Interpret(0, MaxItem, DeleteRules, Final, Final);

        AvSize += NRules;
        AvErrs += Errors[t];

        if ( DeleteRules )
        {
            PRSet[t].SNRules = NRules;
        }
    }

    /*  Print report  */

    printf("\n");
    printf("Trial      Size       Errors\n");
    printf("-----      ----       ------\n");

    ForEach(t, 0, TRIALS)
    {
        if ( t < TRIALS )
        {
            printf("%4d", t);
        }
        else
        {
            printf("  **");
        }
        printf("     %4d  %3d(%4.1f%%)\n",
               PRSet[t].SNRules, Errors[t], 100 * Errors[t] / (MaxItem+1.0));
    }

    AvSize /= TRIALS + 1;
    AvErrs /= TRIALS + 1;
    printf("\t\t\t\tAv size = %.1f,   av errors = %.1f (%.1f%%)\n",
           AvSize, AvErrs, 100 * AvErrs / (MaxItem+1.0));
}
```

```
/**************************************************************************/
/*                                                                        */
/*          Evaluate current ruleset                                      */
/*                                                                        */
/**************************************************************************/

float       Confidence;               /* certainty factor of fired rule */
                                      /* (set by BestRuleIndex) */

ItemNo Interpret(Fp, Lp, DeleteRules, CMInfo, Arrow)
/*         ———————  */
    ItemNo Fp, Lp;
    Boolean DeleteRules, CMInfo, Arrow;
{
    ItemNo i, Tested=0, Errors=0, *Better, *Worse, *ConfusionMat;
    Boolean FoundRule;
    ClassNo AssignedClass, AltClass;
    Attribute Att;
    RuleNo p, Bestr, ri, ri2, riDrop=0, BestRuleIndex();
    float ErrorRate, BestRuleConfidence;

    if ( CMInfo )
    {
        ConfusionMat = (ItemNo *) calloc((MaxClass+1)*(MaxClass+1), sizeof(ItemNo));
    }

    ForEach(ri, 1, NRules)
    {
        p = RuleIndex[ri];
        Rule[p].Used = Rule[p].Incorrect = 0;
    }

    Better = (ItemNo *) calloc(NRules+1, sizeof(ItemNo));
    Worse  = (ItemNo *) calloc(NRules+1, sizeof(ItemNo));

    ForEach(i, Fp, Lp)
    {
        ClearOutcomes();

        /*  Find first choice for rule for this item   */

        ri = BestRuleIndex(Item[i], 1);
        Bestr = ( ri ? RuleIndex[ri]  : 0 );
        FoundRule = Bestr > 0;

        if ( FoundRule )
        {
            Rule[Bestr].Used++;
            AssignedClass = Rule[Bestr].Rhs;
            BestRuleConfidence = Confidence;

            /*   Now find second choice   */

            ri2 = BestRuleIndex(Item[i], ri+1);
            AltClass = ( ri2 ? Rule[RuleIndex[ri2]].Rhs : DefaultClass );
```

```
    if ( AltClass != AssignedClass )
    {
        if ( AssignedClass == Class(Item[i]) )
        {
            Better[ri]++;
        }
        else
        if ( AltClass == Class(Item[i]) )
        {
            Worse[ri]++;
        }
    }
}
else
{
    AssignedClass = DefaultClass;
}

if ( CMInfo )
{
    ConfusionMat[Class(Item[i])*(MaxClass+1)+AssignedClass]++;
}
Tested++;

if ( AssignedClass != Class(Item[i]) )
{
    Errors++;
    if ( FoundRule ) Rule[Bestr].Incorrect++;

    Verbosity(3)
    {
        printf("\n");
        ForEach(Att, 0, MaxAtt)
        {
            printf("\t%s: ", AttName[Att]);
            if ( MaxAttVal[Att] )
            {
                if ( DVal(Item[i],Att) )
                {
                    printf("%s\n", AttValName[Att][DVal(Item[i],Att)]);
                }
                else
                {
                    printf("?\n");
                }
            }
            else
            {
                if ( CVal(Item[i],Att) != Unknown )
                {
                    printf("%g\n", CVal(Item[i],Att));
                }
```

```
                else
                {
                    printf("?\n");
                }
            }
        }
        printf("\t%4d:\tGiven class %s,", i, ClassName[Class(Item[i])]);
        if ( FoundRule )
        {
            printf(" rule %d [%.1f%%] gives class ",
                    Bestr, 100 * BestRuleConfidence);
        }
        else
        {
            printf(" default class ");
        }
        printf("%s\n", ClassName[AssignedClass]);
        }
    }
}

printf("\nRule  Size  Error  Used  Wrong\t          Advantage\n");
printf( "----  ----  -----  ----  -----\t          ---------\n");
ForEach(ri, 1, NRules)
{
    p = RuleIndex[ri];
    if ( Rule[p].Used > 0 )
    {
        ErrorRate = Rule[p].Incorrect / (float) Rule[p].Used;

        printf("%4d%6d%6.1f%%%6d%7d (%.1f%%)\t%6d (%d|%d) \t%s\n",
                p, Rule[p].Size,
                100 * Rule[p].Error, Rule[p].Used, Rule[p].Incorrect,
                100 * ErrorRate,
                Better[ri]-Worse[ri], Better[ri], Worse[ri],
                ClassName[Rule[p].Rhs]);

        /*  See whether this rule should be dropped.  Note: can only drop
            one rule at a time, because Better and Worse are affected.  */

        if ( DeleteRules && ! riDrop && Worse[ri] > Better[ri]  )
        {
            riDrop = ri;
        }
    }
}

cfree(Better);
cfree(Worse);

if ( riDrop )
{
    printf("\nDrop rule %d\n", RuleIndex[riDrop]);
```

```
        ForEach(ri, riDrop+1, NRules)
        {
            RuleIndex[ri-1]  = RuleIndex[ri];
        }
        NRules--;

        Errors = Interpret(Fp, Lp, DeleteRules, false, Arrow);
    }
    else
    {
        printf("\nTested %d, errors %d (%.1f%%)%s\n",
            Tested, Errors, 100 * Errors / (float) Tested,
            ( Arrow ? "   <<" : "" ));
    }

    if ( CMInfo )
    {
        PrintConfusionMatrix(ConfusionMat);
        free(ConfusionMat);
    }

    return Errors;
}


/*************************************************************************/
/*                                                                       */
/*      Find the best rule for the given case.                           */
/*      Assume ClearOutcomes called; leave probability in Confidence.    */
/*                                                                       */
/*************************************************************************/

RuleNo BestRuleIndex(CaseDesc, Start)
/*     ───────────────  */
    Description CaseDesc;
    RuleNo Start;
{
    RuleNo r, ri;
    float Strength();

    ForEach(ri, Start, NRules)
    {
        r = RuleIndex[ri];
        Confidence = Strength(Rule[r], CaseDesc);

        if ( Confidence > 0.1 )
        {
            return ri;
        }
    }

    Confidence = 0.0;
    return 0;
}
```

File consult.c

```
/***********************************************************************/
/*                                                                   */
/*          Classify items interactively using a decision tree       */
/*          ────────────────────────────────────────────            */
/*                                                                   */
/***********************************************************************/


#include "defns.i"
#include "types.i"


                    /*  External data  -- see c4.5.c for meanings  */

short           MaxAtt, MaxClass, MaxDiscrVal;

ItemNo          MaxItem;

Description     *Item;

DiscrValue      *MaxAttVal;

String          *ClassName,
                *AttName,
                **AttValName,
                FileName = "DF";

char            *SpecialStatus;

short           VERBOSITY = 0,
                TRACE   = 0;


        /*  The interview module uses a more complex description of an
            case called a "Range Description." The value of an
            attribute is given by
            - lower and upper bounds (continuous attribute)
            - probability of each possible value (discrete attribute)  */

typedef struct ValRange *RangeDescRec;

struct ValRange
        {
            Boolean     Known,          /* is range known? */
                        Asked;          /* has it been asked? */
            float       LowerBound,     /* lower bound given */
                        UpperBound,     /* upper ditto */
                        *Probability;   /* prior prob of each discr value */
        };

RangeDescRec RangeDesc;

Tree    DecisionTree,                   /* tree being used */
        GetTree();
```

```
float     *LowClassSum,              /* accumulated lower estimates */
          *ClassSum = Nil;           /* accumulated central estimates */

#define Fuzz     0.01                /* minimum weight */


/*************************************************************************/
/*                                                                     */
/*  Classify the extended case description in RangeDesc using the      */
/*  given subtree, by adjusting the values ClassSum and LowClassSum    */
/*  for each class, indicating the likelihood of the case being        */
/*  of that class.                                                     */
/*                                                                     */
/*************************************************************************/


    ClassifyCase(Subtree, Weight)
/*  ─────────────              */
    Tree Subtree;
    float Weight;
{
    DiscrValue v;
    float BranchWeight, Area(), Interpolate();
    Attribute a;
    short s;
    ClassNo c;

    /*  A leaf  */

    if ( ! Subtree->NodeType )
    {
        Verbosity(1)
            printf("\tClass %s weight %g cases %g\n",
                   ClassName[Subtree->Leaf], Weight, Subtree->Items);

        if ( Subtree->Items > 0 )
        {
            /*  Adjust class sum of ALL classes, but adjust low class sum
                of leaf class only  */

            ForEach(c, 0, MaxClass)
            {
                ClassSum[c] += Weight * Subtree->ClassDist[c] / Subtree->Items;
            }

            LowClassSum[Subtree->Leaf] +=
                Weight * (1 - Subtree->Errors / Subtree->Items);
        }
        else
        {
            ClassSum[Subtree->Leaf] += Weight;
        }

        return;
    }

    a = Subtree->Tested;
```

```
    CheckValue(a, Subtree);

    /*  Unknown value  */

    if ( ! RangeDesc[a].Known )
    {
        ForEach(v, 1, Subtree->Forks)
        {
            ClassifyCase(Subtree->Branch[v],
                    (Weight * Subtree->Branch[v]->Items) / Subtree->Items);
        }
        return;
    }

    /*  Known value  */

    switch ( Subtree->NodeType )
    {
        case BrDiscr:  /* test of discrete attribute */

            ForEach(v, 1, MaxAttVal[a])
            {
                BranchWeight = RangeDesc[a].Probability[v];
                if ( BranchWeight > 0 )
                {
                    Verbosity(1)
                        printf("\tWeight %g: test att %s (val %s = %g)\n",
                                Weight, AttName[a], AttValName[a][v],
                                BranchWeight);

                    ClassifyCase(Subtree->Branch[v], Weight * BranchWeight);
                }
            }
            break;

        case ThreshContin:  /* test of continuous attribute */

            BranchWeight =
                RangeDesc[a].UpperBound <= Subtree->Lower ? 1.0 :
                RangeDesc[a].LowerBound > Subtree->Upper ? 0.0 :
                RangeDesc[a].LowerBound != RangeDesc[a].UpperBound ?
                    (Area(Subtree, RangeDesc[a].LowerBound) -
                     Area(Subtree, RangeDesc[a].UpperBound)) /
                    (RangeDesc[a].UpperBound - RangeDesc[a].LowerBound) :
                Interpolate(Subtree, RangeDesc[a].LowerBound) ;

            Verbosity(1)
                printf("\tWeight %g: test att %s (branch weight=%g)\n",
                        Weight, AttName[a], BranchWeight);

            if ( BranchWeight > Fuzz )
            {
                ClassifyCase(Subtree->Branch[1], Weight * BranchWeight);
            }
```

```
            if ( BranchWeight < 1-Fuzz )
            {
                ClassifyCase(Subtree->Branch[2], Weight * (1 - BranchWeight));
            }
            break;

        case BrSubset:  /* subset test on discrete attribute  */

            ForEach(s, 1, Subtree->Forks)
            {
                BranchWeight = 0.0;
                ForEach(v, 1, MaxAttVal[a])
                {
                    if ( In(v, Subtree->Subset[s]) )
                    {
                        BranchWeight += RangeDesc[a].Probability[v];
                    }
                }
                if ( BranchWeight > 0 )
                {
                    Verbosity(1)
                        printf("\tWeight %g: test att %s (val %s = %g)\n",
                                Weight, AttName[a], AttValName[a][v],
                                BranchWeight);

                    ClassifyCase(Subtree->Branch[s], Weight * BranchWeight);
                }
            }
            break;
    }
}


/*************************************************************************/
/*                                                                       */
/*   Interpolate a single value between Lower, Cut, and Upper            */
/*                                                                       */
/*************************************************************************/

float Interpolate(t, v)
/*    ----------           */
    Tree t;
    float v;
{
    float Sum=Epsilon;

    if ( v <= t->Lower )
    {
        return 1.0;
    }

    if ( v <= t->Cut )
    {
        return 1 - 0.5 * (v - t->Lower) / (t->Cut - t->Lower + Epsilon);
    }
```

```c
    if ( v < t->Upper )
    {
        return 0.5 - 0.5 * (v - t->Cut) / (t->Upper - t->Cut + Epsilon);
    }

    return 0.0;
}


/**************************************************************************/
/*                                                                      */
/*  Compute the area under a soft threshold curve to the right of a     */
/*  given value.                                                        */
/*                                                                      */
/**************************************************************************/

float Area(t, v)
/*    ----          */
    Tree t;
    float v;
{
    float Sum=Epsilon, F;

    if ( v < t->Lower )
    {
        Sum += t->Lower - v;
        v = t->Lower;
    }

    if ( v < t->Cut )
    {
        F = (t->Cut - v ) / (t->Cut - t->Lower + Epsilon);

        Sum += 0.5 * (t->Cut - v) + 0.25 * F * (t->Cut - v);
        v = t->Cut;
    }

    if ( v < t->Upper )
    {
        F = (t->Upper - v ) / (t->Upper - t->Cut + Epsilon);

        Sum += 0.25 * (t->Upper - v) * F;
    }

    Verbosity(1) printf("lower=%g  cut=%g  upper=%g  area=%g\n",
                        t->Lower, t->Cut, t->Upper, Sum);

    return Sum;
}
```

```
/************************************************************************/
/*                                                                    */
/*              Process a single case                                 */
/*                                                                    */
/************************************************************************/

    InterpretTree()
/*  ─────────────          */
{
    ClassNo c, BestClass;
    float Uncertainty=1.0;
    char Reply;
    Attribute a;

    /*  Initialise  */

    ForEach(a, 0, MaxAtt)
    {
        RangeDesc[a].Asked = false;
    }

    if ( ! ClassSum )
    {
        /*  The first time through .. allocate class sums  */

        ClassSum = (float *) malloc((MaxClass+1) * sizeof(float));
        LowClassSum = (float *) malloc((MaxClass+1) * sizeof(float));

        printf("\n");
    }
    else
    {
        printf("\n-----------------------------------------\n\n");
    }

    ForEach(c, 0, MaxClass)
    {
        LowClassSum[c] = ClassSum[c] = 0;
    }

    /*  Find the likelihood of an item's being of each class  */

    ClassifyCase(DecisionTree, 1.0);

    /*  Find the best class and show decision made  */

    BestClass = 0;
    ForEach(c, 0, MaxClass)
    {
        Verbosity(1) printf("class %d weight %.2f\n", c, ClassSum[c]);

        Uncertainty -= LowClassSum[c];
        if ( ClassSum[c] > ClassSum[BestClass] ) BestClass = c;
    }
```

```
    printf("\nDecision:\n");
    Decision(BestClass, ClassSum[BestClass],
            LowClassSum[BestClass],
            Uncertainty + LowClassSum[BestClass]);

    /*  Show the other significant classes, if more than two classes  */

    if ( MaxClass > 1 )
    {
        while ( true )
        {
            ClassSum[BestClass]  = 0;
            BestClass = 0;
            ForEach(c, 0, MaxClass)
            {
                if ( ClassSum[c] > ClassSum[BestClass] ) BestClass = c;
            }

            if ( ClassSum[BestClass] < Fuzz ) break;

            Decision(BestClass, ClassSum[BestClass],
                    LowClassSum[BestClass],
                    Uncertainty + LowClassSum[BestClass]);
        }
    }

    /*  Prompt for what to do next  */

    while ( true )
    {
        printf("\nRetry, new case or quit [r,n,q]: ");
        Reply = getchar();
        SkipLine(Reply);
        switch ( Reply )
        {
          case 'r':  return;
          case 'n':  Clear(); return;
          case 'q':  exit(1);
          default:    printf("Please enter 'r', 'n' or 'q'");
        }
    }
}
```

```
/**************************************************************************/
/*                                                                      */
/*   Print the chosen class with certainty factor and range             */
/*                                                                      */
/**************************************************************************/

    Decision(c, p, lb, ub)
/*  ————————        */
    ClassNo c;
    float p, lb, ub;
{
    printf("\t%s", ClassName[c]);

    if ( p < 1-Fuzz || lb < ub - Fuzz )
    {
        printf("   CF = %.2f", p);
        if ( lb < ub - Fuzz )
        {
            printf("   [ %.2f - %.2f ]", lb, ub);
        }
    }

    printf("\n");
}



/**************************************************************************/
/*                                                                      */
/*   Main routine for classifying items using a decision tree           */
/*                                                                      */
/**************************************************************************/

    main(Argc, Argv)
/*  ————             */
    int Argc;
    char *Argv[];
{
    int o;
    extern char *optarg;
    extern int optind;
    Attribute a;

    PrintHeader("decision tree interpreter");

    /*  Process options  */

    while ( (o = getopt(Argc, Argv, "tvf:")) != EOF )
    {
        switch (o)
        {
            case 't':      TRACE = 1;
                           break;
            case 'v':      VERBOSITY = 1;
                           break;
```

```
                case 'f':      FileName = optarg;
                               break;
                case '?':      printf("unrecognised option\n");
                               exit(1);
        }
    }

    /*  Initialise  */

    GetNames();

    DecisionTree = GetTree(".tree");
    if ( TRACE ) PrintTree(DecisionTree);

    /*  Allocate value ranges  */

    RangeDesc = (struct ValRange *) calloc(MaxAtt+1, sizeof(struct ValRange));

    ForEach(a, 0, MaxAtt)
    {
        if ( MaxAttVal[a]  )
        {
            RangeDesc[a].Probability =
                (float *) calloc(MaxAttVal[a]+1, sizeof(float));
        }
    }

    /*  Consult  */

    Clear();
    while ( true )
    {
        InterpretTree();
    }
}
```

File consultr.c

```
/**********************************************************************/
/*                                                                    */
/*          Classify items interactively using a set of rules         */
/*          ─────────────────────────────────────────────            */
/*                                                                    */
/*                                                                    */
/**********************************************************************/
```

```
#include "defns.i"
#include "types.i"
```

```
                    /*   External data   */

short           MaxAtt, MaxClass, MaxDiscrVal;

ItemNo          MaxItem;

Description     *Item;

DiscrValue      *MaxAttVal;

String          *ClassName,
                *AttName,
                **AttValName,
                FileName = "DF";

char            *SpecialStatus;

short           VERBOSITY = 0,
                TRACE   = 0;

Boolean         FirstTime = true;

PR              *Rule;

RuleNo          NRules = 0,
                *RuleIndex;

short           RuleSpace = 0;

ClassNo         DefaultClass;
```

```
        /*   The interview module uses a more complex description of an
             case called a "Range Description" with lower and upper bounds.
             For further information, see consult.c.   */

typedef struct ValRange *RangeDescRec;

struct ValRange
        {
            Boolean Known, Asked;
            float LowerBound, UpperBound, *Probability;
        };
```

```
RangeDescRec RangeDesc;

float Confidence;

#define  MINCF  0.50              /* minimum cf for useable rule */


/*************************************************************************/
/*                                                                     */
/*    Find the best rule for the current case.                         */
/*    Note:  leave probability in Confidence.                          */
/*                                                                     */
/*************************************************************************/

RuleNo BestRule()
/*     ————————            */
{
    RuleNo r;
    float cf, RuleStrength();

    Confidence = 0.0;

    ForEach(r, 1, NRules)
    {
        cf = RuleStrength(Rule[r]);

        if ( cf > 0.5 )
        {
            Confidence = cf;
            return r;
        }
    }

    return 0;
}



/*************************************************************************/
/*                                                                     */
/*    Given a rule, determine the strength with which we can conclude  */
/*    that the current case belongs to the class specified by the RHS  */
/*    of the rule                                                      */
/*                                                                     */
/*************************************************************************/

float RuleStrength(Rule)
/*     ————————————           */
    PR Rule;
{
    short d;
    float RuleProb=1.0, ProbSatisfied();

    ForEach(d, 1, Rule.Size)
    {
        RuleProb *= ProbSatisfied(Rule.Lhs[d]);
```

```
        if ( RuleProb < MINCF )
        {
            return 0.0;
        }
    }

    return ( (1 - Rule.Error) * RuleProb );
}


/**************************************************************************/
/*                                                                        */
/*   Determine the probability of the current case description            */
/*   satisfying the given condition                                       */
/*                                                                        */
/**************************************************************************/


float ProbSatisfied(c)
/*    ─────────────        */
    Condition c;
{
    Attribute a;
    char v;
    float AddProb=0.0;
    Test t;
    DiscrValue i;

    t = c->CondTest;
    a = t->Tested;
    v = c->TestValue;

    CheckValue(a, Nil);

    if ( ! RangeDesc[a].Known )
    {
        return 0.0;
    }

    switch ( t->NodeType )
    {
        case BrDiscr:   /* test of discrete attribute */

            return RangeDesc[a].Probability[v];

        case ThreshContin:   /* test of continuous attribute */

            if ( RangeDesc[a].UpperBound <= t->Cut )
            {
                return ( v == 1 ? 1.0 : 0.0 );
            }
            else
            if ( RangeDesc[a].LowerBound > t->Cut )
            {
                return ( v == 2 ? 1.0 : 0.0 );
            }
            else
```

```
            if ( v == 1 )
            {
                return (t->Cut - RangeDesc[a].LowerBound)  /
                        (RangeDesc[a].UpperBound - RangeDesc[a].LowerBound);
            }
            else
            {
                return (RangeDesc[a].UpperBound - t->Cut)  /
                        (RangeDesc[a].UpperBound - RangeDesc[a].LowerBound);
            }

        case BrSubset:  /* subset test on discrete attribute  */

            ForEach(i, 1, MaxAttVal[a])
            {
                if ( In(i, t->Subset[v]) )
                {
                    AddProb += RangeDesc[a].Probability[i];
                }
            }
            return AddProb;
    }
    return 0.0;
}


/***********************************************************************/
/*                                                                     */
/*                  Process a single case                              */
/*                                                                     */
/***********************************************************************/

    InterpretRuleset()
/*  ──────────────          */
{
    char Reply;
    Attribute a;
    RuleNo r;

    /*  Initialise  */

    ForEach(a, 0, MaxAtt)
    {
        RangeDesc[a].Asked = false;
    }

    if ( FirstTime )
    {
        FirstTime = false;
        printf("\n");
    }
    else
    {
        printf("\n-------------------------------------\n\n");
    }
```

```
    /*  Find the first rule that fires on the item  */

    if ( r = BestRule() )
    {
        printf("\nDecision:\n");
        printf("\t%s", ClassName[Rule[r].Rhs]);

        if ( Confidence < 1.0 )
        {
            printf("   CF = %.2f", Confidence);
        }

        printf("\n");
    }
    else
    {
        printf("\nDecision:\n");
        printf("\t%s (default class)\n", ClassName[DefaultClass]);
    }

    /*  Prompt for what to do next  */

    while ( true )
    {
        printf("\nRetry, new case or quit [r,n,q]: ");
        Reply = getchar();
        SkipLine(Reply);
        switch ( Reply )
        {
          case 'r':  return;
          case 'n':  Clear(); return;
          case 'q':  exit(1);
          default:    printf("Please enter 'r', 'n' or 'q'");
        }
    }
}


/**************************************************************************/
/*                                                                        */
/*  Main routine for classifying items using a set of rules              */
/*                                                                        */
/**************************************************************************/

    main(Argc, Argv)
/*  ————            */
    int Argc;
    char *Argv[];
{
    int o;
    extern char *optarg;
    extern int optind;
    Attribute a;
    RuleNo r;
```

```
    PrintHeader("production rule interpreter");

    /*  Process options  */

    while ( (o = getopt(Argc, Argv, "tvf:")) != EOF )
    {
        switch (o)
        {
            case 't':    TRACE = 1;
                         break;
            case 'v':    VERBOSITY = 1;
                         break;
            case 'f':    FileName = optarg;
                         break;
            case '?':    printf("unrecognised option\n");
                         exit(1);
        }
    }

    /*  Initialise  */

    GetNames();
    GetRules();

    if ( TRACE )
    {
        ForEach(r, 1, NRules)
        {
            PrintRule(r);
        }
        printf("\nDefault class: %s\n", ClassName[DefaultClass]);
    }

    /*  Allocate value ranges  */

    RangeDesc = (struct ValRange *) calloc(MaxAtt+1, sizeof(struct ValRange));

    ForEach(a, 0, MaxAtt)
    {
        if ( MaxAttVal[a] )
        {
            RangeDesc[a].Probability =
                (float *) calloc(MaxAttVal[a]+1, sizeof(float));
        }
    }

    /*  Consult  */

    Clear();
    while ( true )
    {
        InterpretRuleset();
    }
}
```

File userint.c

```
/**********************************************************************/
/*                                                                    */
/*          User interface for consulting trees and rulesets          */
/*          ───────────────────────────────────────────              */
/*                                                                    */
/**********************************************************************/


#include "defns.i"
#include "types.i"
#include "extern.i"


typedef struct   ValRange           *RangeDescRec;
struct    ValRange
          {
              Boolean               Known, Asked;
              float                 LowerBound, UpperBound, *Probability;
          };

extern    RangeDescRec              RangeDesc;

#define Fuzz 0.01


/**********************************************************************/
/*                                                                    */
/*          Ask for the value of attribute Att if necessary           */
/*                                                                    */
/**********************************************************************/


    CheckValue(Att, T)
/*  ──────────  */
    Attribute Att;
    Tree T;
{
    if ( RangeDesc[Att].Asked ) return;

    printf("%s", AttName[Att]);
    if ( RangeDesc[Att].Known )
    {
        printf(" [ ");
        PrintRange(Att);
        printf(" ]");
    }
    printf(": ");

    ReadRange(Att, T);
}
```

```
/**************************************************************************/
/*                                                                        */
/*          Print the range of values for attribute Att                   */
/*                                                                        */
/**************************************************************************/

    PrintRange(Att)
/*  ———————  */
    Attribute Att;
{
    DiscrValue dv;
    Boolean First=true;
    float p;

    if ( MaxAttVal[Att] )  /*  discrete attribute  */
    {
        ForEach(dv, 1, MaxAttVal[Att] )
        {
            if ( (p = RangeDesc[Att].Probability[dv]) > Fuzz )
            {
                if ( ! First )
                {
                    printf(", ");
                }
                First = false;

                printf("%s", AttValName[Att][dv] );
                if ( p < 1-Fuzz )
                {
                    printf(": %.2f", p);
                }
            }
        }
    }
    else  /*  continuous attribute  */
    {
        printf("%g", RangeDesc[Att].LowerBound);
        if ( RangeDesc[Att].UpperBound > RangeDesc[Att].LowerBound + Fuzz )
        {
            printf(" - %g", RangeDesc[Att].UpperBound);
        }
    }
}
```

```
extern    char              Delimiter;
#define  SkipSpace          while ( (c = getchar()) == ' ' || c == '\t' )

/***********************************************************************/
/*                                                                     */
/*         Read a range of values for attribute Att or <cr>            */
/*                                                                     */
/***********************************************************************/

    ReadRange(Att, T)
/*  ——————— */
    Attribute Att;
    Tree T;
{
    char c;

    RangeDesc[Att].Asked=true;

    SkipSpace;

    if ( c == '\n' )
    {
        return;
    }
    if ( c == '?' )
    {
        if ( (c = getchar()) == 't' )
        {
            if ( T ) PrintTree(T);
            SkipLine(c);
            RangeDesc[Att].Asked = false;
            CheckValue(Att, T);
        }
        else
        {
            RangeDesc[Att].Known = false;
            SkipLine(c);
        }
        return;
    }

    ungetc(c, stdin);
    RangeDesc[Att].Known = true;

    if ( MaxAttVal[Att] )
    {
        ReadDiscr(Att, T);
    }
    else
    {
        ReadContin(Att, T);
    }
}
```

```
/****************************************************************************/
/*                                                                        */
/*        Read a discrete attribute value or range                        */
/*                                                                        */
/****************************************************************************/

    ReadDiscr(Att, T)
/*  ————— */
    Attribute Att;
    Tree T;
{
    char Name[500];
    Boolean ReadName();
    DiscrValue dv, PNo;
    float P, PSum;

    ForEach(dv, 1, MaxAttVal[Att])
    {
        RangeDesc[Att].Probability[dv]  = 0.0;
    }

    do
    {
        ReadName(stdin, Name);

        dv = Which(Name, AttValName[Att], 1, MaxAttVal[Att]);
        if ( ! dv )
        {
            printf("\tPermissible values are %s", AttValName[Att][1]);
            ForEach(dv, 2, MaxAttVal[Att])
            {
                printf(", %s", AttValName[Att][dv]);
            }
            printf("\n");

            SkipLine(Delimiter);
            Retry(Att, T);
            return;
        }

        if ( Delimiter == ':' )
        {
            ReadName(stdin, Name);
            sscanf(Name, "%f", &P);        /* get probability */
        }
        else
        {
            P = 1.0;               /*  only one attribute value  */
        }

        RangeDesc[Att].Probability[dv]  = P;
    }
    while ( Delimiter == ',' );
```

```
/*   Check that sum of probabilities is not > 1   */

PNo = MaxAttVal[Att];
PSum = 1.0;
ForEach(dv, 1, MaxAttVal[Att])
{
    if ( RangeDesc[Att].Probability[dv]  > Fuzz )
    {
        PSum -= RangeDesc[Att].Probability[dv];
        PNo--;
    }
}
if ( PSum < 0 || ! PNo && PSum > Fuzz )
{
    printf("Probability values must sum to 1\n");
    SkipLine(Delimiter);
    Retry(Att, T);
    return;
}

/*   Distribute the remaining probability equally among
     the unspecified attribute values   */

PSum /= PNo;
ForEach(dv, 1, MaxAttVal[Att])
{
    if ( RangeDesc[Att].Probability[dv]  < Fuzz )
    {
        RangeDesc[Att].Probability[dv]  = PSum;
    }
}
}
```

```
/**********************************************************************/
/*                                                                    */
/*        Read a continuous attribute value or range                  */
/*                                                                    */
/**********************************************************************/

    ReadContin(Att, T)
/* ———————— */
    Attribute Att;
    Tree T;
{
    char c;

    scanf("%f", &RangeDesc[Att].LowerBound);
    SkipSpace;

    if ( c == '-'  )
    {
        scanf("%f", &RangeDesc[Att].UpperBound);
        SkipSpace;
    }
    else
    {
        RangeDesc[Att].UpperBound = RangeDesc[Att].LowerBound;
    }

    if ( c != '\n' )
    {
        printf("Must be a continuous value or range\n");
        SkipLine(c);
        Retry(Att, T);
    }
}


/**********************************************************************/
/*                                                                    */
/*        Try again to obtain a value for attribute Att               */
/*                                                                    */
/**********************************************************************/

    Retry(Att, T)
/* ——— */
    Attribute Att;
    Tree T;
{
    RangeDesc[Att].Asked = false;
    RangeDesc[Att].Known = false;
    CheckValue(Att, T);
}
```

```
/***********************************************************************/
/*                                                                     */
/*          Skip to the end of the line of input                       */
/*                                                                     */
/***********************************************************************/

    SkipLine(c)
/*  ———— */
    char c;
{
    while ( c != '\n' ) c = getchar();
}



/***********************************************************************/
/*                                                                     */
/*                  Clear the range description                        */
/*                                                                     */
/***********************************************************************/

    Clear()
/*  ——— */
{
    Attribute Att;

    ForEach(Att, 0, MaxAtt)
    {
        RangeDesc[Att].Known = false;
    }
}
```

File header.c

```
/***************************************************************************/
/*                                                                         */
/*          Print header for all C4.5 programs                             */
/*          ─────────────────────────────────                              */
/*                                                                         */
/***************************************************************************/


#define   RELEASE "5"


        PrintHeader(Title)
/*      ───────────    */
        char *Title;
{
        char *ctime(), TitleLine[80];
        long clock, time();
        short Underline;

        clock = time(0);
        sprintf(TitleLine, "C4.5 [release %s]  %s", RELEASE, Title);
        printf("\n%s\t%s", TitleLine, ctime(&clock));

        Underline = strlen(TitleLine);
        while ( Underline-- ) putchar('-');
        putchar('\n');
}
```

File getopt.c

```
/**************************************************************************/
/*                                                                      */
/*    This file is included in case your version of UNIX doesn't include */
/*    the getopt utility.  If it does, discard this file and amend the   */
/*    Makefile accordingly.                                              */
/*                                                                      */
/*    There is no copyright on this file.                                */
/*                                                                      */
/**************************************************************************/

#include <stdio.h>

int optind = 1;
char *optarg;

    getopt(Argc, Argv, Str)
/*  ───────  */
    int Argc;
    char **Argv, *Str;
{
    int Optchar;
    char *Option;

    if ( optind >= Argc ) return EOF;

    Option = Argv[optind++];

    if ( *Option++ != '-' ) return '?';

    Optchar = *Option++;

    while ( *Str && *Str != Optchar ) Str++;
    if ( ! *Str ) return '?';

    if ( *++Str == ':' )
    {
        if ( *Option ) optarg = Option;
        else
        if ( optind < Argc ) optarg = Argv[optind++];
        else
        Optchar = '?';
    }

    return Optchar;
}
```

File getnames.c

```
/************************************************************************/
/*                                                                      */
/*          Get names of classes, attributes, and attribute values      */
/*          ─────────────────────────────────────────────               */
/*                                                                      */
/************************************************************************/


#include "defns.i"
#include "types.i"
#include "extern.i"

#include <sys/types.h>
#include <sys/stat.h>

#define   Space(s)       (s == ' ' || s == '\n' || s == '\t')
#define   SkipComment    while ( ( c = getc(f) ) != '\n' )

char Delimiter;


/************************************************************************/
/*                                                                      */
/*  Read a name from file f into string s, setting Delimiter.           */
/*                                                                      */
/*  -  Embedded periods are permitted, but periods followed by space    */
/*     characters act as delimiters.                                    */
/*  -  Embedded spaces are permitted, but multiple spaces are replaced  */
/*     by a single space.                                               */
/*  -  Any character can be escaped by '\'.                             */
/*  -  The remainder of a line following '|' is ignored.                */
/*                                                                      */
/************************************************************************/


Boolean ReadName(f, s)
/*      ─────────  */
    FILE *f;
    String s;
{
    register char *Sp=s;
    register int c;
    String CopyString();

    /*  Skip to first nonspace character  */

    while ( ( c = getc(f) ) == '|' || Space(c) )
    {
        if ( c == '|' ) SkipComment;
    }
```

```
/*   Return false if no names to read   */

if ( c == EOF )
{
    Delimiter = EOF;
    return false;
}

/*   Read in characters up to the next delimiter   */

while ( c != ':' && c != ',' && c != '\n' && c != '|' && c != EOF )
{
    if ( c == '.' )
    {
        if ( ( c = getc(f) ) == '|' || Space(c) ) break;
        *Sp++ = '.';
    }

    if ( c == '\\' )
    {
        c = getc(f);
    }

    *Sp++ = c;

    if ( c == ' ' )
    {
        while ( ( c = getc(f) ) == ' ' )
            ;
    }
    else
    {
        c = getc(f);
    }
}

if ( c == '|' ) SkipComment;
Delimiter = c;

/*   Strip trailing spaces   */

while ( Space(*(Sp-1)) ) Sp--;

*Sp++ = '\0';
return true;
}
```

```
/*****************************************************************************/
/*                                                                         */
/*  Read the names of classes, attributes, and legal attribute values.     */
/*  On completion, these names are stored in:                              */
/*        ClassName        -  class names                                  */
/*        AttName          -  attribute names                              */
/*        AttValName       -  attribute value names                        */
/*  with:                                                                  */
/*        MaxAttVal        -  number of values for each attribute          */
/*                                                                         */
/*  Other global variables set are:                                        */
/*        MaxAtt           -  maximum attribute number                     */
/*        MaxClass         -  maximum class number                         */
/*        MaxDiscrVal      -  maximum discrete values for any attribute     */
/*                                                                         */
/*  Note:  until the number of attributes is known, the name               */
/*         information is assembled in local arrays                        */
/*                                                                         */
/*****************************************************************************/


    GetNames()
/*  ─────────  */
{
    FILE *Nf, *fopen();
    char Fn[100], Buffer[1000];
    DiscrValue v;
    int AttCeiling=100, ClassCeiling=100, ValCeiling;

    /*  Open names file  */

    strcpy(Fn, FileName);
    strcat(Fn, ".names");
    if ( ! ( Nf = fopen(Fn, "r") ) ) Error(0, Fn, "");

    /*  Get class names from names file  */

    ClassName = (String *) calloc(ClassCeiling, sizeof(String));
    MaxClass = -1;
    do
    {
        ReadName(Nf, Buffer);

        if ( ++MaxClass >= ClassCeiling)
        {
            ClassCeiling += 100;
            ClassName = (String *) realloc(ClassName, ClassCeiling*sizeof(String));
        }
        ClassName[MaxClass] = CopyString(Buffer);
    }
    while ( Delimiter == ',' );

    /*  Get attribute and attribute value names from names file  */

    AttName = (String *) calloc(AttCeiling, sizeof(String));
    MaxAttVal = (DiscrValue *) calloc(AttCeiling, sizeof(DiscrValue));
    AttValName = (String **) calloc(AttCeiling, sizeof(String *));
```

```
SpecialStatus = (char *) malloc(AttCeiling);

MaxAtt = -1;
while ( ReadName(Nf, Buffer) )
{
    if ( Delimiter != ':' )  Error(1, Buffer, "");

    if ( ++MaxAtt >= AttCeiling )
    {
        AttCeiling += 100;
        AttName = (String *) realloc(AttName, AttCeiling*sizeof(String));
        MaxAttVal = (DiscrValue *) realloc(MaxAttVal, AttCeiling*sizeof(DiscrValue));
        AttValName = (String **) realloc(AttValName, AttCeiling*sizeof(String *));
        SpecialStatus = (char *) realloc(SpecialStatus, AttCeiling);
    }

    AttName[MaxAtt] = CopyString(Buffer);
    SpecialStatus[MaxAtt] = Nil;
    MaxAttVal[MaxAtt] = 0;
    ValCeiling = 100;
    AttValName[MaxAtt] = (String *) calloc(ValCeiling, sizeof(String));

    do
    {
        if ( ! ( ReadName(Nf, Buffer) ) ) Error(2, AttName[MaxAtt], "");

        if ( ++MaxAttVal[MaxAtt] >= ValCeiling )
        {
            ValCeiling += 100;
            AttValName[MaxAtt] =
                (String *) realloc(AttValName[MaxAtt], ValCeiling*sizeof(String));
        }

        AttValName[MaxAtt] [MaxAttVal[MaxAtt]] = CopyString(Buffer);
    }
    while ( Delimiter == ',' );

    if ( MaxAttVal[MaxAtt] == 1 )
    {
        /*  Check for special treatment  */

        if ( ! strcmp(Buffer, "continuous") )
        {}
        else
        if ( ! memcmp(Buffer, "discrete", 8) )
        {
            SpecialStatus[MaxAtt] = DISCRETE;

            /*  Read max values, reserve space, and check MaxDiscrVal  */

            v = atoi(&Buffer[8]);
            AttValName[MaxAtt] =
                (String *) realloc(AttValName[MaxAtt], (v+2)*sizeof(String));
            AttValName[MaxAtt] [0] = (char *) v;
            if ( v > MaxDiscrVal ) MaxDiscrVal = v;
        }
```

```
            else
            if ( ! strcmp(Buffer, "ignore") )
            {
                SpecialStatus[MaxAtt] = IGNORE;
            }
            else
            {
                /*  Cannot have only one discrete value for an attribute  */

                Error(3, AttName[MaxAtt], "");
            }

            MaxAttVal[MaxAtt] = 0;
        }
        else
        if ( MaxAttVal[MaxAtt] > MaxDiscrVal ) MaxDiscrVal = MaxAttVal[MaxAtt];
    }

    fclose(Nf);
}


/**************************************************************************/
/*                                                                      */
/*       Locate value Val in List[First]  to List[Last]                 */
/*                                                                      */
/**************************************************************************/

int Which(Val, List, First, Last)
/* ———— */
    String Val, List[];
    short First, Last;
{
    short n=First;

    while ( n <= Last && strcmp(Val, List[n]) ) n++;
    return ( n <= Last ? n : First-1 );
}


/**************************************************************************/
/*                                                                      */
/*       Allocate space then copy string into it                        */
/*                                                                      */
/**************************************************************************/

String CopyString(x)
/*      ——————  */
    String x;
{
    char *s;

    s = (char *) calloc(strlen(x)+1, sizeof(char));
    strcpy(s, x);
    return s;
}
```

```
/*************************************************************************/
/*                                                                       */
/*                          Error messages                               */
/*                                                                       */
/*************************************************************************/
     Error(n, s1, s2)
/*   ———  */
     short n;
     String s1, s2;
{
     static char Messages=0;

     printf("\nERROR:   ");
     switch(n)
     {
         case 0: printf("cannot open file %s%s\n", s1, s2);
                 exit(1);

         case 1:  printf("colon expected after attribute name %s\n", s1);
                 break;

         case 2:  printf("unexpected eof while reading attribute %s\n", s1);
                 break;

         case 3:  printf("attribute %s has only one value\n", s1);
                 break;

         case 4:  printf("case %d's value of '%s' for attribute %s is illegal\n",
                     MaxItem+1, s2, s1);
                 break;

         case 5:  printf("case %d's class of '%s' is illegal\n", MaxItem+1, s2);
     }

     if (  ++Messages > 10 )
     {
         printf("Error limit exceeded\n");
         exit(1);
     }
}
```

File getdata.c

```
/***********************************************************************/
/*                                                                   */
/*        Get case descriptions from data file                       */
/*        ────────────────────────────────                           */
/*                                                                   */
/***********************************************************************/

#include "defns.i"
#include "types.i"
#include "extern.i"

#define Inc 2048


/***********************************************************************/
/*                                                                   */
/*  Read raw case descriptions from file with given extension.       */
/*                                                                   */
/*  On completion, cases are stored in array Item in the form        */
/*  of Descriptions (i.e., arrays of attribute values), and          */
/*  MaxItem is set to the number of data items.                      */
/*                                                                   */
/***********************************************************************/

    GetData(Extension)
/*  ─────────  */
    String Extension;
{
    FILE *Df, *fopen();
    char Fn[100];
    ItemNo i=0, j, ItemSpace=0;
    Description GetDescription();

    /*  Open data file  */

    strcpy(Fn, FileName);
    strcat(Fn, Extension);
    if ( ! ( Df = fopen(Fn, "r") ) ) Error(0, Fn, "");

    do
    {
        MaxItem = i;
```

```
        /*  Make sure there is room for another item   */

        if ( i >= ItemSpace )
        {
            if ( ItemSpace )
            {
                ItemSpace += Inc;
                Item = (Description *)
                        realloc(Item, ItemSpace*sizeof(Description));
            }
            else
            {
                Item = (Description *)
                        malloc((ItemSpace=Inc)*sizeof(Description));
            }
        }

        Item[i]  = GetDescription(Df);

    } while ( Item[i] != Nil && ++i );

    fclose(Df);
    MaxItem = i - 1;
}


/***************************************************************************/
/*                                                                       */
/*  Read a raw case description from file Df.                            */
/*                                                                       */
/*  For each attribute, read the attribute value from the file.         */
/*  If it is a discrete valued attribute, find the associated no.       */
/*  of this attribute value (if the value is unknown this is 0).        */
/*                                                                       */
/*  Returns the Description of the case (i.e., the array of             */
/*  attribute values).                                                  */
/*                                                                       */
/***************************************************************************/


Description GetDescription(Df)
/*          ―――――――――――――  */
    FILE *Df;
{
    Attribute Att;
    char name[500], *endname, *CopyString();
    Boolean ReadName();
    int Dv;
    float Cv;
    Description Dvec;
    double strtod();

    if ( ReadName(Df, name) )
    {
        Dvec = (Description) calloc(MaxAtt+2, sizeof(AttValue));
```

```
ForEach(Att, 0, MaxAtt)
{
    if ( SpecialStatus[Att] == IGNORE )
    {
        /*  Skip this value  */
        DVal(Dvec, Att) = 0;
    }
    else
    if ( MaxAttVal[Att] || SpecialStatus[Att] == DISCRETE )
    {
        /*  Discrete value  */
        if ( ! ( strcmp(name, "?") ) )
        {
            Dv = 0;
        }
        else
        {
            Dv = Which(name, AttValName[Att], 1, MaxAttVal[Att]);
            if ( ! Dv )
            {
                if ( SpecialStatus[Att] == DISCRETE )
                {
                    /*  Add value to list  */
                    Dv = ++MaxAttVal[Att];
                    if ( Dv > (int) AttValName[Att] [0]  )
                    {
                        printf("\nToo many values for %s (max %d)\n",
                               AttName[Att], (int) AttValName[Att] [0]);
                        exit(1);
                    }
                    AttValName[Att] [Dv] = CopyString(name);
                }
                else
                {
                    Error(4, AttName[Att], name);
                }
            }
        }
        DVal(Dvec, Att) = Dv;
    }
    else
    {
        /*  Continuous value  */
        if ( ! ( strcmp(name, "?") ) )
        {
            Cv = Unknown;
        }
        else
        {
```

```
                    Cv = strtod(name, &endname);
                    if ( endname == name || *endname != '\0' )
                        Error(4, AttName[Att], name);
                }
                CVal(Dvec, Att) = Cv;
            }

            ReadName(Df, name);
        }

        if ( (Dv = Which(name, ClassName, 0, MaxClass)) < 0 )
        {
            Error(5, "", name);
            Dv = 0;
        }
        Class(Dvec) = Dv;

        return Dvec;
    }
    else
    {
        return Nil;
    }
}
```

File sort.c

```
/*****************************************************************************/
/*                                                                         */
/*        Sorting utilities                                                */
/*        ───────────────                                                  */
/*                                                                         */
/*****************************************************************************/


#include "defns.i"
#include "types.i"
#include "extern.i"


/*****************************************************************************/
/*                                                                         */
/*        Sort items from Fp to Lp on attribute a                          */
/*                                                                         */
/*****************************************************************************/

    Quicksort(Fp, Lp, Att, Exchange)
/*  ─────────  */
    ItemNo Fp, Lp;
    Attribute Att;
    void (*Exchange)();
{
    register ItemNo Lower, Middle;
    register float Thresh;
    register ItemNo i;

    if ( Fp < Lp )
    {
        Thresh = CVal(Item[Lp], Att);

        /*  Isolate all items with values <= threshold  */

        Middle = Fp;

        for ( i = Fp ; i < Lp ; i++ )
        {
            if ( CVal(Item[i], Att) <= Thresh )
            {
                if ( i != Middle ) (*Exchange)(Middle, i);
                Middle++;
            }
        }
    }
```

```
    /*  Extract all values equal to the threshold  */
    Lower = Middle - 1;
    for ( i = Lower ; i >= Fp ; i-- )
    {
        if ( CVal(Item[i], Att) == Thresh )
        {
            if ( i != Lower )  (*Exchange)(Lower, i);
            Lower--;
        }
    }
    /*  Sort the lower values  */
    Quicksort(Fp, Lower, Att, Exchange);
    /*  Position the middle element  */
    (*Exchange)(Middle, Lp);
    /*  Sort the higher values  */
    Quicksort(Middle+1, Lp, Att, Exchange);
    }
}
```

File trees.c

```
/*************************************************************************/
/*                                                                     */
/*          Routines for displaying, building, saving, and restoring trees */
/*          _____     */
/*                                                                     */
/*                                                                     */
/*************************************************************************/


#include "defns.i"
#include "types.i"
#include "extern.i"


#define  Tab          " |   "
#define  TabSize       4
#define  Width         80        /* approx max width of printed trees */

            /*  If lines look like getting too long while a tree is being
                printed, subtrees are broken off and printed separately after
                the main tree is finished        */

short   Subtree;                 /* highest subtree to be printed */
Tree    Subdef[500];             /* pointers to subtrees */

FILE    *Tf = 0, *fopen();       /* file pointer for tree i/o */
char    Fn[500];                 /* file name */



/*************************************************************************/
/*                                                                     */
/*          Display entire decision tree T                             */
/*                                                                     */
/*************************************************************************/


        PrintTree(T)
/*      _____  */
        Tree T;
    {
        short s;

        Subtree=0;
        printf("Decision Tree:\n");
        Show(T, 0);
        printf("\n");

        ForEach(s, 1, Subtree)
        {
            printf("\n\nSubtree [S%d]\n", s);
            Show(Subdef[s], 0);
            printf("\n");
        }
        printf("\n");
    }
```

```
/******************************************************************/
/*                                                                */
/*        Display the tree T with offset Sh                       */
/*                                                                */
/******************************************************************/

    Show(T, Sh)
/*  ——— */
    Tree T;
    short Sh;
{
    DiscrValue v, MaxV;
    short MaxLine();

    if ( T->NodeType )
    {
        /*  See whether separate subtree needed   */

        if ( T != Nil && Sh * TabSize + MaxLine(T) > Width )
        {
            if ( Subtree < 99 )
            {
                Subdef[++Subtree]  =  T;
                printf(" [S%d]", Subtree);
            }
            else
            {
                printf(" [S??]");
            }
        }
        else
        {
            MaxV = T->Forks;

            /*  Print simple cases first */

            ForEach(v, 1, MaxV)
            {
                if ( ! T->Branch[v]->NodeType )
                {
                    ShowBranch(Sh, T, v);
                }
            }

            /*  Print subtrees  */

            ForEach(v, 1, MaxV)
            {
                if ( T->Branch[v]->NodeType )
                {
                    ShowBranch(Sh, T, v);
                }
            }
        }
    }
}
```

```
    else
    {
        printf(" %s (%.1f", ClassName[T->Leaf], T->Items);
        if ( T->Errors > 0 ) printf("/%.1f", T->Errors);
        printf(")");
    }
}


/*************************************************************************/
/*                                                                       */
/*        Print a node T with offset Sh, branch value v, and continue    */
/*                                                                       */
/*************************************************************************/


    ShowBranch(Sh, T, v)
/*  ———————  */
    short Sh;
    Tree T;
    DiscrValue v;
{
    DiscrValue Pv, Last;
    Attribute Att;
    Boolean FirstValue;
    short TextWidth, Skip, Values=0, i;

    Att = T->Tested;

    switch ( T->NodeType )
    {
        case BrDiscr:

            Indent(Sh, Tab);

            printf("%s = %s:", AttName[Att], AttValName[Att][v]);
            break;

        case ThreshContin:

            Indent(Sh, Tab);

            printf("%s %s %g ",
                    AttName[Att], ( v == 1 ? "<=" : ">" ), T->Cut);

            if ( T->Lower != T->Upper )
            {
                printf(" [%g,%g]", T->Lower, T->Upper);
            }

            printf(":");
            break;
```

```
    case BrSubset:

        /*  Count values at this branch  */
        ForEach(Pv, 1, MaxAttVal[Att])
        {
            if ( In(Pv, T->Subset[v]) )
            {
                Last = Pv;
                Values++;
            }
        }
        if ( ! Values ) return;

        Indent(Sh, Tab);

        if ( Values == 1 )
        {
            printf("%s = %s:", AttName[Att], AttValName[Att][Last]);
            break;
        }

        printf("%s in {", AttName[Att]);
        FirstValue = true;
        Skip = TextWidth = strlen(AttName[Att]) + 5;

        ForEach(Pv, 1, MaxAttVal[Att])
        {
            if ( In(Pv, T->Subset[v]) )
            {
                if ( ! FirstValue &&
                     TextWidth + strlen(AttValName[Att][Pv]) + 11 > Width )
                {
                    Indent(Sh, Tab);
                    ForEach(i, 1, Skip) putchar(' ');

                    TextWidth = Skip;
                    FirstValue = true;
                }

                printf("%s%c", AttValName[Att][Pv], Pv == Last ? '}' : ',');
                TextWidth += strlen(AttValName[Att][Pv]) + 1;
                FirstValue = false;
            }
        }
        putchar(':');
    }

    Show(T->Branch[v], Sh+1);
}
```

```
/***********************************************************************/
/*                                                                     */
/*        Find the maximum single line size for nonleaf subtree St.    */
/*        The line format is                                           */
/*                        <attribute> <> X.xx:[ <class (<Items>)], or  */
/*                        <attribute> = <DVal>:[ <class> (<Items>)]    */
/*                                                                     */
/***********************************************************************/

short MaxLine(St)
/*    ———  */
    Tree St;
{
    Attribute a;
    DiscrValue v, MaxV, Next;
    short LI, MaxLI=0;

    a = St->Tested;

    MaxV = St->Forks;
    ForEach(v, 1, MaxV)
    {
        LI = ( St->NodeType == 2 ? 4 : strlen(AttValName[a][v]) ) + 1;

        /*  Find the appropriate branch  */

        Next = v;

        if ( ! St->Branch[Next]->NodeType )
        {
            LI += strlen(ClassName[St->Branch[Next]->Leaf]) + 6;
        }
        MaxLI = Max(MaxLI, LI);
    }

    return strlen(AttName[a]) + 4 + MaxLI;
}


/***********************************************************************/
/*                                                                     */
/*        Indent Sh columns                                            */
/*                                                                     */
/***********************************************************************/

    Indent(Sh, Mark)
/*  ———  */
    short Sh;
    char *Mark;
{
    printf("\n");
    while ( Sh-- ) printf("%s", Mark);
}
```

```
/**********************************************************************/
/*                                                                    */
/*          Save entire decision tree T in file with extension Extension  */
/*                                                                    */
/**********************************************************************/


    SaveTree(T, Extension)
/*  ─────────  */
    Tree T;
    String Extension;
{
    static char *LastExt="";

    if ( strcmp(LastExt, Extension) )
    {
        LastExt = Extension;

        if ( Tf ) fclose(Tf);

        strcpy(Fn, FileName);
        strcat(Fn, Extension);
        if ( ! ( Tf = fopen(Fn, "w") ) )
            Error(0, Fn, " for writing");
    }

    putc('\n', Tf);
    OutTree(T);
}



/**********************************************************************/
/*                                                                    */
/*          Save tree T as characters                                 */
/*                                                                    */
/**********************************************************************/


    OutTree(T)
/*  ───────  */
    Tree T;
{
    DiscrValue v;
    int Bytes;

    StreamOut((char *) &T->NodeType, sizeof(short));
    StreamOut((char *) &T->Leaf, sizeof(ClassNo));
    StreamOut((char *) &T->Items, sizeof(ItemCount));
    StreamOut((char *) &T->Errors, sizeof(ItemCount));
    StreamOut((char *) T->ClassDist, (MaxClass + 1) * sizeof(ItemCount));

    if ( T->NodeType )
    {
        StreamOut((char *) &T->Tested, sizeof(Attribute));
        StreamOut((char *) &T->Forks, sizeof(short));
```

```
        switch ( T->NodeType )
        {
            case BrDiscr:
                break;

            case ThreshContin:
                StreamOut((char *) &T->Cut, sizeof(float));
                StreamOut((char *) &T->Lower, sizeof(float));
                StreamOut((char *) &T->Upper, sizeof(float));
                break;

            case BrSubset:
                Bytes = (MaxAttVal[T->Tested]>>3) + 1;
                ForEach(v, 1, T->Forks)
                {
                    StreamOut((char *) T->Subset[v], Bytes);
                }
                break;
        }

        ForEach(v, 1, T->Forks)
        {
            OutTree(T->Branch[v]);
        }
    }
}


/*************************************************************************/
/*                                                                       */
/*       Retrieve entire decision tree with extension Extension          */
/*                                                                       */
/*************************************************************************/


Tree GetTree(Extension)
/*   ————————  */
    String Extension;
{
    Tree InTree();
    static char *LastExt="";

    if ( strcmp(LastExt, Extension) )
    {
        LastExt = Extension;

        if ( Tf ) fclose(Tf);

        strcpy(Fn, FileName);
        strcat(Fn, Extension);
        if ( ! ( Tf = fopen(Fn, "r") ) ) Error(0, Fn, "");
    }

    if ( ! Tf  || getc(Tf) == EOF ) return Nil;

    return InTree();
}
```

```
/**************************************************************************/
/*                                                                        */
/*          Retrieve tree from saved characters                           */
/*                                                                        */
/**************************************************************************/


Tree InTree()
/*   ————   */
{
    Tree T;
    DiscrValue v;
    int Bytes;

    T = (Tree) malloc(sizeof(TreeRec));

    StreamIn((char *) &T->NodeType, sizeof(short));
    StreamIn((char *) &T->Leaf, sizeof(ClassNo));
    StreamIn((char *) &T->Items, sizeof(ItemCount));
    StreamIn((char *) &T->Errors, sizeof(ItemCount));

    T->ClassDist = (ItemCount *) calloc(MaxClass+1, sizeof(ItemCount));
    StreamIn((char *) T->ClassDist, (MaxClass + 1) * sizeof(ItemCount));

    if ( T->NodeType )
    {
        StreamIn((char *) &T->Tested, sizeof(Attribute));
        StreamIn((char *) &T->Forks, sizeof(short));

        switch ( T->NodeType )
        {
            case BrDiscr:
                break;
            case ThreshContin:
                StreamIn((char *) &T->Cut, sizeof(float));
                StreamIn((char *) &T->Lower, sizeof(float));
                StreamIn((char *) &T->Upper, sizeof(float));
                break;
            case BrSubset:
                T->Subset = (Set *) calloc(T->Forks + 1, sizeof(Set));
                Bytes = (MaxAttVal[T->Tested]>>3) + 1;
                ForEach(v, 1, T->Forks)
                {
                    T->Subset[v] = (Set) malloc(Bytes);
                    StreamIn((char *) T->Subset[v], Bytes);
                }
        }

        T->Branch = (Tree *) calloc(T->Forks + 1, sizeof(Tree));
        ForEach(v, 1, T->Forks)
        {
            T->Branch[v] = InTree();
        }
    }
    return T;
}
```

```
/**********************************************************************/
/*                                                                    */
/*          Stream characters to/from file Tf from/to an address      */
/*                                                                    */
/**********************************************************************/

    StreamOut(s, n)
/*  ─────────  */
    String s;
    int n;
{
    while ( n-- ) putc(*s++, Tf);
}


    StreamIn(s, n)
/*  ─────────  */
    String s;
    int n;
{
    while ( n-- ) *s++ = getc(Tf);
}



/**********************************************************************/
/*                                                                    */
/*          Free up space taken up by tree Node                       */
/*                                                                    */
/**********************************************************************/

    ReleaseTree(Node)
/*  ─────────  */
    Tree Node;
{
    DiscrValue v;

    if ( Node->NodeType )
    {
        ForEach(v, 1, Node->Forks)
        {
            ReleaseTree(Node->Branch[v]);
        }

        cfree(Node->Branch);

        if ( Node->NodeType == BrSubset )
        {
            cfree(Node->Subset);
        }

    }
    cfree(Node->ClassDist);
    cfree(Node);
}
```

```
/**********************************************************************/
/*                                                                    */
/*        Construct a leaf in a given node                            */
/*                                                                    */
/**********************************************************************/


Tree Leaf(ClassFreq, NodeClass, Cases, Errors)
/*   ——  */
    ItemCount *ClassFreq;
    ClassNo NodeClass;
    ItemCount Cases, Errors;
{
    Tree Node;

    Node = (Tree) calloc(1, sizeof(TreeRec));

    Node->ClassDist = (ItemCount *) calloc(MaxClass+1, sizeof(ItemCount));
    memcpy(Node->ClassDist, ClassFreq, (MaxClass+1) * sizeof(ItemCount));

    Node->NodeType    = 0;
    Node->Leaf        = NodeClass;
    Node->Items       = Cases;
    Node->Errors      = Errors;

    return Node;
}



/**********************************************************************/
/*                                                                    */
/*        Insert branches in a node                                   */
/*                                                                    */
/**********************************************************************/


    Sprout(Node, Branches)
/*  ———  */
    Tree Node;
    DiscrValue Branches;
{
    Node->Forks = Branches;

    Node->Branch = (Tree *) calloc(Branches+1, sizeof(Tree));
}
```

```
/**************************************************************************/
/*                                                                        */
/*        Count the nodes in a tree                                       */
/*                                                                        */
/**************************************************************************/

    TreeSize(Node)
/*  ─────────  */
    Tree Node;
{
    short Sum=0;
    DiscrValue v;

    if ( Node->NodeType )
    {
        ForEach(v, 1, Node->Forks)
        {
            Sum += TreeSize(Node->Branch[v]);
        }
    }

    return Sum + 1;
}



/**************************************************************************/
/*                                                                        */
/*        Return a copy of tree T                                         */
/*                                                                        */
/**************************************************************************/

Tree CopyTree(T)
/*  ─────────  */
    Tree T;
{
    DiscrValue v;
    Tree New;

    New = (Tree) malloc(sizeof(TreeRec));
    memcpy(New, T, sizeof(TreeRec));

    New->ClassDist = (ItemCount *) calloc(MaxClass+1, sizeof(ItemCount));
    memcpy(New->ClassDist, T->ClassDist, (MaxClass + 1) * sizeof(ItemCount));

    if ( T->NodeType )
    {
        New->Branch = (Tree *) calloc(T->Forks + 1, sizeof(Tree));
        ForEach(v, 1, T->Forks)
        {
            New->Branch[v] = CopyTree(T->Branch[v]);
        }
    }

    return New;
}
```

File rules.c

```
/**************************************************************************/
/*                                                                        */
/*          Miscellaneous routines for rule handling                      */
/*          _____                          */
/*                                                                        */
/**************************************************************************/


#include "defns.i"
#include "types.i"
#include "extern.i"
#include "rulex.i"


Test    *TestVec;
short   NTests = 0;

FILE    *Rf = 0, *fopen();      /* rules file */
char    Fn[500];               /* file name */


/**************************************************************************/
/*                                                                        */
/*  Save the current ruleset in rules file in order of the index          */
/*                                                                        */
/**************************************************************************/

    SaveRules()
/*  _____  */
{
    short ri, d, v, Bytes;
    RuleNo r;
    Test Tst;

    if ( Rf ) fclose(Rf);

    strcpy(Fn, FileName);
    strcat(Fn, ".rules");
    if ( ! ( Rf = fopen(Fn, "w") ) ) Error(0, Fn, " for writing");

    RStreamOut((char *) &NRules, sizeof(RuleNo));
    RStreamOut((char *) &DefaultClass, sizeof(ClassNo));

    ForEach(ri, 1, NRules)
    {
        r = RuleIndex[ri];
        RStreamOut((char *) &Rule[r].Size, sizeof(short));
        ForEach(d, 1, Rule[r].Size)
        {
            Tst = Rule[r].Lhs[d]->CondTest;

            RStreamOut((char *) &Tst->NodeType, sizeof(short));
            RStreamOut((char *) &Tst->Tested, sizeof(Attribute));
```

```
                RStreamOut((char *) &Tst->Forks, sizeof(short));
                RStreamOut((char *) &Tst->Cut, sizeof(float));
                if ( Tst->NodeType == BrSubset )
                {
                    Bytes = (MaxAttVal[Tst->Tested]>>3) + 1;
                    ForEach(v, 1, Tst->Forks)
                    {
                        RStreamOut((char *) Tst->Subset[v], Bytes);
                    }
                }
                RStreamOut((char *) &Rule[r].Lhs[d]->TestValue, sizeof(short));
            }
            RStreamOut((char *) &Rule[r].Rhs, sizeof(ClassNo));
            RStreamOut((char *) &Rule[r].Error, sizeof(float));
        }
}


/*************************************************************************/
/*                                                                       */
/*   Put n characters starting from address s to file Rf                 */
/*                                                                       */
/*************************************************************************/


    RStreamOut(s, n)
/*  ----------  */
    String s;
    int n;
{
    while ( n-- ) putc(*s++, Rf);
}


/*************************************************************************/
/*                                                                       */
/*        Get a new ruleset from rules file                              */
/*                                                                       */
/*************************************************************************/


    GetRules()
/*  --------  */
{
    RuleNo nr, r;
    short n, d, v, Bytes;
    Condition *Cond;
    Test Tst, FindTest();
    ClassNo c;
    float e;
    Boolean NewRule();

    if ( Rf ) fclose(Rf);

    strcpy(Fn, FileName);
    strcat(Fn, ".rules");
    if ( ! ( Rf = fopen(Fn, "r") ) ) Error(0, Fn, "");
```

```
    RStreamIn((char *) &nr, sizeof(RuleNo));
    RStreamIn((char *) &DefaultClass, sizeof(ClassNo));

    ForEach(r, 1, nr)
    {
        RStreamIn((char *) &n, sizeof(short));
        Cond = (Condition *) calloc(n+1, sizeof(Condition));
        ForEach(d, 1, n)
        {
            Tst = (Test) malloc(sizeof(struct TestRec));

            RStreamIn((char *) &Tst->NodeType, sizeof(short));
            RStreamIn((char *) &Tst->Tested, sizeof(Attribute));
            RStreamIn((char *) &Tst->Forks, sizeof(short));
            RStreamIn((char *) &Tst->Cut, sizeof(float));
            if ( Tst->NodeType == BrSubset )
            {
                Tst->Subset = (Set *) calloc(Tst->Forks + 1, sizeof(Set));

                Bytes = (MaxAttVal[Tst->Tested]>>3) + 1;
                ForEach(v, 1, Tst->Forks)
                {
                    Tst->Subset[v] = (Set) malloc(Bytes);
                    RStreamIn((char *) Tst->Subset[v], Bytes);
                }
            }

            Cond[d] = (Condition) malloc(sizeof(struct CondRec));
            Cond[d]->CondTest = FindTest(Tst);
            RStreamIn((char *) &Cond[d]->TestValue, sizeof(short));
        }
        RStreamIn((char *) &c, sizeof(ClassNo));
        RStreamIn((char *) &e, sizeof(float));
        NewRule(Cond, n, c, e);
        cfree(Cond);
    }
}


/*************************************************************************/
/*                                                                       */
/*   Get n characters from file Rf into address s and onwards            */
/*                                                                       */
/*************************************************************************/

    RStreamIn(s, n)
/*  ————————  */
    String s;
    int n;
{
    while ( n-- ) *s++ = getc(Rf);
}
```

```
/**************************************************************************/
/*                                                                        */
/*  Find a test in the test vector; if it's not there already, add it     */
/*                                                                        */
/**************************************************************************/

Test FindTest(Newtest)
/*     ————————  */
    Test Newtest;
{
    static short TestSpace=0;
    short i;
    Boolean SameTest();

    ForEach(i, 1, NTests)
    {
        if ( SameTest(Newtest, TestVec[i]) )
        {
            cfree(Newtest);
            return TestVec[i];
        }
    }

    NTests++;
    if ( NTests >= TestSpace )
    {
        TestSpace += 1000;
        if ( TestSpace > 1000 )
        {
            TestVec = (Test *) realloc(TestVec, TestSpace * sizeof(Test));
        }
        else
        {
            TestVec = (Test *) malloc(TestSpace * sizeof(Test));
        }
    }

    TestVec[NTests] = Newtest;

    return TestVec[NTests];
}
```

```
/************************************************************************/
/*                                                                      */
/*        See if test t1 is the same test as test t2                    */
/*                                                                      */
/************************************************************************/


Boolean SameTest(t1, t2)
/*              ————— */
    Test t1, t2;
{
    short i;

    if ( t1->NodeType != t2->NodeType ||
         t1->Tested != t2->Tested )
    {
        return false;
    }

    switch ( t1->NodeType )
    {
        case BrDiscr:       return true;
        case ThreshContin:  return   t1->Cut == t2->Cut;
        case BrSubset:      ForEach(i, 1, t1->Forks)
                            {
                                if ( t1->Subset[i]  != t2->Subset[i]  )
                                {
                                    return false;
                                }
                            }
    }
    return true;
}



/************************************************************************/
/*                                                                      */
/*                Clear for new set of rules                            */
/*                                                                      */
/************************************************************************/


    InitialiseRules()
/*  ————————— */
{
    NRules = 0;
    Rule = 0;
    RuleSpace = 0;
}
```

```
/**************************************************************************/
/*                                                                        */
/*   Clear the outcome fields for the current item in all tests           */
/*                                                                        */
/**************************************************************************/

        ClearOutcomes()
/*      ─────────────  */
{
    short i;

    ForEach(i, 1, NTests)
    {
        TestVec[i]->Outcome = 0;
    }
}




/**************************************************************************/
/*                                                                        */
/*   Add a new rule to the current ruleset, by updating Rule[],           */
/*   NRules, and, if necessary, RuleSpace                                 */
/*                                                                        */
/**************************************************************************/

Boolean NewRule(Cond, NConds, TargetClass, Err)
/*      ───────  */
    Condition Cond[];
    short NConds;
    ClassNo TargetClass;
    float Err;
{
    short d, r;
    Boolean SameRule();

    /*  See if rule already exists  */

    ForEach(r, 1, NRules)
    {
        if ( SameRule(r, Cond, NConds, TargetClass) )
        {
            Verbosity(1) printf("\tduplicates rule %d\n", r);

            /*  Keep the most pessimistic error estimate  */

            if ( Err > Rule[r].Error )
            {
                Rule[r].Error = Err;
            }

            return false;
        }
    }
```

```
    /*   Make sure there is enough room for the new rule   */

    NRules++;
    if ( NRules >= RuleSpace )
    {
        RuleSpace += 100;
        if ( RuleSpace > 100 )
        {
            Rule = (PR *) realloc(Rule, RuleSpace * sizeof(PR));
        }
        else
        {
            Rule = (PR *) malloc(RuleSpace * sizeof(PR));
        }
    }

    /*   Form the new rule   */

    Rule[NRules].Size = NConds;
    Rule[NRules].Lhs = (Condition *) calloc(NConds+1, sizeof(Condition));
    ForEach(d, 1, NConds)
    {
        Rule[NRules].Lhs[d] = (Condition) malloc(sizeof(struct CondRec));

        Rule[NRules].Lhs[d]->CondTest = Cond[d]->CondTest;
        Rule[NRules].Lhs[d]->TestValue = Cond[d]->TestValue;
    }
    Rule[NRules].Rhs = TargetClass;
    Rule[NRules].Error = Err;

    Verbosity(1) PrintRule(NRules);

    return true;
}


/***************************************************************************/
/*                                                                         */
/*   Decide whether the given rule duplicates rule r                       */
/*                                                                         */
/***************************************************************************/

Boolean SameRule(r, Cond, NConds, TargetClass)
/*      ————————      */
    RuleNo r;
    Condition Cond[];
    short NConds;
    ClassNo TargetClass;
{
    short d, i;
    Test SubTest1, SubTest2;

    if ( Rule[r].Size != NConds || Rule[r].Rhs != TargetClass )
    {
        return false;
    }
```

```
ForEach(d, 1, NConds)
{
    if ( Rule[r].Lhs[d]->CondTest->NodeType != Cond[d]->CondTest->NodeType ||
         Rule[r].Lhs[d]->CondTest->Tested != Cond[d]->CondTest->Tested )
    {
        return false;
    }

    switch ( Cond[d]->CondTest->NodeType )
    {
        case BrDiscr:
            if ( Rule[r].Lhs[d]->TestValue != Cond[d]->TestValue )
            {
                return false;
            }
            break;

        case ThreshContin:
            if ( Rule[r].Lhs[d]->CondTest->Cut != Cond[d]->CondTest->Cut )
            {
                return false;
            }
            break;

        case BrSubset:
            SubTest1 = Rule[r].Lhs[d]->CondTest;
            SubTest2 = Cond[d]->CondTest;
            ForEach(i, 1, SubTest1->Forks)
            {
                if ( SubTest1->Subset[i] != SubTest2->Subset[i] )
                {
                    return false;
                }
            }
    }
}

return true;
}
```

```
/**************************************************************************/
/*                                                                        */
/*                  Print the current indexed ruleset                     */
/*                                                                        */
/**************************************************************************/


    PrintIndexedRules()
/*  ———————————  */
{
    short ri;

    ForEach(ri, 1, NRules )
    {
        PrintRule(RuleIndex[ri]);
    }
    printf("\nDefault class: %s\n", ClassName[DefaultClass]);
}



/**************************************************************************/
/*                                                                        */
/*                      Print the rule r                                  */
/*                                                                        */
/**************************************************************************/


    PrintRule(r)
/*  ——————  */
    RuleNo r;
{
    short d;

    printf("\nRule %d:\n", r);
    ForEach(d, 1, Rule[r].Size)
    {
        printf("        ");
        PrintCondition(Rule[r].Lhs[d]);
    }
    printf("\t->  class %s  [%.1f%%]\n",
            ClassName[Rule[r].Rhs], 100 * (1 - Rule[r].Error));
}
```

```
/****************************************************************************/
/*                                                                        */
/*          Print a condition c of a production rule                      */
/*                                                                        */
/****************************************************************************/


        PrintCondition(c)
/*      ───────────   */
        Condition c;
{
        Test tp;
        DiscrValue v, pv;
        Boolean First=true;

        tp = c->CondTest;
        v = c->TestValue;
        printf("\t%s", AttName[tp->Tested]);

        if ( c->TestValue < 0 )
        {
            printf(" is unknown\n");
            return;
        }

        switch ( tp->NodeType )
        {
            case BrDiscr:
                printf(" = %s\n", AttValName[tp->Tested][v]);
                break;

            case ThreshContin:
                printf(" %s %g\n", ( v == 1 ? "<=" : ">" ), tp->Cut);
                break;

            case BrSubset:
                printf(" in ");
                ForEach(pv, 1, MaxAttVal[tp->Tested])
                {
                    if ( In(pv, tp->Subset[v]) )
                    {
                        if ( First )
                        {
                            printf(" {");
                            First = false;
                        }
                        else
                        {
                            printf(", ");
                        }
                        printf("%s", AttValName[tp->Tested][pv]);
                    }
                }
                printf("}\n");
        }
}
```

File confmat.c

```
/**********************************************************************/
/*                                                                    */
/*         Routine for printing confusion matrices                    */
/*         ───────────────────────────────────                        */
/*                                                                    */
/**********************************************************************/

#include "defns.i"
#include "types.i"
#include "extern.i"


    PrintConfusionMatrix(ConfusionMat)
/*  ───────────────────  */
    ItemNo *ConfusionMat;
{
    short Row, Col;

    /*  Print the heading, then each row  */

    printf("\n\n\t");
    ForEach(Col, 0, MaxClass)
    {
        printf("   (%c)", 'a' + Col);
    }
    printf("\t<-classified as\n\t");
    ForEach(Col, 0, MaxClass)
    {
        printf(" ----");
    }
    printf("\n");

    ForEach(Row, 0, MaxClass)
    {
        printf("\t");
        ForEach(Col, 0, MaxClass)
        {
            if ( ConfusionMat[Row*(MaxClass+1) + Col] )
            {
                printf("%5d", ConfusionMat[Row*(MaxClass+1) + Col]);
            }
            else
            {
                printf("     ");
            }
        }
        printf("\t(%c): class %s\n", 'a' + Row, ClassName[Row]);
    }
    printf("\n");
}
```

File stats.c

```
/**************************************************************************/
/*                                                                      */
/*   Statistical routines for C4.5                                      */
/*   ------------------------------                                     */
/*                                                                      */
/**************************************************************************/


#include "defns.i"
#include "types.i"
#include "extern.i"


/**************************************************************************/
/*                                                                      */
/*   Compute the additional errors if the error rate increases to the   */
/*   upper limit of the confidence level.   The coefficient is the      */
/*   square of the number of standard deviations corresponding to the   */
/*   selected confidence level.   (Taken from Documenta Geigy Scientific */
/*   Tables (Sixth Edition), p185 (with modifications).)                */
/*                                                                      */
/**************************************************************************/


float Val[] = {  0,  0.001, 0.005, 0.01, 0.05, 0.10, 0.20, 0.40, 1.00},
      Dev[] = {100,  3.09,  2.58,  2.33, 1.65, 1.28, 0.84, 0.25, 0.00};


float AddErrs(N, e)
/*    ------- */
    ItemCount N, e;
{
    static float Coeff=0;
    float Val0, Pr;

    if ( ! Coeff )
    {
        /*  Compute and retain the coefficient value, interpolating from
            the values in Val and Dev  */

        int i;

        i = 0;
        while ( CF > Val[i] ) i++;

        Coeff = Dev[i-1] +
                (Dev[i] - Dev[i-1]) * (CF - Val[i-1]) /(Val[i] - Val[i-1]);
        Coeff = Coeff * Coeff;
    }

    if ( e < 1E-6 )
    {
        return N * (1 - exp(log(CF) / N));
    }
```

```
    else
    if ( e < 0.9999 )
    {
        Val0 = N * (1 - exp(log(CF) / N));
        return Val0 + e * (AddErrs(N, 1.0) - Val0);
    }
    else
    if ( e + 0.5 >= N )
    {
        return 0.67 * (N - e);
    }
    else
    {
        Pr = (e + 0.5 + Coeff/2
                + sqrt(Coeff * ((e + 0.5) * (1 - (e + 0.5)/N) + Coeff/4)) )
            / (N + Coeff);
        return (N * Pr - e);
    }
}
```

File genlogs.c

```
/*************************************************************************/
/*                                                                     */
/*          Tabluate logs and log factorials (to improve speed)        */
/*          ─────────────────────────────────                          */
/*                                                                     */
/*************************************************************************/

#include "defns.i"
#include "types.i"
#include "extern.i"

float    *LogItemNo;
double   *LogFact;

/*************************************************************************/
/*                                                                     */
/*  Set up the array LogItemNo to contain the logs of integers and     */
/*  the array LogFact to contain logs of factorials (all to base 2)    */
/*                                                                     */
/*************************************************************************/

    GenerateLogs()
/*  ─────────────  */
{
    ItemNo i;

    LogItemNo = (float *) malloc((MaxItem+100) * sizeof(float));
    LogFact = (double *) malloc((MaxItem+100) * sizeof(double));

    LogItemNo[0]  = -1E38;
    LogItemNo[1]  = 0;
    LogFact[0]  = LogFact[1]  = 0;

    ForEach(i, 2, MaxItem+99)
    {
        LogItemNo[i]  = log((float) i)  / Log2;
        LogFact[i]  = LogFact[i-1]  + LogItemNo[i];
    }
}
```

File xval-prep.c

```
/*********************************************************************/
/*                                                                   */
/*          Program to prepare data file for cross-validation        */
/*          ───────────────────────────────────────────────         */
/*                                                                   */
/*          The number of blocks for the cross-validation appears as the  */
/*          First argument.  The data are shuffled and divided into the   */
/*          specified number of blocks, with class distributions as even  */
/*          as possible in each block.                               */
/*                                                                   */
/*********************************************************************/

#include <math.h>
#include <stdio.h>

long      random();
#define  randf                 ((random()&2147483647) / 2147483648.0)
#define  ForEach(var,F,L)      for(var=F; var<=L; ++var)
#define  dig(x)                (x >= '0' && x <= '9')

#define MAXLINE 5000           /* maximum line length */

char      **Item;
int       ItemSpace=1000, MaxItem=0;

     main(argc, argv)
/*   ────  */
     int argc;
     char *argv[];
{
     int i, First=0, Last, Length, Splits;
     char Line[MAXLINE], **ClassPtr, *Temp, *BeginClass();

     sscanf(argv[1], "%d", &Splits);

     Item = (char **) malloc(ItemSpace * sizeof(char *));

     while ( fgets(Line, MAXLINE, stdin) )
     {
         if ( MaxItem >= ItemSpace )
         {
             ItemSpace += 1000;
             Item = (char **) realloc(Item, ItemSpace * sizeof(char *));
         }

         Length = strlen(Line)+2;
         Item[MaxItem] = (char *) malloc(Length);
         memcpy(Item[MaxItem], Line, Length);
         MaxItem++;
     }
```

```c
    if ( ! MaxItem-- )  exit();

Shuffle();

/*  Find classes  */

ClassPtr = (char **) malloc((MaxItem+1) * sizeof(char *));
ForEach(i, 0, MaxItem)
{
    ClassPtr[i] = BeginClass(Item[i]);
}

/*  Sort by class  */

fprintf(stderr, "\nClass frequencies:\n");

while ( First <= MaxItem )
{
    Last = First;

    ForEach(i, First+1, MaxItem)
    {
        if ( ! strcmp(ClassPtr[i], ClassPtr[First]) )
        {
            Last++;
            Temp = Item[Last];
            Item[Last] = Item[i];
            Item[i] = Temp;

            Temp = ClassPtr[Last];
            ClassPtr[Last] = ClassPtr[i];
            ClassPtr[i] = Temp;
        }
    }

    fprintf(stderr, "%6d class %s\n", Last-First+1, ClassPtr[First]);

    First = Last+1;
}
ForEach(First, 0, Splits-1)
{
    for ( i = First ; i <= MaxItem ; i += Splits )
    {
        printf("%s\n", Item[i]);
    }
}
}
```

```
/****************************************************************************/
/*                                                                        */
/*        Find the beginning character of a class name                    */
/*                                                                        */
/****************************************************************************/


char *BeginClass(S)
/*         ─────────  */
    char *S;
{
    char *F;

    F = S - 1;
    do
    {
        S = F + 1;
        while ( *S == ' ' || *S == '\t' || *S == '\n' )  S++;
        F = S;
        while ( *F != ',' && (*F != '.' || dig(*(F+1))) && *F != '\n' )  F++;
    } while ( *F == ',' );

    if ( *F != '.' )    *F = '.';
    *(F+1) = '\0';

    return S;
}




/****************************************************************************/
/*                                                                        */
/*        Shuffle the data items                                          */
/*                                                                        */
/****************************************************************************/


    Shuffle()
/*  ───────  */
{
    int this, alt, left = MaxItem+1;
    char *hold;

    this = 0;
    while ( left )
    {
        alt = this + (left--) * randf;
        if ( alt > MaxItem || alt < this )
        {
            fprintf(stderr, "ERROR!\n");
            exit(1);
        }
        hold = Item[this];
        Item[this++] = Item[alt];
        Item[alt] = hold;
    }
}
```

File average.c

```
/*************************************************************************/
/*                                                                       */
/*          Average results for training and test sets                   */
/*          _____                  */
/*                                                                       */
/*          This is a generic program that averages any numbers found on */
/*          a set of lines of the same pattern.                          */
/*                                                                       */
/*************************************************************************/

#include <stdio.h>

#define  MAXLINE        200      /* max line length */
#define MAXVALS          10      /* max values to be averaged */

main()
{
    char Line[MAXLINE], *p1, *p2;
    int Numbers=0, Lines=0, i, TrainTest;
    float Val, Sum[2][MAXVALS];
    double strtod();

    for ( i = 0 ; i < MAXVALS ; i++ )
    {
        Sum[0][i] = Sum[1][i] = 0;
    }

    while ( fgets(Line, MAXLINE, stdin) )
    {
        i = 0;
        TrainTest = Lines % 2;
        printf("%s", Line);

        /*  Count the numbers appearing on the line   */

        for ( p1 = Line ; *p1 != '\n' ; p1++ )
        {
            if ( *p1 < '0' || *p1 > '9' ) continue;

            Val = strtod(p1, &p2);
            Sum[TrainTest][i++]  += Val;
            p1 = p2-1;
        }

        /*  The number of numbers must match any previous lines   */

        if ( Lines )
        {
            if ( i != Numbers ) exit();
        }
        else
```

```
        {
            Numbers = i;
        }
        Lines++;
    }
    putchar('\n');
    for ( TrainTest = 0 ; TrainTest <= 1 ; TrainTest++ )
    {
        i = 0;
        printf("%s:\t", TrainTest ? "test" : "train");

        for ( p1 = Line ; *p1 != '\n' ; p1++ )
        {
            if ( *p1 < '0' || *p1 > '9' )
            {
                putchar(*p1);
            }
            else
            {
                printf("%.1f", Sum[TrainTest][i++] / (0.5 * Lines));
                strtod(p1, &p2);
                p1 = p2-1;
            }
        }
        putchar('\n');
    }
}
```

File xval.sh

```csh
#csh

#----------------------------------------------------------------------
# N-way cross-validation script
#----------------------------------------------------------------------
#
# invocation:
#   xval filestem N [options for c4.5 and c4.5rules]  [suffix]
#
# individual reults from each block are left in
#      filestem.[rt]o*[suffix],
# averages over all blocks in
#      filestem.[rt]res[suffix]
#----------------------------------------------------------------------

#        sort the options into result suffix and control options for the programs
#        Note: for options with values, there must be no space between the option
#        name and value; e.g. "-v1", not "-v 1"
set treeopts =
set ruleopts =
set suffix =

foreach i ( $argv[3-] )
  switch ( $i )
  case "+*":
    set suffix = $i
    breaksw
  case "-v*":
  case "-c*":
    set treeopts = ($treeopts $i)
    set ruleopts = ($ruleopts $i)
    breaksw
  case "-p":
  case "-t*":
  case "-w*":
  case "-i*":
  case "-g":
  case "-s":
  case "-m*":
    set treeopts = ($treeopts $i)
    breaksw
  case "-r*":
  case "-F*":
    set ruleopts = ($ruleopts $i)
    breaksw
  default:
    echo "unrecognised or inappropriate option" $i
    exit
  endsw
end
```

```
#        prepare the data for cross-validation

cat $1.data $1.test | xval-prep $2 >XDF.data
cp /dev/null XDF.test
ln $1.names XDF.names
rm $1.[rt]o[0-9]*$suffix
set junk = 'wc XDF.data'
set examples = $junk[1]
set large = 'expr $examples % $2'
set segsize = 'expr \( $examples / $2 \) + 1'

#        perform the cross-validation trials

set i = 0
while ( $i < $2 )
  if ( $i == $large ) set segsize = 'expr $examples / $2'
  cat XDF.test XDF.data | split -'expr $examples - $segsize'
  mv xaa XDF.data
  mv xab XDF.test

  c4.5 -f XDF -u $treeopts >$1.to$i$suffix
  c4.5rules -f XDF -u $ruleopts >$1.ro$i$suffix

  @ i++
end

#        remove the temporary files and summarize results

rm XDF.*
cat $1.to[0-9]*$suffix | grep "<<" | average >$1.tres$suffix
cat $1.ro[0-9]*$suffix | grep "<<" | average >$1.rres$suffix
```

Alphabetic index of routines

References and Bibliography

Aha, D. W., Kibler, D., and Albert, M. K. (1991). Instance-based learning algorithms. *Machine Learning 6*, 1, 37–66.

Breiman, L., Friedman, J. H., Olshen, R. A., and Stone, C. J. (1984). *Classification and Regression Trees*. Belmont, CA: Wadsworth.

Buntine, W. (1991). Learning classification trees. Technical Report FIA-90-12-19-01, NASA Ames Research Center, Moffett Field, CA.

Carter, C., and Catlett, J. (1987). Assessing credit card applications using machine learning. *IEEE Expert*, Fall issue, 71–79.

Catlett, J. (1991a). Megainduction: A test flight. *Proceedings of the Eighth International Workshop on Machine Learning* (pp. 596–599). San Mateo, CA: Morgan Kaufmann.

Catlett, J. (1991b). *Megainduction*. PhD Thesis, Basser Department of Computer Science, University of Sydney.

Cestnik, B., Kononenko, I., and Bratko, I. (1987). ASSISTANT 86: A knowledge-elicitation tool for sophisticated users. In I. Bratko and N. Lavrač (eds.), *Progress in Machine Learning*. Wilmslow, UK: Sigma Press.

Clark, P., and Niblett, T. (1989). The CN2 induction algorithm. *Machine Learning 3*, 4, 261–284.

Dieterich, T. G., Hild, H., and Bakiri, G. (1989). A comparative study of ID3 and backpropagation for English text-to-speech mapping. *Proceedings of the Seventh International Conference on Machine Learning* (pp. 24–31). San Mateo, CA: Morgan Kaufmann.

Feigenbaum, E. A., McCorduck, P., and Nii, H. P. (1988). *The Rise of the Expert Company*. New York: Times Books.

Fisher, D. H., and McKusick, K. B. (1989). An empirical comparison of ID3 and back-propagation. *Proceedings of the Eleventh International Joint Conference on Artificial Intelligence* (pp. 788–793). San Mateo, CA: Morgan Kaufmann.

Fisher, D. H., Pazzani, M. J., and Langley, P. (1991). *Concept Formation: Knowledge and Experience in Unsupervised Learning*. San Mateo, CA: Morgan Kaufmann.

Friedman, J. H. (1977). A recursive partitioning decision rule for nonparametric classification. *IEEE Transactions on Computers*, 404–408.

Friedman, J. H. (1988). Multivariate Adaptive Regression Splines. Technical Report 102, Laboratory for Computational Statistics, Stanford University, Stanford, CA.

Hinton, G. E. (1986). Learning distributed representations of concepts. *Proceedings of the Eighth Annual Conference of the Cognitive Science Society*, Amherst, MA. Reprinted in R. G. M. Morris (ed.), *Parallel Distributed Processing: Implications for Psychology and Neurobiology*. Oxford, UK: Oxford University Press.

Holland, J. H. (1986). Escaping brittleness: The possibilities of general-purpose learning algorithms applied to parallel rule-based systems. In R. S. Michalski, J. G. Carbonell, and T. M. Mitchell (eds.), *Machine Learning: An Artificial Intelligence Approach* (Vol. 2). San Mateo, CA: Morgan Kaufmann.

Hunt, E. B., Marin, J., and Stone, P. J. (1966). *Experiments in Induction*. New York: Academic Press.

Hunt, E. B. (1975). *Artificial Intelligence*. New York: Academic Press.

Hyafil, L., and Rivest, R. L. (1976). Constructing optimal binary decision trees is NP-complete. *Information Processing Letters 5*, 1, 15–17.

Langley, P., Bradshaw, G. L., and Simon, H. A. (1983). Rediscovering chemistry with the BACON system. In R. S. Michalski, J. G. Carbonell, and T. M. Mitchell (eds.), *Machine Learning: An Artificial Intelligence Approach*. Palo Alto, CA: Tioga Press.

López de Mántaras, R. (1991). A distance-based attribute selection measure for decision tree induction. *Machine Learning 6*, 1, 81–92.

McClelland, J. L., and Rumelhart, D. E. (1988). *Explorations in Parallel Distributed Processing*. Cambridge, MA: MIT Press.

Michalski, R. S., and Chilausky, R. L. (1980). Learning by being told and learning from examples. *International Journal of Policy Analysis and Information Systems 4*, 2, 125–160.

Michie, D. (1986). *On Machine Intelligence* (2nd ed.). Chichester, UK: Ellis Horwood.

Michie, D. (1987). Current developments in expert systems. In J. R. Quinlan (ed.), *Applications of Expert Systems* (pp. 137–156). Wokingham, UK: Addison-Wesley.

Michie, D. (1989). Problems of computer-aided concept formation. In J. R. Quinlan (ed.), *Applications of Expert Systems* (Vol. 2) (pp. 310–333). Wokingham, UK: Addison-Wesley.

Michie, D. (1991). Use of sequential Bayes with class probability trees. In J. E. Hayes-Michie, D. Michie, and E. Tyugu (eds.), *Machine Intelligence 12*. Oxford, UK: Oxford University Press.

Mingers, J. (1989). An empirical comparison of selection measures for decision-tree induction. *Machine Learning 3*, 4, 319–342.

Mingers, J. (1989). An empirical comparison of pruning methods for decision-tree induction. *Machine Learning 4*, 2, 227–243.

Mitchell, T. M. (1977). Version spaces: A candidate elimination approach to rule learning. *Proceedings of the Fifth International Joint Conference on Artificial Intelligence* (pp. 305–310). San Mateo, CA: Morgan Kaufmann.

Murphy, P. M., and Pazzani, M. J. (1991). ID2-of-3: constructive induction of M-of-N concepts for discriminators in decision trees. *Proceedings of the Eighth International Workshop on Machine Learning* (pp. 183-187). San Mateo, CA: Morgan Kaufmann.

Nilsson, N. J. (1965). *Learning Machines.* New York: McGraw Hill.

Pagallo, G., and Haussler, D. (1990). Boolean feature discovery in empirical learning. *Machine Learning 5*, 1, 71–100.

Paterson, A., and Niblett, T. B. (1982). *ACLS Manual.* Edinburgh: Intelligent Terminals Ltd.

Press, W. H., Flannery, B. P., Teukolsky, S. A., and Vetterling, W. T. (1988). *Numerical Recipes in C.* Cambridge, UK: Cambridge University Press.

Quinlan, J. R. (1979). Discovering rules by induction from large collections of examples. In D. Michie (ed.), *Expert Systems in the Micro Electronic Age*. Edinburgh, UK: Edinburgh University Press.

Quinlan, J. R. (1980). Semi-autonomous acquisition of pattern-based knowledge. *Australian Computer Bulletin*, April 1980. Reprinted in J. E. Hayes, D. Michie, and Y.-H. Pao (eds.), *Machine Intelligence 10*. Chichester, UK: Ellis Horwood.

Quinlan, J. R. (1983a). Learning efficient classification procedures. In R. S. Michalski, J. G. Carbonell, and T. M. Mitchell (eds.), *Machine Learning: An Artificial Intelligence Approach*. Palo Alto, CA: Tioga Press.

Quinlan, J. R. (1983b). INFERNO; a cautious approach to uncertain inference. *Computer Journal 26*, 3, 255–269. Reprinted in P. Klahr and D. A. Waterman (eds.), *Tools for Expert Systems*. Reading, MA: Addison-Wesley.

Quinlan, J. R. (1986a). The effect of noise on concept learning. In R. S. Michalski, J. G. Carbonell, and T. M. Mitchell (eds.), *Machine*

Learning: An Artificial Intelligence Approach (Vol. 2). San Mateo, CA: Morgan Kaufmann.

Quinlan, J. R. (1986b). Induction of decision trees. *Machine Learning 1*, 1, 81–106. Reprinted in J. W. Shavlik and T. G. Dietterich (eds.), *Readings in Machine Learning*. San Mateo, CA: Morgan Kaufmann, 1991. Reprinted in B. G. Buchanan, and D. Wilkins (eds.), *Readings in Knowledge Acquisition and Learning*. San Mateo, CA: Morgan Kaufmann, 1992.

Quinlan, J. R., Compton, P. J., Horn, K. A., and Lazarus, L. A. (1987a). Inductive knowledge acquisition: A case study. In J. R. Quinlan (ed.), *Applications of Expert Systems* (pp. 157–173). Wokingham, UK: Addison-Wesley.

Quinlan, J. R. (1987b). Decision trees as probabilistic classifiers. *Proceedings of the Fourth International Machine Learning Workshop* (pp. 31–37). San Mateo, CA: Morgan Kaufmann.

Quinlan, J. R. (1987c). Generating production rules from decision trees. *Proceedings of the Tenth International Joint Conference on Artificial Intelligence* (pp. 304–307). San Mateo, CA: Morgan Kaufmann.

Quinlan, J. R. (1987d). Induction, knowledge, and expert systems, *Proceedings of the Australian Joint Artificial Intelligence Conference*, Sydney, Australia. Reprinted in J. S. Gero, and R. Stanton (eds.), *Artificial Intelligence Developments and Applications* (pp. 253–271). Amsterdam: North-Holland, 1988. Reprinted in D. Partridge (ed.), *Artificial Intelligence and Software Engineering* (pp. 473–490). Norwood, NJ: Ablex, 1991.

Quinlan, J. R. (1987e). Simplifying decision trees. *International Journal of Man-Machine Studies 27*, 221–234.

Quinlan, J. R. (1988a). An empirical comparison of genetic and decision-tree classifiers. *Proceedings of the Fifth International Machine Learning Conference* (pp. 135–141). San Mateo, CA: Morgan Kaufmann.

Quinlan, J. R. (1988b). Decision trees and multi-valued attributes. In J. E. Hayes, D. Michie, and J. Richards (eds.), *Machine Intelligence 11* (pp. 305–318). Oxford, UK: Oxford University Press.

Quinlan, J. R., and Rivest, R. L. (1989). Inferring decision trees using the Minimum Description Length Principle. *Information and Computation 80*, 3, 227–248.

Quinlan, J. R. (1989). Unknown attribute values in induction. *Proceedings of the Sixth International Machine Learning Workshop* (pp. 164–168). San Mateo, CA: Morgan Kaufmann.

Quinlan, J. R. (1990a). Probabilistic decision trees. In R. S. Michalski, and Y. Kodratoff (eds.), *Machine Learning: An Artificial Intelligence Approach*, (Vol. 3). San Mateo, CA: Morgan Kaufmann.

Quinlan, J. R. (1990b). Decision trees and decision-making. *IEEE Transactions Systems, Man and Cybernetics 20*, 2, 339–346.

Quinlan, J. R. (1990c). Learning logical definitions from relations. *Machine Learning 5*, 3, 239–266.

Quinlan, J. R. (1991). Improved estimates for the accuracy of small disjuncts. *Machine Learning 6*, 1, 93–98.

Quinlan, J. R. (1992). Themes and issues in empirical learning. *Proceedings of the Sixth National Conference of the Japanese Society for Artificial Intelligence*, Tokyo.

Quinlan, J. R. (1993). Comparing connectionist and symbolic learning methods. In S. Hanson, G. Drastal, and R. Rivest (eds.), *Computational Learning Theory and Natural Learning Systems: Constraints and Prospects*. Cambridge, MA: MIT Press.

Rendell, L. A. (1983). A new basis for state-space learning systems and a successful implementation. *Artificial Intelligence 20*, 369–392.

Rendell, L. A., and Cho, H. (1990). Empirical learning as a function of concept character. *Machine Learning 5*, 3, 267–298.

Rissanen, J. (1983). A universal prior for integers and estimation by minimum description length. *Annals of Statistics 11*, 2, 416–431.

Schlimmer, J. C., and Fisher, D. (1986). A case study of incremental concept induction. *Proceedings of the Fifth National Conference on Artificial Intelligence* (pp. 496–501). San Mateo, CA: Morgan Kaufmann.

Shapiro, A. D. (1987). *Structured Induction in Expert Systems*. Wokingham, UK: Addison-Wesley.

Shavlik, J. W., Mooney, R. J., and Towell, G. G. (1991). Symbolic and neural learning algorithms: An experimental comparison. *Machine Learning 6*, 2, 111–144.

Shepherd, B., Piper, J., and Rutovitz, D. (1988). Comparison of ACLS and classical linear methods in a biological application. In J. E. Hayes, D. Michie, and J. Richards (eds.), *Machine Intelligence 11* (pp. 423–434). Oxford, UK: Oxford University Press.

Spackman, K. A. (1988). Learning categorical criteria in biomedical domains. *Proceedings of the Fifth International Machine Learning Conference* (pp. 36–46). San Mateo, CA: Morgan Kaufmann.

Stanfill, C., and Waltz, D. (1986). Toward memory-based reasoning. *Communications of the ACM 29*, 12, 1213–1228.

Thrun, S. B. *et al.* (1991). The Monk's problems: A performance comparison of different learning algorithms. Technical Report CMU-CS-91-197, Computer Science Department, Carnegie Mellon University, Pittsburgh, PA.

Utgoff, P. E. (1989). Incremental induction of decision trees. *Machine Learning 4*, 2, 161–186.

Utgoff, P. E., and Brodley, C. E. (1991). Linear machine decision trees. COINS Technical Report 91-10, University of Massachusetts, Amherst MA.

Weiss, S. M., and Kapouleas, I. (1989). An empirical comparison of pattern recognition, neural nets, and machine learning classification methods. *Proceedings of the Eleventh International Joint Conference on Artificial Intelligence* (pp. 781–787). San Mateo, CA: Morgan Kaufmann.

Weiss, S. M., and Kulikowski, C. A. (1991). *Computer Systems That Learn.* San Mateo, CA: Morgan Kaufmann.

Wilson, S. W. (1987). Classifier systems and the animat problem. *Machine Learning 2*, 3, 199–228.

Winston, P. H. (1992). *Artificial Intelligence* (3rd ed.). Reading, MA: Addison-Wesley.

Wirth, J., and Catlett, J. (1988). Experiments on the costs and benefits of windowing in ID3. *Proceedings of the Fifth International Conference on Machine Learning* (pp. 87–99). San Mateo, CA: Morgan Kaufmann.

Author Index

Subject Index

Advantage, *see* rule advantage

ASSISTANT 86, 17, 29

Attribute, 2, 4, 104
    continuous, *see* continuous attribute
    discrete, *see* discrete attribute
    numeric, *see* continuous attribute
    test on, *see* tests

Attribute value groups, 24, 63, 78, 85, 93, 105

Attribute-value formalism, 2

BACON, 98

Bias, 23, 63, 98

Building trees, *see* decision tree construction

CART, 15, 17, 33, 63, 98, 102, 103

Certainty factor *CF*, 41, 85, 87

χ^2 test, 37

Class, 2, 103
    continuous, *see* continuous class
    default, *see* default class
    distribution, 37, 57, 69, 72
    encoding, 14
    rulesets, *see* rulesets

Class probability trees, 73

CLS, 17, 21, 63, 107

Comments, *see* files, comments

Computation requirement, 26, 53, 58, 60, 61, 64, 66, 67, 102, 106, 107

Conflict resolution, *see* rule ordering

Confusion matrix, 8, 11
    see also error rate on training cases,
    error rate on test cases

Constructive induction, 101

Contingency table, 48
    see also significance test

Continuous attribute, 4
    test on, *see* tests, continuous attribute

Continuous class, 2, 103

Cross-validation, 40, 42, 89, 92

Data, 83
    amount of, 3, 63, 85, 89, 98, 106
    noise, 85
    repository, *see* UCI Data Repository
    structured, 2

Decision node, 5, 18

Decision tree, 5, 7
    accuracy, *see* error rate on test cases
    construction, 17, 35, 98
    leaf, 5, 17, 32
    multiple, *see* windowing
    number of possible, 20
    simplifying, *see* pruning
    test, *see* tests

Default class, 9, 50, 54, 79

Dependent variable, *see* class

Description space, 95, 98, 100

DF (default filestem), 85, 87

Discrete attribute, 4, 104

299